The Ultimate
Instant Pot
Cookbook for Beginners

Easy & Excellent Instant Pot Recipes Take You on an Exploration of
Delicious Breakfasts, Lunches, Dinners, Appetizers, and Desserts

Jodi Gutierrez

Table of Contents

1   Introduction

11   4-Week Meal Plan

13   Chapter 1 Breakfast Recipes

25   Chapter 2 Vegetable and Sides

36   Chapter 3 Soup, Stew, and Chili

49   Chapter 4 Poultry Mains Recipes

61   Chapter 5 Fish and Seafood Recipes

73   Chapter 6 Meat Mains

86   Chapter 7 Dessert Recipes

100 Conclusion

101 Appendix 1 Measurement Conversion Chart

102 Appendix 2 Recipes Index

Introduction

Instant Pot Duo is a versatile multi-use pressure cooker. You can call it with another name, "genius or miracle pot." It is a secret weapon in your kitchen. Instant Pot Duo mini is a great kitchen appliance for busy people and helps them to save time, energy, and money. No doubt, Instant Pot Duo mini can change the way of life.

Cooking with Instant Pot Duo is super easy and fun. Everyone is excited and enjoys the versatility and ease of getting mouthwatering and creative meals on the dining table in a hurry. It is a great cooking appliance that saves you many hours every week.

With this Instant Pot Duo mini cooking appliance, you can cook flavorful, healthy, and quick meals with little effort. It has various cooking functions, accessories, and user-friendly operating buttons. In this cookbook, you will get delicious and healthy recipes. You can prepare them at any time or on any occasion.

The Instant Pot Duo makes our life easier. It cooks food in very less time. You can spend many hours with your family. You can prepare any meal like chicken, beef, lamb, pork, vegetables, appetizer, soup, stews, dips, sauces, grains, beans, rice, yogurt, fish/seafood, dessert, snacks, and many more. You don't need any other appliance because it offers all cooking functions.

It is safe to use and easy to understand. It provides the families and households with everything they need from the Instant pot, but at the accurate settings and possible size. Let's find out more about this wonderful Instant Pot Duo mini cooking appliance that can make you fall in love with cooking all over again!

What Is Instant Pot Duo Mini?

The Instant Pot Duo mini is a wonderful kitchen appliance. It comes with two smart programs: Pressure cooking includes steam, pressure cook, porridge, soup/broth, rice, meat/stews, bean/chili, etc. No pressure cooking includes slow cook, sauté, yogurt, and keep warm, etc. It comes with useful accessories, including the top lid, bottom lid, inner pot, cooker base, steam rack (with handles), condensation collector, and control panel. It has user-friendly operating buttons. Using Instant Pot Duo mini cooking appliance, prepare chicken, beef, lamb, pork, seafood, vegetables, dessert, appetizer/snacks, soups/broth, yogurt, beans, rice meals. It makes life comfortable.

The Instant pot is wonderful for the family budget. You didn't need to bring a complex shopping list. In this cookbook, you will find simple and regular ingredients for each recipe. You can create different meals using your favorite ingredients and spices.

Benefits of Using Instant Pot Duo Mini

Here are some benefits of using the Instant duo mini cooking pot:

Time, Money, And Energy Saving Pot:

Pressure cooking is one of the most affordable ways to cook large budget-friendly foods. It saves your time and takes you some hours in the week. It doesn't allow you to bring complex shopping for cooking meals. You will spend 4 to 5 hours with your family and cook food within 1 hour. You didn't need to purchase separate kitchen appliances such as pans/skillet, rice cooker, steamer, or slow cooker. It is the best pot for busy people. In the morning, you can prepare breakfast in very little time. Then, you can go on your work.

Multi-Functions:

The Instant Pot Duo mini offers many useful functions such as steam, pressure cook, porridge, soup/broth, rice, meat/stews, bean/chili, slow cook, sauté, yogurt, and keep warm, etc. Now, you can prepare any meal using these cooking functions. Using this cooking appliance, you will get tender, healthy, and delicious meals.

It Comes with Cool Accessories:

When you purchase this appliance, you will gift some cool accessories, which you can use in everyday cooking. The accessories include a measuring cup, steam rack (without handle), inner pot, cooker base, condensation collector, top lid, and bottom lid, etc. It is an excellent way to get started cooking. You don't need to purchase additional accessories before you start cooking. The cleaning process of these accessories is super easy.

Safe to Use:

High pressure or high temperature can make you afraid of using this appliance, especially children. However, Instant pot has created a safety mechanism, which almost certainly guarantees that the appliance will continue to cook without any problems. There is nothing that kids and adults should be afraid of. The best way is to read about this appliance before cooking. I added all information, including safety tips, in my cookbook. You can read it before cooking food.

Before First Use

When you purchase an Instant Pot Duo appliance, remove all the cooker and accessories packaging.

Cleaning Before the First Use:

Remove the inner pot from the cooker base and rinse it with hot and soapy water. Wash with warm and clean water and use a soft cloth or dry the exterior of the pot or you can put the inner pot in the dishwasher.

Wipe the heating element with a soft cloth before returning the inner pot to the cooker base. Make sure that there are no dust and package particles present. The inner pot is a main part of the Instant Pot. The food is placed into the inner pot, not directly in the cooker base. t

If you see the deformed or damaged inner pot, return it because it will cause personal injury or damage the appliance.

Install Condensation Collector:

Dry the inner pot, cooker base, and accessories before returning to the main unit. When all parts are inserted in the main pot, install the condensation collector at the rear of the cooker by aligning the top of the collector and press in. When done, place the steam release handle on the lid.

Before Using Instant Pot:

If you want to remove the lid, hold the handle, turn the lid counterclockwise, and lift the lid.

Remove the inner pot from the main unit. Place food and liquid into the inner pot according to the recipe instructions. Place the steam rack if using the steam cooking function onto the bottom of the inner pot first. Wipe outside of the unit and make sure that there is no food debris on the bottom side of the inner pot.

Return the inner pot to the unit and rotate slightly. Check and make sure that the sealing ring rack is completely set on the inner side of the sealing ring. Check and make sure that there is no deformation on the sealing ring rack. Close the lid.

Ensure that the steam release valve, float valve, and anti-block shield are dust-free and debris-free. After putting a lid on, ensure that the float valve drops down. Do not put the lid on if you use a sauté cooking function.

Initial Test:

Add 3 cups of water into the inner pot. Close the lid.

After that, turn the steam release handle to the sealing position. Then, press the "steam" button onto the control panel. Adjust the time for two minutes. It will take ten seconds to preheat. The display shows "ON" on the screen. The steam will release until the float valve pops up. The steam cooking function will start when pressure is reached. The instant pot will beep when cooking time is completed and turn to the "KEEP WARM" button.

Introduction to Pressure Cooking

Pressure cooking is a versatile method to cook any meal. It is an efficient way to cook food quickly. You can cook your favorite meals using pressure cooking.

The pressure cooker has three stages when pressure cooking:

Preheating and Pressurization: Select desired cooking program in pressure cooking. The main unit will take ten seconds to ensure you have selected the cooking function. The display shows "ON" onto the screen to signify it has started preheating. When the Instant pot is preheated, the liquid is vaporized in the inner pot to build steam. When the steam has built up, the float valve pops up. It would be best if you locked the lid for safe cooking.

When the float valve pops up, the silicone cap attached to the bottom of the float valve seals the steam inner side of the cooking chamber. Allow the pressure to rise. If pressure is high, then it means that the cooking temperature is high.

High pressure = High temperature

Cooking: When the float valve pops up, the main unit needs a few minutes to build pressure. When desired pressure level is reached, cooking starts. The display shows "ON" onto the screen in HH: MM (hours: mins)

Smart program settings – pressure level (HI or Lo), Temperature, Cooking time, and Keeping warm will automatically be on or off. You can adjust at any time during cooking.

Depressurizing the Cooker (Venting Methods)

When pressure cooking is completed, read the recipe instructions for depressurization of the main unit. If automatic keep warm is on, the display shows counting automatically. If not, adjust the cooking time. When cooking time is completed, the display shows "END."
There are three methods for the venting process:
1. Natural release method: Some recipes call the natural release method to release steam or pressure. Leave the steam releases to handle in the sealing position. If the cooking temperature is dropped, the unit depressurizes naturally. The depressurization time increases vary based on the quantity of food and liquid. When the cooker has depressurized, the float valve drops in the lid of the main unit.
2. Quick-release method: Some recipes call the quick release method to release steam or pressure. Turn the steam releases handle from the sealing position to the venting position. Use the natural release method to vent the remaining pressure/steam.
3. 10-minutes Natural release: Leave the steam releases to handle in the sealing position for ten minutes after cooking is completed, then turn the steam release handle to the venting position.

Main Functions of Instant Pot Duo Mini

There are two programs in the Instant Pot Duo mini cooking appliance: Pressure cooking and Non-pressure cooking.
Pressure cooking has the following cooking functions:
  • Pressure cook, Soup/Broth, Meat/Stew, Bean/Chili, Rice, Multigrain, Poultry, Porridge, and Steam
The non-pressure cooking has the following cooking functions:
  • Slow cook, Sauté, Yogurt, and Keep warm, etc.

Pressure Cooking

Pressure Cook

Pressure cooking is the most used cooking function. It cooks food under high pressure. It takes 30 minutes to prepare a meal.
Cooking method using pressure cook:
  • Place steam rack in the bottom of the inner pot.
  • Add liquid to the inner pot. Place ingredients onto the steam rack.
  • Insert the inner pot in the cooker base. Close lid.
  • Select "pressure cook" cooking function.
  • Select "HI" or "Lo" pressure level. Press "Keep warm" to turn the automatic "keep warm" setting on or off.
  • Press the start button to begin cooking.
  • Follow the direction of the recipe to choose the exact venting method.

Cooking function	Setting	Suggested use	Imp note
Pressure cook	Less/normal/more	Manual programming	Press pressure level to toggle between high and low pressure Press +/- button to select cooking time Adjust according to the recipe instruction

Note: You can use the following liquids using the pressure cooking method: Stock, soup, broth, juice, water, filter water, etc.

Steam

The steam cooking method is mostly used for vegetables. You can steam any vegetable. Insert steam rack in the bottom of the inner pot.
Cooking method using steam:
  • Place steam rack in the bottom of the inner pot.
  • Add liquid/broth/water/stock in the inner pot. Place ingredients onto the steam rack.
  • Insert the inner pot in the cooker base. Close lid.
  • Select "steam" cooking function.

- Select "HI" or "Lo" pressure level. Press "Keep warm" to turn automatic keep the warm setting on or off.
- Press the start button to begin cooking.
- Follow the direction of the recipe to choose the exact venting method.

Cooking function	Setting	Suggested use	Imp note
Steam	Less/normal/more	Vegetables/Fish and Seafood/ Meat	Insert steam rack in the bottom of the inner pot to elevate food from cooking liquid Use quick-release method to prevent food from burning/overcooking

Rice

You can cook white rice, basmati rice, short-grain, and jasmine rice using the rice cooking method. It prefers high pressure to cook rice.

Cooking method using rice:

- Add liquid/broth/water/stock in the inner pot. Place rice into the pot.
- Insert the inner pot in the cooker base. Close lid.
- Select "rice" cooking function.
- Select "HI" or "Lo" pressure level. Press "Keep warm" to turn automatic keep the warm setting on or off.
- Press the start button to begin cooking.
- Follow the direction of the recipe to choose the exact venting method.

Cooking function	Setting	Suggested use	Imp note
Rice	Less/normal/more	Tender/Normal texture/ Soft texture	Automated cooking smart program. Depending upon the quantity of rice, adjust the cooking time- the cooking range is 8-15 minutes. When cooking time is done, wait for ten minutes. Use quick method to release pressure or release remaining pressure using natural release method

Bean/Chili

Using the bean/chili cooking method, you can cook various beans, including black-eyed peas, kidney beans, and white beans. It prefers high pressure to cook bean/chili.

Cooking method using bean/chili:

- Add liquid/broth/water/stock in the inner pot. Place bean/chili into the pot.
- Insert the inner pot in the cooker base. Close lid.
- Select the "bean/chili" cooking function.
- Select "HI" or "Lo" pressure level. Press "Keep warm" to turn the automatic "keep warm" setting on or off.
- Press the start button to begin cooking.
- Follow the direction of the recipe to choose the exact venting method.

Cooking function	Setting	Suggested use	Imp note
Bean/chili	Less/normal/more	Firm texture/Soft texture/ Very soft texture	Insert steam rack in the bottom of the inner pot to elevate food from cooking liquid Use a quick-release method to prevent food from burning/overcooking

Soup/Broth

Using the soup/broth cooking method, you can prepare soup, stock, or broth. You need to select the "Soup" cooking function.

Cooking method using soup/broth:

- Add liquid to the inner pot. Place ingredients into the pot.
- Insert the inner pot in the cooker base. Close lid.
- Select "soup/broth" cooking function.
- Select "HI" or "Lo" pressure level. Press "Keep warm" to turn the automatic "keep warm" setting on or off.
- Press the start button to begin cooking.
- Follow the direction of the recipe to choose the exact venting method.

Cooking function	Setting	Suggested use	Imp note
Soup/Broth	Less/normal/more	Soup without meat/soup with meat/bone broth	The Liquid remains clear because there is less boiling motion Use natural release method always when coup has a high starch content

Porridge

Using the porridge cooking method, you can cook different kinds of grains. This cooking method prefers high pressure.

Cooking method using porridge:

- Add liquid to the inner pot. Place ingredients into the pot.
- Insert the inner pot in the cooker base. Close lid.
- Select "porridge" cooking function.
- Select "HI" or "Lo" pressure level. Press "Keep warm" to turn the automatic "keep warm" setting on or off.
- Press the start button to begin cooking.
- Follow the direction of the recipe to choose the exact venting method.

Cooking function	Setting	Suggested use	Imp note
Porridge	Less/normal/more	Rice porridge/ White rice, porridge/Oatmeal, rolled, steel-cut	Adjust cooking time according to the recipe's instructions. Use natural release method to release pressure when foods expand

Meat/Stew

Using the meat/stew cooking method, you can cook chicken, beef, lamb, pork, and seafood and make different stews, including chicken stews, beef stew, vegetable stew, lamb stew, and sausage stew, and fish stew, etc.

Cooking method using meat/stews:

- Add liquid to the inner pot. Place ingredients into the pot.
- Insert the inner pot in the cooker base. Close lid.
- Select the "meat/stews" cooking function.
- Select "HI" or "Lo" pressure level. Press "Keep warm" to turn the automatic "keep warm" setting on or off.
- Press the start button to begin cooking.
- Follow the direction of the recipe to choose the exact venting method.

Cooking function	Setting	Suggested use	Imp note
Meat/stew	Less/normal/more	Soft texture/Very soft texture/Fall off bone	Choose a setting on meat texture as you want. Adjust cooking time manually. Let rest the meat for 5 to 30 minutes until tender or succulent

Non-Pressure Cooking

Slow Cook

Slow cook is a non-pressure cooking method. It takes a lot of time to cook food but gives tender and delicious meals. This cooking method is best for meats including chicken, beef, lamb, seafood, pork, etc.

Cooking method using slow cook:

- Remove inner pot from cooker base.
- Place liquid and ingredients into the inner pot. Insert it into the cooker base. Close the lid or use a glass lid with a venting hole.
- After that, turn the steam release handle to the venting position.
- Select the "slow cook" cooking function.
- Press the cooking function again to adjust the temperature according to the recipe's instructions.
- Press +/- button to adjust the cooking time according to the recipe's instructions.
- Press "Keep Warm" to toggle the keep warm setting on or off.
- The display shows time in counting while cooking.
- When cooking time is completed, the display shows "END" onto the screen.

Cooking function	Setting	Suggested use	Imp note
Slow cook	Less/normal/more	Low setting/Medium setting/High setting	Follow the recipe's instructions for slow cooking. Cooking time should be set for a minimum of ten hours for best results

Sauté

Sauté cooking method is used for sautéing meats, vegetables, and many more. You don't need to use water for this setting. Pour oi into the inner pot.

Cooking method using Sauté:

- Insert the inner pot into the cooker base. But, don't put the lid.
- Select "sauté" cooking function.

- Press sauté mode again to adjust the cooking temperature.
- Wait for ten seconds; then display shows "ON" to indicate that it has started preheating.
- Place food in the inner pot when the display shows "HOT" onto the screen.
- When cooking time is completed, the display shows "END" onto the screen.

Cooking function	Setting	Suggested use	Imp note
Sauté	Less/normal/more	Simmering/sautéing or searing/ stir-frying	The display shows "Hot" to "ON" indicates the main unit is maintaining the cooking temp 30 minutes is perfect cooking time for safety

Deglaze the inner pot (Turn pressure cooking to sauté mode):

You should sauté the meat and vegetables before pressure cooking because it is the perfect way to boost the flavor. If you are using sauté cooking mode after pressure cooking, deglaze the inner pot to ensure meal ingredients do not burn. Remove the ingredients from the inner pot and add water to the hot bottom surface to deglaze.

Yogurt

Using yogurt function, you can make yogurt at home. You can add it to different dishes.

Cooking method using yogurt:

- Select "yogurt" cooking function.
- Press yogurt cooking mode again to select cooking time.
- Press +/- button to select the fermentation time if you want.
- Wait for ten seconds the unit begins preheating.
- The display shows cooking time in counting.
- When fermentation is completed, the unit beeps, and the display shows "END."

Cooking function	Setting	Suggested use	Imp note
Yogurt	Less/normal/more	For low temperature fermentation/Fermenting milk after cultured has been included/Pasteurizing milk	Fermentation time is 24 hours Adjust the fermentation time according to the recipe's instructions. Pasteurizing time cannot be preset. When yogurt program is running, the display shows "BOIL." If you want extra thick yogurt, do pasteurize two times.

Buttons and User Guide of Instant Pot Duo Mini

The Instant Pot Duo series has user-friendly operating buttons.

Pressure Cooking Temperature:

Select the cooking function and press "Pressure level" to toggle between HI and Lo pressure levels.

Pressure Cooking Time:

Select the cooking function, and then press the smart program button again to adjust the less, normal, and more cooking time options. Press +/- button to increase or decrease the time if you want.

Non-Pressure Cooking Temperature:

Select the non-pressure cooking functions, and then presses the smart program button again to less, normal and more cooking temperature levels if you want.

Non-Pressure Cooking Time:

Select the non-pressure cooking functions, and then presses +/- button to adjust the cooking time. The cooking time can be changed during cooking.

Cancel and Standby mode:

When the unit is plugged in, the display shows "OFF" to indicate "Standby mode."
Press the "Cancel" button to stop the cooking function at any time. The main unit returns to standby mode.

Turn Sound ON/OFF:

Sound ON: When the main unit is in standby mode, press the + button until the displays show "ON" onto the screen.
Sound OFF: When the main unit is in standby mode, press and hold – button until the display shows "OFF" onto the screen.

Keep Warm:

The "keep warm" mode automatically turns on all cooking functions except yogurt and sauté.

Reset:

When the main unit is in standby mode, press the "cancel" button to reset cooking functions, temperature, pressure level, cooking time, etc.

Cooking Lid:

When the display shows "lid", it indicates that the pressure lid is not adequately secured or missing.

Preheat:

When the display shows "ON", it indicates that the main unit is preheating.

Display Timer:

The display shows "Time" onto the screen in the following:
- When the cooking function is running, the display timer is a countdown to indicate the cooking time remaining in the cooking function.
- The display timer countdown until the cooking function begins when the delay starts.
- When keep warm is running, the display timer counts to indicate how long food has been warming.

Auto:

The display shows "Auto" to indicate that the rice cooking function is running.

Boil:

The display shows "Boil" to indicate that the yogurt function is pasteurizing.

Hot:

The display shows "Hot" to indicate that food should be placed in the inner pot – (In sauté cooking function).

End:

The display shows "End" to indicate that cooking time is completed.

Food burn:

The display shows "Food burn" to indicate that food is burnt in the inner pot.

The Instant Pot Duo mini comes with different accessories.

Pressure Cooking Lid

The pressure cooking lid is made with stainless steel. The pressure cooking lid is used in many cooking methods.

Open and remove the pressure lid:
- Grip the upper lid handle, turn it counterclockwise, and lift it.

Close the pressure lid:
- Turn the lid clockwise until the symbol present on the lid aligns with the symbol of the cooker base.

Steam Release Handle

Turn the steam release handle from sealing to venting and vice versa, open and close the valve, venting, sealing the cooker as you want. When the unit releases pressure, steam is removed from the top of the steam release handle. It is the main accessory for your safety and pressure cooking. It must be installed before cooking.

Remove the steam release valve:
- Lift the steam release valve and wait until all steam is removed.
- Install the steam release handle
- Put steam release handle on steam release pipe and press down tightly.

Anti-Block Shield

The anti-block shield should be installed because it is necessary to prevent food particles from the steam release pipe. It is an essential accessory for your safety.

Remove the anti-block shield:
- Lift the lid tightly and press firmly against the side of the anti-block shield with your thumbs.
- Install the anti-block shield:
- Put anti-block shield over prongs and press it down.

Sealing Ring

You should install a sealing ring to create a tight sealing between the lid and cooker base. You should install a sealing ring before cooking. It should be cleaned after every use. You should install 1 sealing ring while using the unit.

Remove the sealing ring:
- Lift the edges of the silicone rubber and pull the sealing ring out. When the sealing ring is removed, check the rack to ensure it is secured.

Install the sealing rings:
- Put sealing ring over the sealing ring rack and press it firmly.

Float Valve

The float valve shows that pressure is built up within the inner pot and appears in two positions.

Pressurized:
- The float valve is appeared and pops up with the lid.

Depressurized:
- The float valve is pinched into the lid.

Inner Pot

The inner pot is an essential accessory in the Instant Pot Duo mini appliance. Place food in the inner pot. Close the lid.

Cooker Base

The cooker base is present at the bottom of the main unit. The inner pot is inserted into the cooker base. Don't place food directly in the cooker base.

Cleaning and Maintenance of Instant Pot Duo

The cleaning process of Instant Pot Duo mini is super easy. You should clean it after every use.
- Remove all accessories from the main unit, including the cooker base.
- Don't use chemical detergents, scouring pads or powdered on accessories.
- Rinse condensation collector after every use.
- Rinse sealing ring, anti-block shield, silicone cap, steam release valve, and float valve under hot and soapy water. You can put them in the dishwasher.
- Remove all small parts from the lid before cleaning.
- When the steam release valve is removed, clean the inner part of the steam release pipe to prevent clogging.
- Hold it vertically and turn it 360 degrees to remove water from the lid.
- If there is tough food residue stuck at the bottom, soak it in hot water for a few hours.
- If there is an odor present in the pot, combine 1 cup of white vinegar and 1 cup of water, run pressure cook for 5 to 10 minutes, and then use a quick method to release pressure.
- When all parts get dried, return to the main unit.
- Don't put the main unit in the dishwasher. Wipe the main unit with a soft cloth.
- Wipe the exterior part of the main unit with a moist and soft cloth.

Troubleshooting

Problem – 1
If you face difficulty in closing the lid
Possible reason
The sealing ring is not installed correctly.
May be contents in the Instant pot is still hot.
Solution
Again install the sealing ring properly
Turn the steam release handle to the venting position and slowly lower the lid on the cooker base.
Problem – 2
If you face difficulty in opening the lid
Possible reason
Pressure is present inside the unit
Solution
Release pressure according to the recipe's instructions.
Problem – 3
Steam is leaked from the side of the pressure lid
Possible reason
The lid is closed properly
The sealing ring is not installed
The sealing ring is damaged
Solution
Install the sealing ring
Replace the sealing ring
Open and then close the lid
Clean the sealing ring thoroughly

Meals Cooking Time in Instant Pot Duo Mini

Vegetable:

FOOD	COOKING TIME
Sweet potato – cubed	2-4 minutes
Sweet potato – whole	12-15 minutes
Corn	3-5 minutes
Carrots	6-8 minutes
Butternut squash	4-6 minutes
Cauliflower	2-3 minutes
Brussels sprouts	2-3 minutes
Cabbage	2-3 minutes
Asparagus	1-2 minutes
Broccoli	1-2 minutes

Meats and eggs:

FOOD	COOKING TIME
Eggs	5 minutes
Pork ribs	15-20 minutes
Lamb leg	15 minutes
Chicken breast	6-8 minutes
Chicken stock	40-45 minutes
Beef stew	20 minutes
Beef ribs	20-25 minutes
Whole chicken	8 minutes

Beans and lentils:

FOOD (soaked)	COOKING TIME
Soybeans	18-20 minutes
Lima beans	6-10 minutes
Yellow lentils	1-2 minutes
Green lentils	8-10 minutes
Kidney beans	6-9 minutes
Chickpeas	10-15 minutes
Black-eyed peas	4-5 minutes
Black beans	6-8 minutes

Seafood and fish:

FOOD	COOKING TIME
Fish stock	7-8 minutes
Shrimp or prawn	1-3 minutes
Mussels	1-2 minutes
Whole fish	4-5 minutes

4-Week Meal Plan

Week 1

Day 1:
Breakfast: Cheese and Sausage Egg Muffins
Lunch: Simple Sicilian Steamed Leeks
Dinner: Homemade Chicken Hawaiian
Dessert: Mini Monkey Breads with Cereal

Day 2:
Breakfast: Mushrooms and Goat Cheese Frittata
Lunch: Cheese Summer Squash and Zucchini
Dinner: Chickpea Curry with Patota
Dessert: Chocolate Cookies Cheesecake

Day 3:
Breakfast: Yummy Bacon Corn Grits
Lunch: Cheese Buffalo Potatoes
Dinner: Pork Roast with Apples and Plums
Dessert: Sweet Bread Pudding with Pomegranates

Day 4:
Breakfast: Greek Quiche with Kalamata Olives
Lunch: Tomato-Based Spaghetti Squash with Olives
Dinner: Nutritious Salsa Chicken Tacos
Dessert: Vanilla Pudding Cups

Day 5:
Breakfast: Homemade Delicious Gravy
Lunch: Tasty Rice Pilaf with Mushrooms
Dinner: Steamed Mussels with Pepper
Dessert: Coconut Banana Bread with Chocolate Chips

Day 6:
Breakfast: Creamy Strawberry Oats
Lunch: Fresh Spiced Beets
Dinner: Chuck Roast with Vegetables
Dessert: Apple Sauce with Pear and Sweet Potato

Day 7:
Breakfast: Nutty Chocolate Banana Quinoa
Lunch: Garlic Ham and Black-Eyed Peas
Dinner: Healthy Vegetable and Beef Soup
Dessert: Yummy Coconut Brownies

Week 2

Day 1:
Breakfast: Peanut Butter and Strawberry Jelly Oatmeal
Lunch: Smoked Ham and White Beans
Dinner: Potato and Chicken Thigh Casserole
Dessert: Simple Chai Spice Rice Pudding

Day 2:
Breakfast: Cheesy Yellow Squash Frittata
Lunch: Classic Chickpea Tagine
Dinner: Herbed Poached Salmon with Carrots
Dessert: Pumpkin Cheesecake with Granola

Day 3:
Breakfast: Cheesy Ham and Egg Muffins
Lunch: Easy Cob-Styled Corn
Dinner: Pork Chops and Acorn Squash
Dessert: Cinnamon Raisin-Filled Apples

Day 4:
Breakfast: Pecan and Apple Oatmeal
Lunch: Simple Sweet Potatoes
Dinner: Cheesy Rice and Chicken Thighs
Dessert: Pumpkin Spice Cheese

Day 5:
Breakfast: Classic French Toast-Cinnamon Roll Casserole
Lunch: Cheesy Zucchini Fritters
Dinner: Simple Steamed Tilapia
Dessert: Sweet Apple Crisp Doughnut

Day 6:
Breakfast: Best Nutty Zucchini Bread
Lunch: Lemony Artichoke with Dipping Sauce
Dinner: Red Beans and Ham Hocks with Rice
Dessert: Lemony Raspberry Curd

Day 7:
Breakfast: Healthy Mixed-Berry Syrup
Lunch: Green Beans with Shallot
Dinner: Creamy Chicken Rice Soup
Dessert: Easy Cranberry-Pear Crisp

Week 3

Day 1:
Breakfast: Creamy Buttermilk Corn Bread
Lunch: Easy Curried Cauliflower
Dinner: Homemade Honey Sriracha Chicken Breast
Dessert: Simple Honey Lemon Curd

Day 2:
Breakfast: Savory Goat Cheese and Bacon Muffins
Lunch: Quick Salty Potatoes
Dinner: Parmesan Haddock Fillets
Dessert: Perfect Chocolate Cake

Day 3:
Breakfast: Chocolate-Hazelnuts French Toast Casserole
Lunch: Garlicky Broccoli
Dinner: Classic Beef Biryani
Dessert: Hot Spiced Apple-Cranberry Cider

Day 4:
Breakfast: Sweet Strawberry Jam with Chia Seeds
Lunch: Honey-Glazed Carrots
Dinner: Homemade Chicken Wings
Dessert: Quick Vanilla Custard

Day 5:
Breakfast: Homemade Peaches Steel-Cut Oats
Lunch: Creamy Mashed Cauliflower
Dinner: Lemony Butter Crab Legs
Dessert: Delicious Dulce De Leche

Day 6:
Breakfast: Peanut Butter and Raisin Granola Bars
Lunch: Traditional Sweet Corn Tamalito
Dinner: Rosemary Pork Tenderloin
Dessert: Savory Butterscotch Pudding

Day 7:
Breakfast: Fresh Mixed Fruit
Lunch: Homemade Corn Bread
Dinner: Simple and Quick Meatloaf
Dessert: Sweet Coconut Rice with Fresh Mango

Week 4

Day 1:
Breakfast: Delicious Maple and Cinnamon Cereal Bowls
Lunch: Cheesy Corn Zucchini Casserole
Dinner: Coconut Tomato Chicken Curry
Dessert: Classic Sugar Flan

Day 2:
Breakfast: Apple Cinnamon Crumb Muffins
Lunch: Savory Red Potato Salad
Dinner: Buttered Lobster Claws
Dessert: Traditional Noodle Kugel

Day 3:
Breakfast: Coconut Banana Oat Cake
Lunch: Summer Vegetable Tian
Dinner: Tasty Barbecued Ribs
Dessert: Buttery Caramel Pears

Day 4:
Breakfast: Easy Traditional Shakshuka
Lunch: Steamed Lemony Artichokes
Dinner: Authentic Adobo Chicken Drumstick
Dessert: Fluffy Eggnog Cheesecake

Day 5:
Breakfast: Classic Huevos Ranchero
Lunch: Italian-Style Asparagus
Dinner: Swiss Steak with Potato and Carrot
Dessert: Banana Cake with Almonds

Day 6:
Breakfast: Soft-Boiled Eggs with Lemony Shredded Kale
Lunch: Refreshing Balsamic-Maple Parsnips
Dinner: Delicious Mediterranean Squid
Dessert: Yummy Key Lime Cake Soufflé

Day 7:
Breakfast: Mini Quiches with Cheese and Mushroom
Lunch: Cider-Braised Brussels Sprouts
Dinner: Mushroom Pork Ragout
Dessert: Soft Lemon Sponge Cake

Chapter 1 Breakfast Recipes

Mushrooms and Goat Cheese Frittata 14

Greek Quiche with Kalamata Olives 14

Cheesy Yellow Squash Frittata 14

Cheesy Ham and Egg Muffins 15

Cheese and Sausage Egg Muffins 15

Apple Cinnamon Crumb Muffins 15

Yummy Bacon Corn Grits 16

Homemade Delicious Gravy 16

Peanut Butter and Strawberry Jelly Oatmeal 16

Pecan and Apple Oatmeal 16

Nutty Chocolate Banana Quinoa 17

Savory Goat Cheese and Bacon Muffins 17

Vanilla Raisin Muffins with Pecans 17

Sweet Bananas Corn Muffins 18

Homemade Peaches Steel-Cut Oats 18

Classic French Toast-Cinnamon Roll Casserole 18

Chocolate-Hazelnuts French Toast Casserole 19

Best Nutty Zucchini Bread 19

Creamy Buttermilk Corn Bread 19

Healthy Mixed-Berry Syrup 20

Sweet Strawberry Jam with Chia Seeds ... 20

Creamy Strawberry Oats..................... 20

Soft-Boiled Eggs with Lemony Shredded Kale 20

Peanut Butter and Raisin Granola Bars ... 21

Fresh Mixed Fruit 21

Delicious Maple and Cinnamon Cereal Bowls 21

Cheese Spinach Frittatas..................... 22

Coconut Banana Oat Cake 22

Easy Traditional Shakshuka 22

Cheesy Leek and Asparagus Frittata 23

Classic Huevos Ranchero 23

Yummy Huevos Rancheros Casserole ... 23

Classic Middle Eastern Baked Eggs 24

Authentic Spanish Omelet 24

Mini Quiches with Cheese and Mushroom 24

Mushrooms and Goat Cheese Frittata

Prep Time: 10 minutes | Cook Time: 13 minutes | Serves: 4

6 large eggs
¼ cup chopped fresh basil leaves
½ cup crumbled goat cheese
½ teaspoon salt
¼ teaspoon ground black pepper

1 tablespoon olive oil
2 cups sliced baby bella mushrooms
1 small yellow onion, peeled and diced
1 cup water

1. Combine the eggs, basil, salt, goat cheese, and pepper in a medium bowl. Place aside. 2. Heat the oil in a pan for 30 seconds and stir fry mushrooms and onions in it for 5 minutes, or until onions are transparent. 3. Place the cooked mushroom mixture in a glass bowl measuring cups, coat it with the cooking spray or oil, and let it cool for 5 minutes. Add the whisked eggs to the cooked mixture, and then toss everything together. 4. Add the water to the instant pot inner pot and insert the steam rack. Put the glass dish with the egg mixture on the steam rack. Lock the lid. 5. Press Pressure Cook button and set time to 8 minutes and level to high. 6. When the timer beeps, allow the steam to release on the seal position and open the lid. 7. Take the dish out of the pot and let it sit for 10 minutes so the eggs can set. Slice and warmly serve.
Per Serving: Calories 182; Fat: 15.17g; Sodium 404mg; Carbs: 2.87g; Sugars: 1.03g; Protein 8.39g

Greek Quiche with Kalamata Olives

Prep Time: 10 minutes | Cook Time: 8 minutes | Serves: 6

6 large eggs
¼ cup whole milk
2 teaspoons chopped fresh dill
½ teaspoon salt
¼ teaspoon ground black pepper
1 Roma tomato, seeded and diced

¼ cup diced jarred artichokes, drained
¼ cup sliced pitted Kalamata olives
¼ cup crumbled feta cheese
¼ cup peeled and diced red onion
2 cups water

1. Whisk the eggs, salt, milk, dill, and pepper in a medium bowl. Add onion, feta cheese, tomato, artichokes, and olives. Place aside. 2. Grease a 7-cup glass dish with the oil or cooking spray and fill it with the egg mixture. 3. Fill the Instant Pot with the water. Put in the steam rack. Place the egg mixture dish on the steam rack. Lid locked. 4. Press Pressure Cook button. Set 8 minutes for the cook time and select level high. When the timer beeps, let the pressure to naturally release for 10 minutes on the seal position, and then quick-release any remaining pressure on the vent position. Then open the lid. 5. Remove the dish from the pot and let it sit for 10 minutes. Slice and warmly serve.
Per Serving: Calories 98; Fat: 6.91g; Sodium 314mg; Carbs: 4.94g; Sugars: 2.47g; Protein 4.51g

Cheesy Yellow Squash Frittata

Prep Time: 10 minutes | Cook Time: 8 minutes | Serves: 4

6 large eggs
2 tablespoons whole milk
2 slices gluten-free bread, cubed
1 teaspoon salt
½ teaspoon ground black pepper

¼ cup shredded Cheddar cheese
3 cups shredded yellow squash (approximately 1 large)
¼ cup peeled and diced sweet onion
1 cup water

1. Mix the eggs and milk together in a medium bowl. Add the bread cubes and let them absorb some of the liquid. Add the cheese, squash, salt, onion, and pepper. 2. Place the egg mixture in a 7-cup glass bowl coated with the cooking oil or cooking spray. 3. Insert the steam rack and add the water to the Instant Pot. Put the glass bowl with the egg mixture on the steam rack. Lock lid. 4. Press Pressure Cook button and set 8 minutes for the cook time and level to High. 5. When the timer beeps, allow the steam to naturally release on the seal position and then open the lid. Take the bowl out of the pot and let it set for 10 minutes until the eggs are set. Slice and warmly serve.
Per Serving: Calories 170; Fat: 8.9g; Sodium 860mg; Carbs: 14.33g; Sugars: 4.95g; Protein 8.61g

Cheesy Ham and Egg Muffins

Prep Time: 10 minutes | Cook Time: 8 minutes | Serves: 6

4 large eggs
½ cup small-diced cooked ham
½ cup grated Swiss cheese
2 teaspoons Dijon mustard

½ teaspoon salt
½ teaspoon ground black pepper
1 cup water

1. Mix the eggs, ham, salt, cheese, Dijon mustard, and pepper in a medium bowl. Spread the egg mixture evenly among the six silicone cupcake liners gently oiled or sprayed with the cooking oil. 2. Add the water to the inner pot of instant pot. Insert the steam rack. Place the muffin cups in the steam rack carefully. Lock lid. 3. Press Pressure Cook button and set 8 minutes for the cook time and level to High. 4. When the timer beeps, quickly release the pressure steam on the vent position and then open the lid. 4. Remove the egg muffins and then serve warm.
Per Serving: Calories 101; Fat: 6.84g; Sodium 493mg; Carbs: 1.46g; Sugars: 0.23g; Protein 8.37g

Cheese and Sausage Egg Muffins

Prep Time: 10 minutes | Cook Time: 13 minutes | Serves: 6

1 tablespoon olive oil
½ small yellow onion, peeled and diced
¼-pound ground pork sausage
4 large eggs

¼ cup grated mozzarella cheese
⅛ teaspoon salt
½ teaspoon ground black pepper
1 cup water

1. Heat the oil in the Instant Pot for 30 seconds by pressing the Sauté button. Add the sausage and onion. Stir-fry the sausage and onions for 5 minutes, or until they begin to brown. Transfer mixture to a small bowl to cool. 2. Whisk the eggs, cheese, salt, and pepper in a medium bowl. Add the egg mixture to the cooled onion mixture. Spread the egg mixture evenly among the six silicone cupcake liners gently oiled or sprayed with the cooking oil. 3. Add the water to the inner pot and insert the steam rack. Place the cupcake liners in the steam rack carefully. Lock lid. 4. Press Pressure Cook button and set 8 minutes for the cook time and level to High. 5. When the timer beeps, quickly release the pressure steam on the vent position and then open the lid. 6. Remove the egg muffins and then serve warm.
Per Serving: Calories 122; Fat: 9.2g; Sodium 107mg; Carbs: 1.28g; Sugars: 0.38g; Protein 8.24g

Apple Cinnamon Crumb Muffins

Prep Time: 10 minutes | Cook Time: 9 minutes | Serves: 6

Muffins
1¼ cups gluten-free all-purpose flour
2 teaspoons gluten-free baking powder
½ teaspoon baking soda
1 teaspoon ground cinnamon
⅛ teaspoon salt
1 cup water
Crumb Topping
2 tablespoons gluten-free all-purpose flour
¼ cup light brown sugar
⅛ teaspoon ground cinnamon

½ teaspoon vanilla extract
3 tablespoons unsalted butter, melted
2 large eggs
¼ cup granulated sugar
¼ cup grated, peeled red apple

⅛ teaspoon salt
2 tablespoons unsalted butter, softened

1. Combine the flour, baking soda, cinnamon, salt, and baking powder in a big bowl. 2. Combine the apple, butter, eggs, sugar, and vanilla in a medium bowl. 3. Add the wet ingredients to the dry ingredients. Mix the ingredients gently. Avoid overmixing. Fill six silicone cupcake liners with the mixture and gently coat with the oil or cooking spray. 4. Use a fork to stir the ingredients for the crumb topping in a small bowl, working the butter into the dry ingredients to produce a crumbly consistency. Sprinkle the mixture on top after evenly distributing this among the cupcakes. 5. Add the water to the Instant Pot and insert the steam rack. Place the cupcake liners on the rack. Lock lid. 6. Select the Pressure Cook button, then set the level to High and timer for the 9 minutes. 7. When the timer beeps, quickly release the pressure steam on the vent position and then open the lid. 8. Take the muffins out of the pot and let them cool for 5 minutes before serving.
Per Serving: Calories 352; Fat: 8.54g; Sodium 114mg; Carbs: 60.91g; Sugars: 13.69g; Protein 7.52g

Yummy Bacon Corn Grits

Prep Time: 5 minutes | Cook Time: 15 minutes |Serves: 6

4 slices bacon, diced
5 cups water
1 cup coarse corn grits

2 tablespoons unsalted butter
½ teaspoon salt
½ cup shredded sharp Cheddar cheese

1. Choose the Sauté button on the Instant Pot. Add the bacon to the pot. Stir for 5 minutes until the bacon is crispy. Then place the bacon on a small dish lined with paper towels to cool. 2. Combine the salt, butter, water, and grits in the Instant Pot inner pot. Lock lid. 3. Press Pressure Cook button and set level to High and timer to 10 minutes. 4. When the timer beeps, quickly release the pressure steam on the vent position and then open the lid. Whisk the grits in the pot for 5 minutes until they thicken. Add the cheese and fried bacon. 5. Spoon the grits into the dishes and serve.
Per Serving: Calories 171; Fat: 13.18g; Sodium 652mg; Carbs: 7.8g; Sugars: 1.77g; Protein 5.74g

Homemade Delicious Gravy

Prep Time: 5 minutes | Cook Time: 17 minutes |Serves: 10

2 tablespoons unsalted butter
1-pound ground pork sausage
1 small sweet onion, peeled and diced
¼ cup chicken broth
¼ cup gluten-free all-purpose flour

1 tablespoon cornmeal
1½ cups whole milk
½ teaspoon salt
1 tablespoon ground black pepper

1. Choose the Sauté button on the Instant Pot. Melt the butter in the pot by heating it for 1 minute. Add the onion and sausage. Stir-fry for 5 minutes or until onions are transparent. 2. Place the chicken broth into the Instant Pot. Lock lid. 3. Press Pressure Cook button and set level to high and time to 1 minute. 4. When the timer beeps, quickly release the pressure steam on the vent position and then open the lid. 5. Add the milk, cornmeal, salt, flour, and pepper while whisking. Press the Keep Warm button. 6. After 10 minutes, stir the gravy once or twice to help the sauce thicken. 7. Remove gravy from heat and serve warm.
Per Serving: Calories 307; Fat: 15.6g; Sodium 237mg; Carbs: 23.48g; Sugars: 18.92g; Protein 17.76g

Peanut Butter and Strawberry Jelly Oatmeal

Prep Time: 5 minutes | Cook Time: 7 minutes |Serves: 2

1 cup old-fashioned oats
1¼ cups water
⅛ teaspoon salt

2 teaspoons smooth peanut butter
2 tablespoons strawberry jelly
¼ cup whole milk

1. Add the salt, water, and oats to the Instant Pot. Lock lid. 2. Press Pressure Cook button and set level to Low and time to 7 minutes. 3. After the timer beeps, allow the steam to naturally release on the seal position and then open the lid. 4. Divide the oatmeal into two dishes. Add peanut butter and jelly and stir. Add milk. Serve hot.
Per Serving: Calories 173; Fat: 5.24g; Sodium 258mg; Carbs: 40.12g; Sugars: 9.09g; Protein 9.5g

Pecan and Apple Oatmeal

Prep Time: 5 minutes | Cook Time: 7 minutes |Serves: 2

1 cup old-fashioned oats
1¼ cups water
1 peeled and cored Granny Smith apple, diced
¼ teaspoon ground cinnamon
⅛ teaspoon salt

2 tablespoons light brown sugar
¼ teaspoon vanilla extract
¼ cup chopped pecans
4 tablespoons whole milk

1. Add the oats, water, apple, cinnamon, and salt to the Instant Pot inner pot. Lock lid. 2. Press Pressure Cook button and set level to Low and time to 7 minutes. 3. When the timer beeps, allow the steam to naturally release on the seal position and then open the lid. 4. Add the vanilla and brown sugar to stir. Divide the oatmeal into two dishes. Garnish with pecans over the oatmeal and pour in milk. Serve hot.
Per Serving: Calories 336; Fat: 13.29g; Sodium 181mg; Carbs: 63.05g; Sugars: 27.57g; Protein 10.54g

Nutty Chocolate Banana Quinoa

Prep Time: 5 minutes | Cook Time: 20 minutes | Serves: 4

1 cup quinoa
1¼ cups water
1½ cups whole milk, divided
2 tablespoons unsalted butter
1 teaspoon unsweetened cocoa

1 tablespoon light brown sugar
½ teaspoon salt
2 tablespoons semisweet chocolate chips
2 medium bananas, diced
¼ cup chopped pecans

1. Add the quinoa, water, half a cup of milk, butter, chocolate, sugar, and salt to the Instant Pot. Stir well. Lock lid. 2. Select the Pressure Cook button, then set the level to High and timer for 20 minutes. 3. When the timer beeps, quickly release the pressure steam on the vent position and then open the lid. 4. Transfer the quinoa to a serving dish and fluff it with a fork. Add the chocolate chips, then toss three times. Garnish with the diced bananas and chopped pecans over the quinoa, then pour the remaining 1 cup of milk. Serve right away.
Per Serving: Calories 596; Fat: 23.18g; Sodium 447mg; Carbs: 82.03g; Sugars: 50.1g; Protein 17.43g

Savory Goat Cheese and Bacon Muffins

Prep Time: 5 minutes | Cook Time: 15 minutes | Serves: 6

4 slices bacon, diced
½ small yellow onion, peeled and diced
1 cup buckwheat flour
2 teaspoons gluten-free baking powder
½ teaspoon baking soda

½ teaspoon ground black pepper
3 tablespoons unsalted butter, melted
2 large eggs, whisked
½ cup crumbled goat cheese
1 cup water

1. Choose the Sauté button on the Instant Pot. Add bacon and onion to the pot. Stir-fry for 5 minutes, or until bacon is crisp and onions begin to brown. Transfer the mixture to a small bowl lined with paper towels to cool before using. 2. Combine the flour, butter, eggs, pepper, baking soda, and baking powder in a medium bowl. Combine the cooled bacon mixture with the goat cheese. Spread the mixture evenly into six silicone cupcake liners gently oiled or sprayed with the cooking spray. 3. Add the water to the inner pot and insert the steam rack. Place the cupcake liners in the steam rack carefully. Lock lid. 4. Press Pressure Cook button and set 8 minutes for the cook time and level to High. 5. When the timer beeps, quickly release the pressure steam on the vent position and then open the lid. 6. Remove the egg muffins and then serve warm.
Per Serving: Calories 236; Fat: 16.14g; Sodium 157mg; Carbs: 16.03g; Sugars: 1g; Protein 8.61g

Vanilla Raisin Muffins with Pecans

Prep Time: 10 minutes | Cook Time: 9 minutes | Serves: 6

¾ cup gluten-free all-purpose flour
¼ cup old-fashioned oats
¼ cup raisins
2 tablespoons chopped pecans
1 tablespoon salted sunflower seeds
1 tablespoon peanut butter chips
¼ cup granulated sugar
2 teaspoons gluten-free baking powder

½ teaspoon baking soda
¼ teaspoon ground cinnamon
⅛ teaspoon salt
1 teaspoon vanilla extract
4 tablespoons unsalted butter, melted and cooled
2 large eggs, whisked
1 cup water

1. Mix the flour, oats, raisins, pecans, sunflower seeds, peanut butter chips, sugar, baking soda, cinnamon, and salt in a large bowl. 2. Combine the eggs, butter, and vanilla in a medium bowl. 3. Add the wet ingredients to the dry ingredients. Mix the ingredients gently. Avoid overmixing. Fill six silicone cupcake liners with the mixture and gently coat with the oil or cooking spray. 4. Add the water to the Instant Pot and insert the steam rack. Place the muffin cups on the steam rack. Lid locked. 5. Select the Pressure Cook button, then set the level to High and timer for the 9 minutes. 6. When the timer beeps, quickly release the pressure steam on the vent position and then open the lid. 7. Take the muffins out of the pot and let them cool for 5 minutes before serving.
Per Serving: Calories 192; Fat: 10.77g; Sodium 119mg; Carbs: 21.44g; Sugars: 5.13g; Protein 4.37g

Sweet Bananas Corn Muffins

Prep Time: 10 minutes | Cook Time: 9 minutes | Serves: 6

¾ cup gluten-free all-purpose flour
½ cup self-rising cornmeal
2 tablespoons granulated sugar
2 teaspoons gluten-free baking powder
½ teaspoon baking soda
⅛ teaspoon salt

½ teaspoon vanilla extract
3 tablespoons unsalted butter, melted
2 large eggs
2 ripe medium bananas, mashed with fork
1 cup water

1. Combine the flour, cornmeal, sugar, baking powder, baking soda, and salt in a large bowl. 2. Combine the vanilla, butter, eggs, and bananas in a medium bowl. 3. Add the wet ingredients to the dry ingredients. Mix the ingredients gently. Avoid overmixing. Fill six silicone cupcake liners with the mixture and gently coat with the oil or cooking spray. 4. Add the water to the Instant Pot and insert the steam rack. Place the muffin cups on the steam rack. Lock lid. 5. Select the Pressure Cook button, then set the level to High and timer for the 9 minutes. 6. When the timer beeps, quickly release the pressure steam on the vent position and then open the lid. 7. Take the muffins out of the pot and let them cool for 5 minutes before serving.
Per Serving: Calories 199; Fat: 5.85g; Sodium 215mg; Carbs: 33.2g; Sugars: 7.54g; Protein 4.14g

Homemade Peaches Steel-Cut Oats

Prep Time: 5 minutes | Cook Time: 4 minutes | Serves: 4

2 cups steel-cut oats
4 cups water
1 pound frozen sliced peaches

½ teaspoon ground cinnamon, plus more for serving (optional)
¼ cup pure maple syrup
½ cup full-fat coconut milk, plus more for serving (optional)

1. Stir the water and steel-cut oats together in Instant Pot and then add the peaches, cinnamon, and maple syrup. Move the steam release valve to seal position and close the lid. Choose Pressure Cook for 4 minutes, cook under high pressure. 2. After the cooking cycle is over, allow the pressure to naturally relax for 15 minutes. To discharge any leftover steam pressure, turn the steam release valve to the vent position. Remove the lid after the floating valve drops. 3. Stir in the coconut milk, then taste and adjust any seasonings. If preferred, top with more cinnamon or coconut milk and serve warm. Oats may be kept in the refrigerator for five days in an airtight container. Serve them chilled, or quickly reheat them using the Sauté function of your Instant Pot.
Per Serving: Calories 343; Fat10.6g; Sodium 20mg; Carbs: 74g; Sugars: 39g; Protein 9g

Classic French Toast-Cinnamon Roll Casserole

Prep Time: 10 minutes | Cook Time: 25 minutes | Serves: 4

Casserole
4 cups cubed gluten-free bread, dried out overnight
2 cups whole milk
3 large eggs
1 teaspoon vanilla extract
2 tablespoons pure maple syrup
1 teaspoon ground cinnamon
Cream Cheese Drizzle
1 tablespoon whole milk
1 tablespoon powdered sugar

⅛ teaspoon salt
¼ cup raisins
2 tablespoons chopped pecans
2 tablespoons unsalted butter, melted and cooled
1 cup water

2 tablespoons cream cheese

1. Add the bread to a 7-cup glass dish greased with the oil or cooking spray. Place aside. 2. Mix the milk, eggs, vanilla, maple syrup, cinnamon, and salt in a medium bowl. Pour onto the bread in the glass bowl. Spread the bread with the raisins, pecans, and butter evenly distributed. 3. Add the water to the Instant Pot and put in the steam rack. Then place the glass dish on rack. Lock lid. 4. Press the Pressure Cook button and adjust cook time to 25 minutes and level to high. When the timer beeps, quickly release the pressure steam on the vent position and then open the lid. 5. Remove the glass bowl, place on a rack, and cool for 10 minutes. 6. In a small bowl, mix the milk, cream cheese, and sugar. Pour over the casserole. Serve dish by portioning it into four bowls.
Per Serving: Calories 516; Fat: 17.59g; Sodium 593mg; Carbs: 70.09g; Sugars: 25.74g; Protein 18.86g

Chocolate-Hazelnuts French Toast Casserole

Prep Time: 10 minutes | Cook Time: 25 minutes | Serves: 4

4 cups cubed gluten-free bread, dried out overnight
4 tablespoons chocolate hazelnut spread
2 cups whole milk
3 large eggs
1 teaspoon vanilla extract

2 tablespoons granulated sugar
⅛ teaspoon salt
3 tablespoons unsalted butter, cut into 6 pats
1 cup water
2 tablespoons powdered sugar

1. Add the bread to a 7-cup glass dish greased with the oil or cooking spray. Place aside. 2. Mix the chocolate hazelnut spread, milk, eggs, sugar, vanilla, and salt in a medium bowl. Pour onto the bread in the glass bowl. Add the butter pats on top. 3. Add the water to the Instant Pot and put in the steam rack. Then place the glass dish on the steam rack. Lock lid. 4. Select the Pressure Cook button, then set the level to High and timer for the 25 minutes. 5. When the timer beeps, quickly release the pressure steam on the vent position and then open the lid. 5. Take the glass bowl out of the pot, place on a rack, and cool for 10 minutes. 6. Serve the dish with a dusting of powdered sugar.
Per Serving: Calories 683; Fat: 26.12g; Sodium 564mg; Carbs: 91.12g; Sugars: 45.13g; Protein 20.1g

Best Nutty Zucchini Bread

Prep Time: 10 minutes | Cook Time: 30 minutes | Serves: 6

2 large eggs
4 tablespoons whole milk
4 tablespoons unsalted butter, melted and cooled
½ cup grated zucchini (approximately 1 medium)
1⅓ cups gluten-free all-purpose flour
1½ teaspoons gluten-free baking powder

½ teaspoon baking soda
½ cup granulated sugar
½ teaspoon ground cinnamon
⅛ teaspoon salt
¼ cup chopped pecans
1 cup water

1. Set aside a 7"springform pan lightly greased with the cooking spray or oil. 2. Mix the eggs, milk, and butter in a medium bowl before adding the zucchini. 3. Combine the flour, baking powder, baking soda, sugar, cinnamon, and salt in a large basin. Do not overmix as some lumps are OK. 4. Add the wet ingredients to the dry ingredients and stir until incorporated. Fold in the pecans. 5. Put the mixture in the oiled pan. 6. Add the water to the Instant Pot and put in the steam rack. Then place the pan on the steam rack. Lock lid. 7. Select the Pressure Cook button, then set the level to High and timer for the 30 minutes. 8. When the timer beeps, quickly release the pressure steam on the vent position and then open the lid. 9. Unlock the pan and let cool for 10 minutes. Slice and serve.
Per Serving: Calories 409; Fat: 10.4g; Sodium 64mg; Carbs: 69.8g; Sugars: 8.56g; Protein 9.52g

Creamy Buttermilk Corn Bread

Prep Time: 10 minutes | Cook Time: 30 minutes | Serves: 4

1 large egg
1½ cups self-rising buttermilk cornmeal mix
½ cup creamed corn
⅓ cup peeled and diced sweet onion
½ cup whole milk

1 tablespoon unsalted butter, melted
½ teaspoon granulated sugar
⅛ teaspoon salt
⅛ teaspoon ground pepper
1 cup water

1. Set aside a 7"springform pan lightly greased with the cooking spray or oil. 2. Combine the egg, cornmeal, creamed corn, onion, milk, butter, sugar, salt, and pepper in a big bowl. 3. Put the mixture in the oiled pan. 4. Add the salt, water to the Instant Pot and put in the steam rack. Then place the pan on the steam rack. Lock lid. 5. Select the Pressure Cook button, then set the level to High and timer for the 30 minutes. 6. When the timer beeps, quickly release the pressure steam on the vent position and then open the lid. 7. Unlock the pan. Slice and serve.
Per Serving: Calories 819; Fat: 8.27g; Sodium 2663mg; Carbs: 164g; Sugars: 5.8g; Protein 16.86g

Healthy Mixed-Berry Syrup

Prep Time: 5 minutes | Cook Time: 3 minutes |Serves: 1

1 pound frozen mixed berries
1 tablespoon unsalted butter
½ cup pure maple syrup
¼ cup freshly squeezed orange juice

1 tablespoon orange zest
¼ teaspoon vanilla extract
⅛ teaspoon salt

1. Combine all the ingredients to the Instant Pot. Lock lid. 2. Press the Pressure Cook button and set level to high and adjust cook time to 3 minutes. 3. When the timer beeps, quickly release the pressure steam on the vent position and then open the lid. 4. Serve hot or cold.
Per Serving: Calories 1097; Fat: 24.23g; Sodium 621mg; Carbs: 213g; Sugars: 192g; Protein 14.66g

Sweet Strawberry Jam with Chia Seeds

Prep Time: 5 minutes | Cook Time: 20 minutes |Serves: 15

1 pound frozen strawberries
¼ cup pure maple syrup

Pinch of fine sea salt
2 tablespoons chia seeds

1. Combine the salt, maple syrup, and frozen strawberries in the Instant Pot. Lock the lid. Select Pressure Cook and turn the steam release valve to the seal position. Set time to 1 minute and level to high pressure. 2. After the cooking cycle is over, release the pressure naturally on the seal position for 10 minutes, then switch the steam release valve to vent position to allow any residual pressure out. Remove the lid and click Cancel to end the cooking cycle when the floating valve descends. 3. Add the chia seeds and then press the Sauté button. Simmer the jam for about 5 minutes, stirring often to prevent it from sticking to the bottom of pan. 4. Press Cancel button to halt the cooking process after the mixture has somewhat thickened or if the jam begins to adhere to the pan. Put the jam in a 16-ounce glass jar with a lid and then place it in the refrigerator so that it may chill and thicken. The jam should keep in the fridge for 2 weeks.
Per Serving: Calories 1202; Fat: 107g; Sodium 1994mg; Carbs: 50g; Sugars: 11.73g; Protein 17.13g

Creamy Strawberry Oats

Prep Time: 5 minutes | Cook Time: 7 minutes |Serves: 2

1 cup old-fashioned oats
1 cup water
½ cup whole milk
2 cups diced fresh strawberries, hulled

2 tablespoons granulated sugar
¼ teaspoon vanilla extract
¼ teaspoon ground cinnamon
⅛ teaspoon salt

1. Fill the Instant Pot with the oats, water, milk, strawberries, sugar, vanilla, cinnamon, and salt and mix well. Lock lid. 2. Press Pressure Cook button. Set level to High and timer to 7 minutes. 3. When the timer beeps, quickly release the pressure steam on the vent position and then open the lid. 4. Stir well, then pour the oatmeal into two dishes. Serve hot.
Per Serving: Calories 250; Fat: 5.6g; Sodium 188mg; Carbs: 58.3g; Sugars: 23.4g; Protein 10.92g

Soft-Boiled Eggs with Lemony Shredded Kale

Prep Time: 5 minutes | Cook Time: 5 minutes |Serves: 4

4 large eggs
4 cups shredded kale
Juice of 1 lemon

Extra-virgin olive oil, for serving
Pinch flaky sea salt
Salsa Verde, for serving (optional)

1. Add 1 cup of water to the Instant Pot and put the steam rack inside. 2. Place the eggs in a row on the rack. Lock the lid by closing it. 3. Choose Pressure Cook and cook for 5 minutes at low pressure for a hard-boiled egg or 3 minutes at low pressure for a soft-boiled egg with a runny yolk. 4. While the eggs are cooking, in a mixing dish, combine the kale with the lemon juice, olive oil, and sea salt. 5. After cooking is finished, release the steam from the vent position and carefully remove the lid. Give the eggs a thorough rinse in the cold water and then peel them. 6. Place the dressed kale, two halves of an egg, and salsa verde on each platter.
Per Serving: Calories 65; Fat 4.6g; Sodium 14mg; Carbs: 2.87g; Sugars: 1.03g; Protein 3.39g

Peanut Butter and Raisin Granola Bars

Prep Time: 5 minutes | Cook Time: 20 minutes | Serves: 10

cup quick-cooking oats
⅓ cup pure maple syrup
½ cup all-natural peanut butter
tablespoon extra-virgin olive oil

¼ teaspoon fine sea salt
⅓ cup dried cranberries or raisins
½ cup raw pumpkin seeds (pepitas)

. Line a 7-inch round pan with parchment paper. 2. In a large bowl, combine the oats, maple syrup, peanut butter, olive oil, and salt and stir well. Fold in the dried fruit and pumpkin seeds. Then pour the batter into the ready pan and press the mixture into the bottom of the pan with a spatula. 3. Add 1 cup of water to the Instant Pot and place the steam rack in it. Put the pan on top of the rack. To shield the granola bars from condensation, place another piece of parchment or an upside-down plate over the pan. Move the steam release valve to the seal position and tighten the lid. Choose Pressure Cook and set timer to 20 minutes at high pressure. 4. After the timer beeps, allow the pressure to drop naturally for 10 minutes on the seal position, then switch the steam release valve to the vent position. After the floating valve has drops, remove the lid. Lift the rack and the pan from the pot using oven mitts. Allow at least an hour for the granola to cool fully in the pan. 5. Cut the chilled granola into 10 pieces. The bars will have various sizes because to the circular pan, but if you'd like, you may cut them into consistent wedges. They may be kept in the refrigerator for two weeks by individually wrapping them in the plastic wrap or putting them in an airtight container.
Per Serving: Calories 154; Fat: 8.7g; Sodium 166mg; Carbs: 16.6g; Sugar 8.73g; Protein 7g

Fresh Mixed Fruit

Prep Time: 5 minutes | Cook Time: 1 minutes | Serves: 6

pound sliced frozen peaches
pound frozen pineapple chunks
cup frozen and pitted dark sweet cherries
2 ripe pears, sliced

¼ cup pure maple syrup
1 teaspoon curry powder, plus more as needed
Steel-cut oatmeal, for serving (optional)

. Combine the peaches, pineapple, cherries, pears, maple syrup, and curry powder in the Instant Pot. Cover the pot. Select Pressure Cook and turn the steam release valve to the seal position. Set time to 1 minute, and level to high pressure. 2. Once the cooking cycle is over, move the steam release valve to vent position to swiftly remove the steam pressure. Remove the lid when the floating valve drops and thoroughly stir the mixture. If you like your food spicy, add more curry powder. 3. Add the warm fruit to the oatmeal or served as a side dish. When this meal is finished, submerge the fruit in the liquid. Scoop it with a slotted spoon and let the juices drain back into the pot before serving. Store leftovers in an airtight container in the fridge for 5 days.
Per Serving: Calories 217; Fat 0.32g; Sodium 8mg; Carbs: 55g; Sugars: 50g; Protein 1.41g

Delicious Maple and Cinnamon Cereal Bowls

Prep Time: 5 minutes | Cook Time: 1 minutes | Serves: 6

cups buckwheat groats, soaked for at least 20 minutes and up to
overnight
cups water
teaspoon ground cinnamon
¼ cup pure maple syrup

1 teaspoon vanilla extract
¼ teaspoon fine sea salt
Almond milk, for serving
Chopped or sliced fresh fruit, for serving

. Rinse the buckwheat and drain. Then add the buckwheat to the Instant Pot along with water, salt, cinnamon, maple syrup, vanilla, and vanilla extract. Select Pressure Cook and turn the steam release valve to the Seal position. Set time to 1 minute and level to high pressure. 2. Before switching the steam release valve to vent position, let the pressure to naturally dissipate for 10 minutes on the seal position. Carefully remove the lid and stir the cooked grains when the floating valve descends. 3. You may immediately serve the buckwheat with the almond milk and fruit, or you can store approximately 1 cup of the cooked grains in each of several airtight containers and keep them in the refrigerator for a week, serving them cold or warm for a quick weekday breakfast.
Per Serving: Calories 89; Fat: 0.3g; Sodium 103mg; Carbs: 20g; Sugar 8.5g; Protein 1.9g

Cheese Spinach Frittatas

Prep Time: 10 minutes | Cook Time: 20 minutes | Serves: 4

6 eggs
½ teaspoon fine sea salt
1 red bell pepper, seeded and chopped
3 green onions, tender white and green parts only, chopped

1 cup chopped spinach
¼ cup crumbled feta cheese
Freshly ground black pepper

1. In a mixing dish, combine the eggs, salt, feta, bell pepper, green onions, spinach, and a few grinds of black pepper. Stir thoroughly. 2. Divide the mixture equally among the four 8-ounce Mason jars lightly greased with the olive oil. 3. Add 1 cup of water and place the steam rack on the bottom of the Instant Pot. Arrange the four jars in a single layer on the rack and lock the lids. Select Pressure Cook and turn the steam release valve to the seal position. Set time to 8 minutes and cook under high pressure. Allow the pressure to drop naturally for 10 minutes on the seal position before turning the steam release valve to the vent position to let out any leftover steam. 4. Use oven mitts to remove the jars. Tip the frittatas out of the jars and onto plates to serve warm, or cover the jars and store in the fridge for 5 days. Enjoy these frittatas chilled or reheat them, if desired.
Per Serving: Calories 240; Fat 16.78g; Sodium 554mg; Carbs: 6g; Sugars: 4.03g; Protein 15.39g

Coconut Banana Oat Cake

Prep Time: 10 minutes | Cook Time: 40 minutes | Serves: 8

½ cup mashed ripe banana (1 large banana)
½ cup almond butter
½ cup coconut sugar
2 eggs

½ teaspoon baking soda
½ teaspoon cinnamon
¼ teaspoon fine sea salt
1 cup quick-cooking oats

1. Put a piece of parchment paper into a 7-inch circular pan and put it aside. 2. Combine the banana, almond butter, eggs, baking soda, coconut sugar, cinnamon, and salt in a big basin. Thoroughly stir to remove any lumps, then add the oats. Pour the batter into the prepared pan and level the top with a spatula. 3. Add 1 cup of water to the Instant Pot, and place the steam rack on the bottom, and place the pan on top of the rack. Cover the cake with an upside-down dish or some more parchment paper to prevent condensation. 4. Close the lid, then switch the pressure valve to the seal position. Choose Pressure Cook for 40 minutes at high pressure, then allow the pressure drop naturally for 10 minutes. To vent any residual steam, turn the steam release valve to the vent position. Remove the lid after the floating valve drops. 5. Lift the rack and the pan from the pot using oven mitts. Let the cake firm up fully in the pan for around 30 minutes, then remove it from the pan. Slice and serve refrigerated or at room temperature. For a week, keep leftovers in the refrigerator in an airtight container.
Per Serving: Calories 172; Fat: 11.17g; Sodium 213mg; Carbs: 14g; Sugars: 8.03g; Protein 6.39g

Easy Traditional Shakshuka

Prep Time: 10 minutes | Cook Time: 5 minutes | Serves: 4

1 tablespoon extra-virgin olive oil
½ yellow onion, chopped
2 cloves garlic, minced
Fine sea salt
¼ cup water
2½ cups marinara sauce

1 cup chopped kale, stems removed
4 eggs
Freshly ground black pepper
Crumbled feta or grated Parmesan cheese, for garnish (optional)
Chopped fresh flat-leaf parsley or basil, for garnish (optional)
Toast slices, for serving (optional)

1. Add the olive oil to the Instant Pot and select Sauté. Add the garlic, onion, and a bit of salt but not smoking oil and sauté for about 5 minutes or until the vegetables are tender. Add the water, marinara sauce, and kale. Then, with a wooden spoon, thoroughly mix to scraping the pot's bottom to prevent anything from sticking. 2. Select Cancel. Create four perfectly spaced little wells in the marinara sauce using the spoon, and then delicately crack an egg into each one of them. Add the pepper and salt to the eggs as desired. 3. Move the steam release valve to the seal position and fasten the lid. Choose Pressure Cook for 2 minutes under high pressure. When the timer beeps, quickly release the pressure by immediately moving the steam release valve to the vent position. 4. Take off the lid until the floating valve drops, then scoop the eggs, sauce, and a good amount of the cooked vegetables into a small serving dish. Serve immediately as is or with a couple slices of bread, garnished with the cheese and chopped parsley.
Per Serving: Calories 244; Fat: 14.17g; Sodium 184mg; Carbs: 15.87g; Sugars: 10.3g; Protein 11.39g

Cheesy Leek and Asparagus Frittata

Prep Time: 10 minutes | Cook Time: 10 minutes |Serves: 4

5 eggs
¼ teaspoon fine sea salt
Freshly ground black pepper
8 ounces asparagus spears, woody stems removed, cut into 1-inch pieces

1 cup thinly sliced leeks
¼ cup grated Parmesan cheese
Chopped green onions, for garnish
Fresh flat-leaf parsley, for garnish

1. To avoid sticking, thoroughly grease a 7-inch circular pan with the olive oil. Add the salt, a few pinches of black pepper, and the eggs, then beat the eggs thoroughly with a fork in a large mixing basin. Add the Parmesan, leeks, and asparagus and pour the mixture into the prepared pan. 2. Add 1 cup of water to the Instant Pot, and place the steam rack on the bottom, and place the pan on top of the rack. Move the steam release valve to seal and fasten the lid. Choose Pressure Cook for 10 minutes at high pressure. After 10 minutes of natural pressure release, turn the steam release valve to the vent position to let off any leftover pressure. Take the lid off when the floating valve drops. 3. Use the oven mitts to lift the rack and the pan out of the pot. Before cutting and serving, allow the frittata to cool in the pan for 5 minutes. For 5 days, keep leftovers in the refrigerator in an airtight container.
Per Serving: Calories 322; Fat: 21g; Sodium 755mg; Carbs: 10.7g; Sugars: 2.03g; Protein 22.39g

Classic Huevos Ranchero

Prep Time: 5 minutes | Cook Time: 6 minutes |Serves: 6

1 tablespoon extra-virgin olive oil
½ red onion, chopped
1 green bell pepper, seeded and chopped
1 teaspoon ground cumin
⅛ teaspoon cayenne pepper (optional)
1½ cups cooked black beans, or one 15-ounce can black beans, drained and rinsed

1½ cups prepared salsa, plus more for serving
½ cup water
6 eggs
Fine sea salt and freshly ground black pepper
6 corn tortillas
Chopped green onions, crumbled feta cheese, sliced avocado, and chopped fresh cilantro, for garnish (optional)

1. Add the olive oil to the Instant Pot and select Sauté. Place in the onion and bell pepper to the heated but not smoking oil and sauté for about 6 minutes, or until soft. Press the Cancel button, then, while the pot is still hot, mix in the cumin and cayenne. 2. Fill the pot with the water, add the beans, and stir thoroughly, scraping the bottom to make sure nothing sticks. Keeping the eggs at least an inch apart, carefully cracks them into the salsa. Sprinkle with the salt and black pepper over every egg. 3. Secure the lid and move the steam release valve to the seal position. Select Pressure Cook and cook on high pressure for 2 minutes. 4. When the timer beeps, quickly release the pressure steam on the vent position and then open the lid. 5. Use a slotted spoon to scoop the eggs and portion of the salsa mixture onto a tortilla after timer beeps. Serve immediately after adding more salsa and your preferred toppings.
Per Serving: Calories 171; Fat: 11g; Sodium 583mg; Carbs: 7.87g; Sugars: 3.03g; Protein 10.39g

Yummy Huevos Rancheros Casserole

Prep Time: 10 minutes | Cook Time: 10 minutes |Serves: 4

Cooking spray
2 corn tortillas
1 (15-ounce) can black beans, drained or 1¾ cups cooked black beans
Salt
Freshly ground black pepper
Salsa Roja or store-bought salsa, for serving

4 large eggs

Fresh cilantro leaves, chopped, for serving
Herby Queso Fresco, crema, or sour cream for serving (optional)

1. Add 1 cup of water to the Instant Pot and put the steam rack inside. 2. Place the tortillas on the bottom of a 7-inch circular baking dish sprayed with cooking spray. 3. On top of the tortillas, pour the black beans. Create four holes in the beans with a spoon, and then carefully crack the eggs into the holes. Add salt and pepper to taste. 4. Place aluminum foil over the dish before carefully setting it down on the rack. Lock the lid by closing it. 5. Choose the Pressure Cook mode, and cook at high pressure for 7 minutes. Once the food has finished cooking, quickly remove the steam on the seal position. Carefully unlock and remove the lid. 6. Carefully remove the dish from the pot and remove the foil. Serve, topped with the salsa roja, chopped cilantro, and queso fresco (if using).
Per Serving: Calories 207; Fat: 6g; Sodium 24mg; Carbs: 31.87g; Sugar0.89g; Protein 7.39g

Classic Middle Eastern Baked Eggs

Prep Time: 10 minutes | Cook Time: 10 minutes | Serves: 6

2 cups Sofrito Base Sauce
6 large eggs
Salt

Freshly ground black pepper
1 teaspoon sumac
Fresh cilantro leaves, chopped, for garnish

1. Add 1 cup of water to the Instant Pot and put the steam rack inside. 2. Add the sofrito sauce to a 7-inch baking dish. Make six indentations in the sofrito using a wooden spoon. Be cautious not to crack the yolks when you crack each egg into one of the indentations. 3. Add the pepper and salt to the eggs as desired. Place the dish on the steam rack with the foil covering it. Put the lid on. 4. Choose the Pressure Cook, for a set egg cook continuously for 7 minutes at low pressure. For a runnier yolk, cook continuously for 2 minutes at low pressure. Once the food has finished cooking, quickly remove the steam on the vent position. Take off the lid. 5. Remove the foil before carefully removing the dish from the pot. Sprinkle the sumac and chopped cilantro on top, and serve.
Per Serving: Calories 217; Fat: 17g; Sodium 794mg; Carbs: 4.87g; Sugars: 0.1g; Protein 11.39g

Authentic Spanish Omelet

Prep Time: 10 minutes | Cook Time: 30 minutes | Serves: 6

Cooking spray
2 tablespoons extra-virgin olive oil
2 cups julienned onions
2 medium waxy potatoes (like red potatoes or fingerling potatoes), cut

into thin rounds
8 large eggs
Salt

1. Spray the cooking oil in a 7-inch baking dish. 2. Add the potatoes, onions, and olive oil, then choose the Sauté option. Add a bit of salt to help the onions release their moisture and start cooking. When the potatoes and onions are tender and transparent, add a little extra oil if they become too dry. Reduce the heat if they begin to turn brown and cover them for a while so they can release more moisture. You don't want them to get caramelized or brown. 3. For about 15 minutes, until the mixture is soft, keep stirring and moving it with a wooden spoon so it doesn't stick to the bottom of the pan. When finished, take the potatoes and onions out of the pot and place them aside to cool. 4. Whip the eggs in a medium bowl in the meanwhile. 5. Combine the eggs with the potato and onion mixture and pour into the prepared baking dish. Use aluminum foil to protect. 6. Add 1½ cup of water to the Instant Pot and put in the steam rack. Place the baking pan very gently on the rack. Close the lid. 7. Choose the Pressure Cook mode, and cook at high pressure for 15 minutes. After cooking is finished, let the steam out naturally on the seal position. Carefully remove the cover after unlocking. 8. Remove the dish from the pot carefully. Unmold the frittata onto a platter after removing the foil. Serve.
Per Serving: Calories 132; Fat: 8.17g; Sodium 58mg; Carbs: 10.87g; Sugars: 3.03g; Protein 4.39g

Mini Quiches with Cheese and Mushroom

Prep Time: 10 minutes | Cook Time: 15 minutes | Serves: 4

2 tablespoons extra-virgin olive oil
3 cups sliced button mushrooms
Salt
8 large eggs

1 cup shredded Cheddar cheese
Freshly ground black pepper
Cooking spray
Fresh spinach, torn, for garnish

1. Choose the Sauté option. 2. Add the mushrooms and olive oil. Add salt, stir, and simmer for 2 minutes to release moisture. 3. Till the mushrooms are cooked through, continue sautéing for an additional 3 minutes while stirring often. 4. Take the mushrooms out of the pot and set aside. 5. Beat the eggs just a little bit in a medium bowl. Add the cheese and mushrooms to the same bowl and mix. Add salt and pepper to taste. 6. Apply the cooking spray to four 6-ounce ramekins, then fill each with a quarter cup of the egg mixture. Place aluminum foil over each ramekin. 7. Add 1 cup of water to the Instant Pot and put the steam rack inside. Place the ramekins on the rack carefully. Close the lid. 8. Choose the Pressure Cook button and give it 7 minutes at high pressure. Once the food has finished cooking, quickly remove the steam on vent position. Carefully remove the cover. 9. Carefully remove the ramekins from the pot and remove the foil. Serve with the spinach for garnish.
Per Serving: Calories 274; Fat: 18.17g; Sodium 774mg; Carbs: 11.87g; Sugars: 7.03g; Protein 17.39g

Chapter 2 Vegetable and Sides

Cheese Summer Squash and Zucchini ... 26

Simple Sicilian Steamed Leeks 26

Garlic Buttered Mashed Potatoes 26

Steamed Lemony Artichokes 26

Cheese Buffalo Potatoes 27

Tasty Rice Pilaf with Mushrooms 27

Honey-Glazed Carrots 27

Green Beans with Shallot 27

Fresh Spiced Beets 28

Garlic Ham and Black-Eyed Peas 28

Classic Chickpea Tagine 28

Smoked Ham and White Beans 29

Easy Cob-Styled Corn...................... 29

Simple Sweet Potatoes 29

Quick Salty Potatoes 29

Savory Red Potato Salad.................... 30

Cheesy Zucchini Fritters.................... 30

Tomato-Based Spaghetti Squash with Olives... 30

Baked Sweet Potatoes with Marshmallows   31

Lemony Artichoke with Dipping Sauce ... 31

Yummy Homemade Dressing 31

Easy Curried Cauliflower 32

Garlicky Broccoli 32

Apple Strawberry Sauce 32

Super-Easy Sweet Potatoes................. 32

Creamy Mashed Cauliflower 33

Traditional Sweet Corn Tamalito 33

Homemade Corn Bread 33

Cheesy Corn Zucchini Casserole 34

Summer Vegetable Tian 34

Primavera Spaghetti Squash with Peas ... 34

Italian-Style Asparagus 35

Refreshing Balsamic-Maple Parsnips...... 35

Coconut Creamed Kale 35

Cider-Braised Brussels Sprouts 35

Cheese Summer Squash and Zucchini

Prep Time: 20 minutes | Cook Time: 5 minutes | Serves: 8

1 lb. medium yellow summer squash
1 lb. medium zucchini
2 medium tomatoes, chopped
1 cup vegetable broth
¼ cup thinly sliced green onions

½ tsp. salt
¼ tsp. pepper
1½ cups Caesar salad croutons, coarsely crushed
½ cup shredded cheddar cheese
4 bacon strips, cooked and crumbled

1. Slice the squash into 14-inch-thick pieces and Place in the Instant pot. Add the broth, green onions, tomatoes, salt, zucchini, and pepper. Close the lid. Adjust to Pressure Cook for 1 minute on high. Rapidly release pressure on valve to vent and unlock the lid. Use a slotted spoon to remove the squash. 2. Add the cheese, bacon, and croutons to serve.
Per Serving: Calories 307; Fat: 30g; Sodium 384mg; Carbs: 7g; Sugars: 3g; Protein 5g

Simple Sicilian Steamed Leeks

Prep Time: 10 minutes | Cook Time: 5 minutes | Serves: 6

1 large tomato, chopped
1 small navel orange, peeled, sectioned and chopped
2 Tbsp. minced fresh parsley
2 Tbsp. sliced Greek olives
1 tsp. capers, drained
1 tsp. red wine vinegar

1 tsp. olive oil
½ tsp. grated orange zest
½ tsp. pepper
6 medium leeks (white portion only), halved lengthwise, cleaned
Crumbled feta cheese

1. Combine the first nine ingredients and set aside. Pour 1 cup of water into the Instant Pot and put the steam rack inside. Place the leeks on the rack. Close the lid. Set to Pressure Cook for 2 minutes on high. Quickly release pressure on the vent position. 2. Leeks should be moved to a serving plate. Top with the tomato mixture and cheese, then spoon it on.
Per Serving: Calories 82; Fat: 1g; Sodium 74mg; Carbs: 16.87g; Sugars: 6.03g; Protein 2.39g

Garlic Buttered Mashed Potatoes

Prep Time: 10 minutes | Cook Time: 8 minutes | Serves: 4

2½ pounds russet potatoes, peeled
1 cup chicken broth
½ teaspoon salt

¾ cup whole milk, warm
2 tablespoons butter
5 cloves garlic, minced

1. Add the salt, stock, and potatoes to the Instant Pot. 2. Set the pressure release to seal position and close the lid. 3. Set the timer to 8 minute and press the Pressure Cook button. 4. When the timer beeps, quickly release the pressure on the vent position, then open the lid and take it off. 5. Spit out the broth. 6. Mash the potatoes in the pot using a potato masher. Add the warm milk and stir. 7. Melt the butter before adding it. Add the garlic and fold. 8. Serve warm.
Per Serving: Calories 417; Fat: 12g; Sodium 618mg; Carbs: 60g; Sugars: 7g; Protein 20g

Steamed Lemony Artichokes

Prep Time: 2 minutes | Cook Time: 30 minutes | Serves: 2

2 medium to large artichokes, tops and stems trimmed
1 lemon

½ teaspoon garlic salt

1. Add 1½ cup of water to the Instant Pot and put the steam rack inside. 2. Place the artichokes stem-side down and standing up on the rack. 3. Squeeze the juice from half a lemon over artichokes and sprinkle the garlic salt over each artichoke. Try to get some of the spice under the leaves. 4. Seal the valve and lock the lid. Choose Pressure Cook. Cook for 25 minutes at high pressure. When the timer beeps, quickly reduce the pressure in the pot on the vent position, then remove the lid. 5. Take the artichokes out of the pot with the tongs and served.
Per Serving: Calories 104; Fat: 3g; Sodium 445mg; Carbs: 18g; Sugars: 1g; Protein 4g

Cheese Buffalo Potatoes

2 lbs. Yukon Gold potatoes, cut into 1-in. cubes
1 small sweet yellow pepper, chopped
½ small red onion, chopped
Optional toppings: Crumbled cooked bacon, sliced green onions and sour cream

¼ cup Buffalo wing sauce
½ cup shredded cheddar cheese

1. Pour 1 cup of water into the Instant Pot and put the steam rack inside. Put the potatoes, onion, and yellow pepper on the rack. Close the pressure-release valve and lock the lid. Adjust to Pressure Cook on high for 3 minutes. Quickly release the pressure on the vent position. Select Cancel. 2. Take out the veggies and pour the cooking liquid away. Stir the veggies in the Buffalo wing sauce until evenly coated. Grate some cheese on top. For 1-2 minutes, while the cheese melts, cover and leave out. Add the bacon, green onions, and sour cream as desired.
Per Serving: Calories 187; Fat: 3g; Sodium 290mg; Carbs: 32g; Sugars: 2.03g; Protein 7g

Tasty Rice Pilaf with Mushrooms

¼ cup butter
1 cup medium grain rice
½ lb. sliced baby portobello mushrooms
5 green onions, chopped

2 garlic cloves, minced
1 cup water
4 tsp. beef base

1. Choose the Instant Pot's sauté setting. Put the butter in. Cook and stir the rice for 3 to 5 minutes while butter is still hot. Select Cancel. Add the garlic, green onions, and mushrooms. In a small bowl, whisk the water and beef base and pour over the rice mixture. 2. Close the pressure-release valve and lock the lid. Adjust to Pressure Cook on high for 4 minutes. Allow the pressure to release naturally on the seal position. Serve with more green onions if desired.
Per Serving: Calories 218; Fat: 9.17g; Sodium 73mg; Carbs: 29.87g; Sugars: 4.03g; Protein 4.39g

Honey-Glazed Carrots

⅓ cup olive oil
1 pound carrots, cut into ½" slices
1 teaspoon cumin

½ teaspoon salt
¼ teaspoon black pepper
¼ cup honey

1. Click the Sauté button. Add the oil and heat it for 1 minute. 2. Add the cumin, salt, pepper, and carrots. Stirring periodically, cook for 10 minutes with lid on. 3. Add the honey, then combine before capping. Allow it simmer for a further 5 minutes while stirring periodically. 4. Remove from heat and serve hot.
Per Serving: Calories 288; Fat: 18g; Sodium 373mg; Carbs: 28g; Sugars: 22g; Protein 1.23g

Green Beans with Shallot

1 cup water
¼ teaspoon salt, divided
1 pound green beans, trimmed

2 tablespoons olive oil
1 medium shallot, peeled and minced
½ teaspoon black pepper

1. Add the water and ½ teaspoon salt to the Instant Pot and put the steam rack inside. Place the green beans on steam rack. 2. Set the pressure release to the seal position and close the lid. 3. Set the time to 10 minutes, press the Pressure Cook button on low. 4. When the timer beeps, quickly release the pressure, then open the lid and take it off. Remove the green beans. Drain the water. 5. Add the oil to the pot and press the Sauté button. 6. Add the green beans and shallot. Cook for 6 minutes while periodically stirring. 7. Add the final ¼ teaspoon of salt and pepper to taste. Remove from heat and serve.
Per Serving: Calories 86; Fat: 7g; Sodium 440mg; Carbs: 5g; Sugars: 1g; Protein 1g

Fresh Spiced Beets

Prep Time: 20 minutes | Cook Time: 20 minutes |Serves: 8

5 large fresh beets (about 3½ lbs.)
1 Tbsp. olive oil
1 medium red onion, chopped
2 garlic cloves, minced
1 medium orange, peeled and chopped
⅓ cup honey
¼ cup white balsamic vinegar

1 Tbsp. minced fresh rosemary or 1 tsp. dried rosemary, crushed
2 tsp. minced fresh thyme or ¾ tsp. dried thyme
¾ tsp. salt
½ tsp. Chinese five-spice powder
½ tsp. coarsely ground pepper
1 cup crumbled feta cheese

1. Pour 1 cup of water into to the Instant Pot and put the steam rack inside. Scrub the beets and cut their tops off at 1 inch. Close the pressure-release valve and lock the lid. Adjust to Pressure Cook on high for 20 minutes. Allow the pressure to release naturally. Select Cancel. 2. When cool enough to handle, remove the beets. Eliminate the steam rack and throw away cooking fluids. Wipe the pot dry. Peel the beets and slice into wedges. 3. Choose the sauté option. Cook the oil and red onion and stir for 4-5 minutes after the oil is heated. For a further minute, add the garlic. Heat through the addition of the orange, honey, vinegar, rosemary, thyme, salt, Chinese five-spice, and beets. Select Cancel. Serve hot, or cool and store in the fridge. Add the cheese before serving with a slotted spoon.
Per Serving: Calories 138; Fat: 5g; Sodium 432mg; Carbs: 18.87g; Sugars: 16g; Protein 3g

Garlic Ham and Black-Eyed Peas

Prep Time: 10 minutes | Cook Time: 20 minutes |Serves: 10

1 pkg. (16 oz.) dried black-eyed peas
4 cups water
1 cup cubed fully cooked ham
1 medium onion, finely chopped

3 garlic cloves, minced
2 tsp. seasoned salt
1 tsp. pepper
Thinly sliced green onions, optional

1. Sort the black-eyed peas and rinse. Transfer them to the Instant pot. Stir in the ham, onion, garlic, seasoned salt, water and pepper. Close the pressure-release valve and lock the lid. Adjust to Pressure Cook on high for 18 minutes. Allow any leftover pressure to naturally release for ten minutes on the seal position before quick-releasing it on vent position. 2. Serve with a slotted spoon. Add some thinly sliced green onions if desired.
Per Serving: Calories 40; Fat: 1g; Sodium 788mg; Carbs: 2.87g; Sugars: 1g; Protein 4g

Classic Chickpea Tagine

Prep Time: 30 minutes | Cook Time: 5 minutes |Serves: 12

2 Tbsp. olive oil
2 garlic cloves, minced
2 tsp. paprika
1 tsp. ground ginger
1 tsp. ground cumin
½ tsp. salt
¼ tsp. pepper
¼ tsp. ground cinnamon
1 small butternut squash (about 2 lbs.), peeled and cut into ½-in. cubes
2 medium zucchini, cut into ½-in. pieces

1 can (15 oz.) chickpeas or garbanzo beans, rinsed and drained
1 medium sweet red pepper, coarsely chopped
1 medium onion, coarsely chopped
12 dried apricots, halved
½ cup water
2 to 3 tsp. harissa chili paste
2 tsp. honey
1 can (14.5 oz.) crushed tomatoes, undrained
¼ cup chopped fresh mint leaves
Plain Greek yogurt, optional

1. Choose the Instant Pot's sauté setting. Add the oil, and when the oil is heated, add the garlic, paprika, ginger, cumin, salt, pepper, and cinnamon. Cook and stir for approximately 1 minute, or until fragrant. Select Cancel. 2. Add the water, harissa, honey, onion, red pepper, zucchini, squash, chickpeas, and apricot halves. Close the pressure-release valve and lock the lid. Adjust to Pressure Cook on high for 3 minutes. Rapidly release pressure on the vent position. Select Cancel. Add the tomatoes and mint, stirring gently, and heat through. 3. If desired, top with the yogurt and additional mint, olive oil and honey.
Per Serving: Calories 386; Fat: 3g; Sodium 283mg; Carbs: 91g; Sugars: 73g; Protein 8.39g

Smoked Ham and White Beans

Prep Time: 15 minutes | Cook Time: 30 minutes | Serves: 10

1 lb. dried great northern beans
3 smoked ham hocks (about 1½ lbs.)
3 cans (14½ oz. each) reduced-sodium chicken or beef broth
2 cups water
1 large onion, chopped

1 Tbsp. onion powder
1 Tbsp. garlic powder
2 tsp. pepper
Thinly sliced green onions, optional

1. Sort and rinse the beans. Add to the Instant Pot. Toss in the ham hocks. Add the spices, water, onion, and broth. Close the pressure-release valve and lock the lid. Adjust to Pressure Cook on high for 30 minutes. Allow the pressure to naturally dissipate for 10 minutes, quickly release any lingering pressure. Select Cancel. 2. Remove the meat from bones once it is cold enough to handle. Chop up the ham into bite-sized pieces and put back in the Pressure Cook. Use a slotted spoon before serving. If desired, garnish with the green onions.
Per Serving: Calories 500; Fat: 12.17g; Sodium 2884mg; Carbs: 36g; Sugars: 2g; Protein 63g

Easy Cob-Styled Corn

Prep Time: 5 minutes | Cook Time: 5 minutes | Serves: 4

1 cup water
¼ teaspoon salt

4 ears corn

1. Add 1 cup of water and salt to the Instant Pot and put the steam rack inside. Put the corn on the rack. 2. Set the pressure release to seal position and close the lid. 3. Press Pressure Cook button and adjust time to 5 minutes. 4. When the timer beeps, quickly release the pressure steam on the vent position and then open the lid. 5. Take the corn out of the pot and serve corn.
Per Serving: Calories 282; Fat: 2.17g; Sodium 222mg; Carbs: 15.87g; Sugars: 1.03g; Protein 1.39g

Simple Sweet Potatoes

Prep Time: 5 minutes | Cook Time: 15 minutes | Serves: 4

1 cup water

4 medium sweet potatoes

1. Add the water to the Instant Pot and put the steam rack inside. 2. On the top and bottom, pierce sweet potatoes with a fork on both sides. Cover the rack with the sweet potatoes. 3. Set the pressure release to seal position and close the lid. 4. Set the timer to 15 minutes and press the Pressure Cook button. 5. When the timer beeps, quickly release the pressure steam on the vent position and then open the lid. 6. Take the sweet potatoes out of the pot and serve.
Per Serving: Calories 115; Fat: 1g; Sodium 40mg; Carbs: 26g; Sugars: 8.03g; Protein 2.39g

Quick Salty Potatoes

Prep Time: 5 minutes | Cook Time: 20 minutes | Serves: 4

1 cup water
½ teaspoon salt

4 medium russet potatoes

1. Add the water and salt to the Instant Pot and put the steam rack inside. 2. On the top and bottom, pierce potatoes with a fork on all sides. Put potatoes on the rack. 3. Set the pressure release to seal position and close the lid. 4. Set the timer to 20 minutes and press the Pressure Cook button. 5. When the timer beeps, quickly release the pressure steam on the vent position and then open the lid. 6. Take the potatoes out of the pot and serve.
Per Serving: Calories 110; Fat: 1.17g; Sodium 404mg; Carbs: 12.87g; Sugars: 7.3g; Protein 2.39g

Savory Red Potato Salad

1 cup water
2½ pounds medium red potatoes, peeled and cut into 1" cubes
½ cup mayonnaise
2 tablespoons yellow mustard
1 tablespoon apple cider vinegar

½ teaspoon salt
½ teaspoon black pepper
½ teaspoon paprika
4 medium green onions, sliced

1. Add the water to the Instant Pot and put the steam rack inside. 2. Arrange the potato cubes on the steam rack. 3. Set the pressure release to sea position and close the lid. 4. Set the timer to 4 minutes and press the Pressure Cook button. 5. When the timer beeps, quickly release the pressure steam on the vent position, open the lid, and remove the potato cubes from the pot. 6. Place the potatoes in a dish of cold water and let it sit for 10 minutes. 7. Combine the mayonnaise, pepper, mustard, vinegar, salt, and paprika in a small basin. 8. Remove the potatoes from the cold bath and place in a big, dry dish. 9. Add the sauce to the potatoes and toss to cover well. Add the green onions in slices to the potato salad. 10. Chil until ready to serve.
Per Serving: Calories 204; Fat: 6g; Sodium 440mg; Carbs: 32g; Sugars: 3g; Protein 5g

Cheesy Zucchini Fritters

4 cups shredded zucchini
1 teaspoon salt
1 large egg, beaten
⅓ cup all-purpose flour

⅓ cup shredded Parmesan cheese
2 cloves garlic, minced
½ teaspoon black pepper
6 tablespoons olive oil

1. Salt the zucchini and place it in a colander. Wait for 10 minutes. 2. Take the zucchini out of the colander and cover it in a fresh kitchen towel Wring and squeeze the water out of the zucchini. 3. Combine the zucchini with the egg, flour, Parmesan, garlic, and pepper in a large bowl Blend well. 4. Press the Instant Pot's Sauté button. Fill the Instant Pot with 2 tablespoons of oil. 5. Put heaping teaspoons of zucchini in the Pressure Cook. Using the back of a spoon, flatten into 2½" rounds. Make three fritters at a time while working in batches. 6. After 4 minutes turn the food. Cook the second side for a further 4 minutes. 7. Using a slotted spatula, remove the zucchini fritters. Cook the zucchini in batches using more oil as needed, until all are consumed. 8. Serve hot.
Per Serving: Calories 296; Fat: 12g; Sodium 810mg; Carbs: 26g; Sugars: 0.03g; Protein 6g

Tomato-Based Spaghetti Squash with Olives

1 medium spaghetti squash, halved lengthwise, seeds removed
1 can (14 oz.) diced tomatoes, drained
¼ cup sliced green olives with pimientos
1 tsp. dried oregano
¼ cup minced fresh basil

½ tsp. salt
½ tsp. pepper
½ cup shredded cheddar cheese

1. Pour 1 cup of water into to the Instant Pot and put the steam rack inside. Overlap the squash as necessary to fit it on the rack. Close the lid Adjust to Pressure Cook for 7 minutes on high. Quickly release pressure on the vent position. Select Cancel. 2. Remove the squash and rack then drain cooking liquid from pot. Cut the squash into spaghetti-like strands and discard squash skin. 3. Return the squash to the pot. Add the salt, pepper, oregano, tomatoes, and olives to the mixture. Choose the sauté option. For approximately 3 minutes, stir and cook until well cooked Add the cheese and basil on top. 4. When cooking is finished, serve.
Per Serving: Calories 40; Fat: 1g; Sodium 304mg; Carbs: 4g; Sugars: 2.03g; Protein 2.39g

Baked Sweet Potatoes with Marshmallows

Prep Time: 10 minutes | Cook Time: 23 minutes |Serves: 6

I cup water
3 (15-ounce) cans sweet potatoes, drained
½ cup packed brown sugar
¼ cup butter, melted

3 tablespoons orange juice
⅛ teaspoon ground cinnamon
1 (10-ounce) bag mini marshmallows

1. Add the steam rack and fill the Instant Pot with the water. Organize a 7-inch cake pan with grease. 2. Combine the sweet potatoes, brown sugar, butter, orange juice, and cinnamon in a big basin. Completely mix by blending. 3. Fill the cake pan with the sweet potato mixture. Add the remaining bag of small marshmallows on top. 4. Cover the cake pan with foil and a dry paper towel. To prevent the paper towel from slipping, secure foil over the pan. 5. Make a foil sling, gently place the covered cake pan inside the Instant Pot, and cover the cake pan with the ends of the sling. 6. Set the pressure release to seal position and close the lid. 7. Set the timer to 20 minutes and press the Pressure Cook button. 8. When the timer beeps, quickly release the pressure on the vent position, then open the lid and take it off. Utilizing a foil sling, carefully remove the cake pan. Remove the paper towel and foil. 10. Top the dish with the remaining half of the small marshmallows. 11. Casserole in the oven for 2 to 3 minutes, or until marshmallows start to turn golden. To prevent marshmallows from burning, keep a close eye on them. Serve.
Per Serving: Calories 495; Fat: 14.17g; Sodium 280mg; Carbs: 116g; Sugars: 66g; Protein 3g

Lemony Artichoke with Dipping Sauce

Prep Time: 10 minutes | Cook Time: 15 minutes |Serves: 4

2 large artichokes
I medium lemon
I cup water
3 cloves garlic, crushed

¾ teaspoon salt, divided
3 tablespoons mayonnaise
¼ teaspoon chili powder
⅛ teaspoon black pepper

1. Rinse each artichoke and slice the top half an inch off. 2. Half a lemon, please. Set aside one half. Wedge-cut the remaining half. 3. Add the water, garlic, lemon wedges, and ½ teaspoon salt to the Instant Pot. 4. Place the steam rack in the Instant Pot and arrange the artichokes on the rack. If necessary, cut the artichoke stems so the lid will shut. 5. Set the pressure release to seal position and close the lid. 6. Set the timer to 15 minutes and press the Pressure Cook button. 7. When the timer beeps, quickly release the pressure on the vent position, then open the lid and take it off. Remove the artichokes. 8. Mix the remaining juice from ½ a lemon, ¼ teaspoon of salt, chili powder, and pepper in a small dish with the mayonnaise. 9. Cut artichokes in half and serve with the sauce.
Per Serving: Calories 81; Fat: 3g; Sodium 606mg; Carbs: 11g; Sugars: 1g; Protein 3g

Yummy Homemade Dressing

Prep Time: 15 minutes | Cook Time: 10 minutes |Serves: 8

2 Tbsp. olive oil
I medium celery rib, chopped
I small onion, chopped
2 cups reduced-sodium chicken broth

1 tsp. poultry seasoning
¼ tsp. salt
¼ tsp. pepper
8 cups unseasoned stuffing cubes

1. Choose Sauté setting on the Instant Pot. Add the oil. Add the celery and onion to cook and stir in the heated oil for 3 to 4 minutes, or until crisp-tender. Select "Cancel." Stir in the seasonings and broth. Add the stuffing cubes and mix just until combined. Transfer to a 1½ qt. oiled baking pan. 2. Pour 1 cup of water into the Instant Pot and put the steam rack inside. Cover the baking dish with foil. An 18x12-inch strip of foil is folded into thirds along its length to create a sling. Lower the dish onto the rack using the sling. 3. Close lid. Adjust to Pressure Cook on high for 15 minutes. Allow any leftover pressure to naturally release for 10 minutes on the seal position before quick-releasing it on the vent position. Carefully remove the baking dish using foil sling. Let stand 10 minutes.
Per Serving: Calories 270; Fat: 10g; Sodium 344mg; Carbs: 2g; Sugars: 1.03g; Protein 38.39g

Easy Curried Cauliflower

2 tablespoons olive oil
1 medium head cauliflower, cut into florets
½ teaspoon curry powder

⅛ teaspoon salt
⅛ teaspoon black pepper

1. Click the Sauté button. Add the oil and heat for 1 minute. 2. Stir in the cauliflower, curry powder, salt, and pepper. Now cook for 12 minutes under cover with occasional stirring. 3. Remove from heat and serve hot.
Per Serving: Calories 77; Fat: 7g; Sodium 93mg; Carbs: 3g; Sugars: 1.03g; Protein 1g

Garlicky Broccoli

3 tablespoons olive oil
2 medium heads broccoli, cut into florets
½ teaspoon salt

½ teaspoon black pepper
4 cloves garlic, crushed

1. Click the Sauté button. Add the oil, heat for 1 minute. 2. Add the broccoli, seasonings, and stir. With the lid on, heat for 4 minutes while stirring now and then. 3. Add the garlic and cover the lid. Allow it simmer for a further 4 minutes while stirring periodically. 4. Remove from heat and serve hot.
Per Serving: Calories 95; Fat: 10g; Sodium 291mg; Carbs: 2g; Sugars: 0.03g; Protein 0.39g

Apple Strawberry Sauce

6 cups roughly chopped Gala apples
4 cups frozen strawberries
½ cup granulated sugar

½ cup water
¼ teaspoon salt

1. In the Instant Pot, add the strawberries and apples. 2. Add the salt, water, and sugar. Blend well. 3. Set the pressure release to seal position and close the lid. 4. Press Pressure Cook button and adjust time to 5 minutes on low. 5. When the timer beeps, allow the steam to naturally release on the seal position, then open the lid, and take it off. 6. Blend the ingredients with an immersion blender until it's smooth. 7. Chill in the refrigerator 2 hours. Serve cold.
Per Serving: Calories 146; Fat: 1g; Sodium 5mg; Carbs: 36g; Sugars: 26g; Protein 1g

Super-Easy Sweet Potatoes

4 medium sweet potatoes
Ghee (optional)
Chopped chives or scallions, both white and green parts (optional)

Avocado slices (optional)
Chopped, cooked bacon (optional)

1. Add ½ cup of water to the Instant Pot and put the steam rack inside. 2. Wash each sweet potato and make vents by poking them numerous times. Put on the rack, stacked as necessary. 3. Seal the vent and lock the lid. Choose Pressure Cook on high pressure for 20 minutes. When the timer beeps, release the pressure naturally for 10 minutes on the seal position. Remove the lid after quickly release any leftover pressure in the pot on vent position. If some of the cooked sweet potatoes aren't soft enough for you, add additional 3 to 5 minutes of cooking time with at least 1 cup of water, depending on how soft you want them. 4. When cool enough to handle, slice open the potatoes. If using, top with the ghee, chives, avocado slices, and bacon.
Per Serving: Calories 140; Fat: 5g; Sodium 70mg; Carbs: 20g; Sugars: 6g; Protein 2g

Creamy Mashed Cauliflower

Prep Time: 10 minutes | Cook Time: 2 minutes | Serves: 4

cup water
medium head cauliflower, cut into florets
cup whole milk, warm

1 tablespoon unsalted butter
¼ teaspoon salt

. Fill the Instant Pot with water and put the rack inside. 2. On top of the steam rack, arrange the cauliflower. 3. Set the pressure release to seal position and close the lid. 4. Press Pressure Cook button and adjust time to 2 minutes on high. 5. When the timer beeps, quickly release the pressure steam on the vent position, then open the lid, and take it off. 6. Drain the water, then take the steam rack off. 7. In the Instant Pot bottom, put the cauliflower. Use a potato masher to thoroughly mash the cauliflower. 8. Mix in the warm milk and stir until cauliflower absorbs milk. 9. Fold in the butter and salt. Mix until butter is melted. Serve warm.
Per Serving: Calories 90; Fat: 4g; Sodium 48mg; Carbs: 12g; Sugars: 9.1g; Protein 3.2g

Traditional Sweet Corn Tamalito

Prep Time: 15 minutes | Cook Time: 50 minutes | Serves: 6

tablespoons butter, melted
¼ cup masa harina
½ cup granulated sugar
2½ cups water, divided
2 cups frozen corn kernels, thawed, divided

½ cup cornmeal
4 teaspoons whole milk
1 teaspoon baking powder
½ teaspoon salt

. Mix the sugar, masa harina, and butter in a large basin until well-combined. 2. Combine ½ cup water, 1 cup corn, and ¼ cup cornmeal in a blender. Until smooth, blend. 3. Combine the masa mixture with the pureed corn. 4. Add the remaining 1 cup of corn, milk, baking soda, and salt while whisking. Stir well to mix. 5. Pour the batter into a 7-cup metal basin. Place a paper towel on the bowl and seal the bowl with the foil. 6. Add the final 2 cups of water to the Instant Pot and put the steam rack inside. Carefully put the bowl into the Instant Pot, use a foil sling. 7. Set to seal position and close the lid. 8. Click the Steam button, then set the timer to 50 minutes. 9. When the timer beeps, quickly release the pressure steam on the vent position, then open the lid, and take it off. 10. Using a foil sling, remove the bowl. Remove the foil and paper towels. 11. Stir before serving.
Per Serving: Calories 227; Fat: 10g; Sodium 81mg; Carbs: 30g; Sugars: 9g; Protein 2g

Homemade Corn Bread

Prep Time: 10 minutes | Cook Time: 25 minutes | Serves: 6

cup water
½ cups all-purpose flour
¼ cup cornmeal
2 cups granulated sugar
2 teaspoons baking powder

½ teaspoon salt
1 large egg, beaten
1 cup whole milk
½ cup vegetable oil
½ cup frozen corn kernels, thawed

. Add the water to the Instant Pot and put the steam rack inside. Grease a 6-cup Bundt pan and set aside. 2. Mix the flour, cornmeal, sugar, baking soda, and salt in a large basin. 3. Create a well in the center of the dry ingredients, then add the milk, oil, and egg. Just mix the dry components with the wet ones by folding. 4. Mix in the corn until it is spread evenly. 5. Fill the Bundt pan with the corn bread batter. Cover the pan with a paper towel before foil. 6. Delicately lower the pan into the Instant Pot using a foil sling. 7. Set the pressure release to seal position and close the lid. 8. Press Pressure Cook button and set the timer for 25 minutes on high. 9. Once the timer beeps, allow pressure to naturally relax on seal position for 10 minutes, then quickly remove any leftover pressure on vent position. Remove the lid by unlocking it. Using a foil sling, remove the pan from the Instant Pot. 10. Let cool on a wire rack before serving.
Per Serving: Calories 534; Fat: 20g; Sodium 217mg; Carbs: 81g; Sugars: 38g; Protein 6g

Cheesy Corn Zucchini Casserole

Prep Time: 15 minutes | Cook Time: 65 minutes |Serves: 6

1½ cups water
1½ cups all-purpose flour
¾ cup cornmeal
2 teaspoons baking powder
1 teaspoon salt
¼ teaspoon black pepper

2 large eggs, beaten
1 cup whole milk
¼ cup vegetable oil
4 cups shredded zucchini
1½ cups Monterey jack cheese

1. Add the steam rack and fill the Instant Pot with water. Organize a 7-inch cake pan with grease. 2. Mix the flour, cornmeal, baking powder, salt, and pepper in a big basin. 3. Make a well in the dry ingredients and add the egg, milk, and oil. Mix thoroughly. 4. Add the zucchini and blend well. Add the cheese after that. 5. Fill the cake pan with the casserole batter. Add a paper towel on top and carefully wrap the foil around the pan's top. Delicately lower the pan into the Instant Pot using a foil sling. 6. Set the pressure release to seal position and close the lid. 7. Set the timer to 65 minutes and press the Pressure Cook button on high. 8. When the timer beeps, quickly release pressure and then unlock lid and remove it. Remove pan from Instant Pot using foil sling. 9. Serve hot.
Per Serving: Calories 508; Fat: 27g; Sodium 712mg; Carbs: 45g; Sugars: 6g; Protein 19g

Summer Vegetable Tian

Prep Time: 10 minutes | Cook Time: 30 minutes |Serves: 4

1 tablespoon olive oil
½ medium yellow onion, peeled and diced
2 cloves garlic, minced
1 cup water
1 medium yellow squash, cut into ½"-thick slices
1 medium zucchini, cut into ½"-thick slices

2 Roma tomatoes, cut into ½"-thick slices
1 large russet potato, cut into ½"-thick slices
¼ teaspoon salt
⅛ teaspoon black pepper
½ cup shredded mozzarella cheese
¼ cup grated Parmesan cheese

1. Press Sauté button on the Instant Pot. 2. Add the onion and oil. Cook for 4 minutes, or until softened. 3. Place in the garlic and cook for 30 seconds or until fragrant. 4. Then spread the onion and garlic on the bottom of a 7-inch cake pan. 5. Place the cleaned inner pot inside the Instant Pot once again. Add the water to the Instant Pot and put the steam rack inside. 6. Around the perimeter of the cake pan, arrange the sliced veggies in a pattern of squash, zucchini, tomato, and potato. Once all of the veggies have been utilized, continue in the middle of the pan. 7. Add a paper towel on top and carefully wrap the foil around the top of pan. Delicately lower the pan into the Instant Pot using a foil sling. 8. Set the pressure release to seal position and close the lid. 9. Press Pressure Cook button and adjust time to 30 minutes. 10. Once the timer beeps, allow 10 minutes for the pressure to naturally release on the seal position. Release any residual pressure quickly on the vent position, then open the lid and take it off. 11. Using a foil sling, remove the pan from the Instant Pot. On top, grate the mozzarella, Parmesan, salt, and pepper. Serve warm.
Per Serving: Calories 135; Fat: 4g; Sodium 400mg; Carbs: 13g; Sugars: 1g; Protein 10g

Primavera Spaghetti Squash with Peas

Prep Time: 5 minutes | Cook Time: 20 minutes |Serves: 4

1 spaghetti squash
2 tablespoons extra-virgin olive oil, divided
2 garlic cloves, minced
1 cup peas

3 tablespoons nutritional yeast
½ teaspoon sea salt
¼ teaspoon freshly ground black pepper
1 cup cherry tomatoes, halved

1. Add ½ cup of water to the Instant Pot and put the steam rack inside. Cut the spaghetti squash in half crosswise and scoop out the seeds. Arrange both halves, stacking if necessary, on the rack. 2. Close the lid. Choose Pressure Cook and cook on high pressure for 7 minutes. When the timer beeps, quickly release the pressure in the pot on the vent position and remove the lid. Select Cancel. Cook the squash under high pressure for a further 1 to 3 minutes if you want it more tender. 3. Remove the squash and put aside to cool. Remove the bowl's water and empty it. 4. Choose Sauté. Heat 1 teaspoon of oil till shimmering. Place in the garlic and cook for 30 seconds. Add the peas and cooked for 1 to 2 minutes, stirring regularly, until tender. 5. Scrape the squash threads off the skin with a fork, then add them back to the saucepan. Throw away the skin. Add the remaining 1 tablespoon of oil, pepper, and salt, along with the nutritional yeast. Add the cherry tomatoes and stir gently. Serve and enjoy!
Per Serving: Calories 154; Fat: 4g; Sodium 800mg; Carbs: 26g; Sugars: 12g; Protein 5g

Italian-Style Asparagus

-pound asparagus spears, woody ends trimmed
tablespoon extra-virgin olive oil
½ teaspoon Italian seasoning

½ teaspoon sea salt
¼ teaspoon freshly ground black pepper

. Add 1½ cup of water to the Instant Pot and put the steam rack inside. 2. Add the oil and arrange the asparagus in the rack. Add some salt, pepper, and Italian seasoning. 3. Close the lid. Choose Pressure Cook on high pressure for 1 minute. When the timer beeps, quickly release the pressure in the pot on the vent position and remove the lid. 4. Using tongs, remove the asparagus and serve.

Per Serving: Calories 25; Fat: 1g; Sodium 232mg; Carbs: 3g; Sugars: 2.03g; Protein 1.6g

Refreshing Balsamic-Maple Parsnips

2 or 3 parsnips, peeled and cut into ½-inch pieces
2 garlic cloves, minced
½ cup applesauce
¼ cup maple syrup

2 tablespoons balsamic vinegar
2 tablespoons extra-virgin olive oil
½ teaspoon dried thyme
¼ teaspoon sea salt

1. Combine the parsnips, garlic, applesauce, maple syrup, vinegar, oil, thyme, and salt in the Instant Pot. 2. Close the lid. Select Pressure Cook on high pressure for 2 minutes. When the timer beeps, quickly release the pressure in the pot on the vent position and remove the lid. 3. Cook the parsnips for an additional minute under high pressure if they are too hard for your tastes.

Per Serving: Calories 100; Fat: 3g; Sodium 210mg; Carbs: 18g; Sugars: 16g; Protein 1g

Coconut Creamed Kale

tablespoon extra-virgin olive oil
3 garlic cloves, minced
bunch kale, stemmed and torn into bite-size pieces

¼ teaspoon sea salt
⅛ teaspoon freshly ground black pepper
1 cup full-fat coconut milk

1. Select Instant Pot Sauté option. Heat the oil until it shimmers. 2. Stirring continuously, add the garlic and sauté for 30 seconds. Add the pepper and salt and stir in the greens. Over the top, pour the coconut milk. Select Cancel. 3. Seal the valve and lock the lid. Select Pressure Cook on high pressure for 5 minutes. When the timer beeps, quickly release the pressure in the pot on the vent position and remove the lid. 4. After stirring the kale, transfer it to a serving bowl with the tongs or a slotted spoon. Serve and enjoy!

Per Serving: Calories 157; Fat: 16g; Sodium 186mg; Carbs: 4g; Sugars: 2g; Protein 2g

Cider-Braised Brussels Sprouts

tablespoon extra-virgin olive oil
shallot, diced
cup apple cider or juice
tablespoon Dijon mustard

1 teaspoon dried thyme
½ teaspoon sea salt
¼ teaspoon freshly ground black pepper
1 pound Brussels sprouts, trimmed and halved

1. Select Instant Pot Sauté option. Heat the oil until it shimmers. 2. Add the shallot and cook it for 2 to 3 minutes, stirring often, until it is tender and translucent. Add the salt, pepper, mustard, thyme, and apple cider. To blend, stir. Add the Brussels sprouts and stir well. Select Cancel. 3. Seal the valve and lock the lid. Choose Pressure Cook on high pressure for 10 minute. When the timer beeps, quickly release the pressure in the pot on the vent position and remove the lid. 4. Place the Brussels sprouts to a serving bowl using a slotted spoon.

Per Serving: Calories 62; Fat: 2g; Sodium 263mg; Carbs: 12g; Sugars: 5g; Protein 2g

Chapter 3 Soup, Stew, and Chili

Creamy Onion Soup 37

Vegetable and Chicken Noddle Soup 37

Garlicky Bacon and Cabbage Soup 37

Healthy Vegetable and Beef Soup 38

Ham and Split Pea Soup 38

Classic Italian Soup......................... 38

Healthy Barley Soup with Beans 39

Classic Heart Healthy Soup 39

Authentic Carrot Potato Soup with Broccoli 39

Cheesy Carrot and Broccoli Soup 40

Creamy Tomato Soup with Basil 40

Creamy Chicken Rice Soup 40

Pinto Bean and Tortilla Soup 41

Lemony Shredded Chicken and Rice Soup 41

Fresh Tomato Basil Soup 41

Broccoli and Cheese Soup 42

Delicious Beef Noodle Soup 42

Homemade Tomato Lentil Soup 42

Creamy Baked Potato Soup 43

Kale Tomato Tortellini Soup with Parsley 43

Classic Lasagna Soup 43

Wisconsin Brats and Cheddar Chowder ... 44

Perfect Chicken Enchilada Soup............ 44

Spicy Red Chili 44

Cheesy Beany Pasta 45

Classic Beef Chili 45

Ground Beef Chili with Beans 45

Traditional Beef and Sweet Potato Chili... 46

Savory Chipotle Beer Chili.................. 46

Authentic Cincinnati-Style Chili............ 46

Mouthwatering Bean Soup 47

Yummy Buffalo Chicken Chili 47

Flavorful Chili Macaroni and Cheese...... 47

Simple Vegetarian Chili 48

Southwest Chili with Black Beans and Corn 48

Creamy Onion Soup

tablespoons salted butter, divided
pounds sweet onions, peeled and sliced
tablespoon light brown sugar
¼ cup white wine
cloves garlic, peeled and smashed
tablespoon balsamic vinegar
bay leaf

½ teaspoon dried thyme
¼ teaspoon ground black pepper
4 cups Beef Stock
4 cups Beef Broth
8 (1"-thick) slices French baguette
1 cup grated Gruyère cheese

. Press the Sauté button and melt 3 tablespoons of butter in the Instant Pot. Add the brown sugar and onions. Cook for about 5 minutes, or until onions are barely soft. Press the Cancel button. Close the lid, set the steam release to seal position, select Pressure Cook, and set the timer for 15 minutes. When the timer beeps, quickly release the steam on the vent position, then click Cancel. 2. Drain the inner pot of any extra liquid. Put the inner pot back in the pot and choose Sauté. Adding the remaining butter, sauté the onions for 15 to 20 minutes, flipping regularly, until they are caramelized and browned. 3. Add the wine to the pot after scraping out any browned pieces. Press the Cancel button. Pepper, stock, vinegar, bay leaf, thyme, garlic, and vinegar to the pot. Close the lid, set the steam release to seal position, select Pressure Cook, and set the timer for 20 minutes. Allow pressure to naturally relax for around 20 minutes on seal position after the timer chimes. Open the lid, press the Cancel button, and mix well. Get rid of the bay leaf. 4. To thicken the soup, select the Sauté button and boil it for 10 minutes while stirring often. 5. Put the soup in the heat-resistant bowls. Distribute the cheese on each bowl and place a slice of bread on it. Broil for 3-5 minutes, or until bubbling and browned. Add 1 cup of water to the Instant Pot and put the steam rack inside. Cook the cheese on low pressure by choosing Pressure Cook. Serve warm.
Per Serving: Calories 147; Fat: 10.17g; Sodium 97mg; Carbs: 13.87g; Sugars: 8.9g; Protein 1.56g

Vegetable and Chicken Noddle Soup

(3½-pound) chicken, cut into pieces
stalks celery, chopped
medium carrots, peeled and chopped
medium yellow onion, peeled and chopped
clove garlic, peeled and smashed
bay leaf

1 teaspoon poultry seasoning
½ teaspoon dried thyme
1 teaspoon salt
¼ teaspoon ground black pepper
4 cups low-sodium chicken broth
4 ounces dried egg noodles

. In the Instant Pot, combine the chicken, celery, carrots, onion, garlic, bay leaf, poultry seasoning, thyme, salt, and pepper. Press the Soup button, close the lid, set the steam release to seal position, and cook the soup for the preset 20 minutes. 2. Once the timer beeps, allow the pressure to naturally for 20 to 25 minutes on seal. Press the Cancel button and open lid. 3. Get rid of the bay leaf. Move the chicken to a cutting board using the tongs or a slotted spoon. Delicately shred the chicken, skin and bones removed. Stir the chicken back into the pot. Add the noodles, secure the cover, set the steam release to the seal position, select Pressure Cook, and set the timer for 4 minutes. 4. Once the timer beeps, quickly release the pressure on the vent position, take off the lid, and thoroughly stir. Serve warm.
Per Serving: Calories 560; Fat: 16g; Sodium 1023mg; Carbs: 9g; Sugars: 3g; Protein 89g

Garlicky Bacon and Cabbage Soup

tablespoons vegetable oil
slices thick-cut bacon, chopped
medium yellow onions, peeled and chopped
large head cabbage, cored and chopped
cloves garlic, peeled and minced

4 cups Vegetable Broth
1 cup Bone Broth
¼ teaspoon crushed red pepper flakes
½ teaspoon salt
½ teaspoon ground black pepper

. Press the Sauté button and heat the oil in the Instant Pot. Add the bacon and cook for approximately 8 minutes, or until the edges are just beginning to brown. Add the onions and simmer for 5 minutes or until they are soft. Cook the garlic and cabbage together for approximately a minute, or until aromatic. Press the Cancel button. 2. Mix in the broths and red pepper flakes. Stir thoroughly, fasten the lid, select Pressure Cook, and set the timer for 3 minutes on high. 3. When the timer beeps, allow the steam to naturally release for 20 to 25 minutes on the seal position. Open the lid and add the salt and pepper. Serve hot.
Per Serving: Calories 1072; Fat: 117g; Sodium 294mg; Carbs: 8.72g; Sugars: 4.03g; Protein 9.39g

Healthy Vegetable and Beef Soup

Prep Time: 20 minutes | Cook Time: 20 minutes |Serves: 8

2 pounds boneless chuck roast, cut into 1" pieces
¼ cup all-purpose flour
1 teaspoon salt, divided
1 teaspoon ground black pepper, divided
2 tablespoons vegetable oil, divided
2 medium yellow onions, peeled and chopped
2 medium carrots, peeled and chopped

2 stalks celery, chopped
2 cloves garlic, peeled and minced
¼ teaspoon dried thyme
1 russet potato, peeled and cut into ½" cubes
1 (14-ounce) can diced tomatoes, undrained
4 cups Vegetable Broth
2 cups water

1. Fill a big zip-top plastic bag with the meat, flour, and ½ teaspoon of salt and pepper each. Make sure the steak is uniformly covered and shake thoroughly. 2. Press the Sauté button and heat 1 tablespoon of oil in the Instant Pot. Make sure there is enough space between each piece of meat before adding the first half to the saucepan. Each side for two to three minutes. Transfer the hamburger to a dish and repeat with the remaining oil and meat. 3. Add the onions, celery, and carrots to the pot. Cook for approximately 5 minutes, or until barely tender. Cook for about 30 seconds or until the garlic and thyme are aromatic. Press the Cancel button. 4. Return the beef to pot. Add the broth, water, tomato sauce, and potato. Stir well, being sure to scrape off any food remnants from the pot's bottom. Close lid, set steam release to seal position, press the Soup button, and cook for the default time of 20 minutes. 5. When the timer beeps, let the pressure release naturally on the seal position, about 15 minutes. Open lid and stir in the remaining ½ teaspoon each salt and pepper. Serve hot.
Per Serving: Calories 1394; Fat: 138g; Sodium 456mg; Carbs: 18g; Sugars: 3.4g; Protein 32.39g

Ham and Split Pea Soup

Prep Time: 10 minutes | Cook Time: 20 minutes |Serves: 8

4 tablespoons unsalted butter
1 medium yellow onion, peeled and finely diced
2 stalks celery, finely diced
2 cups diced ham steak
2 cloves garlic, peeled and minced

1 pound dried green split peas
6 cups Ham Stock or Chicken Stock
1 bay leaf
½ teaspoon salt
½ teaspoon ground black pepper

1. Press the Sauté button and melt the butter in the Instant Pot. Add the ham, onion, and celery. 3 minutes for sautéing. Add the garlic and heat for 30 seconds or until fragrant. Press the Cancel button. 2. Add the peas, stock, bay leaf, salt, and pepper to the pot. Close the lid, select Pressure Cook, and set the timer for 20 minutes. Once the timer beeps, release the pressure quickly on the vent position. Open the lid, press the Cancel button, then throw out the bay leaf. 3. Blend one-third of the soup until smooth, then add it back to the pot and thoroughly mix. Serve warm.
Per Serving: Calories 968; Fat: 25.17g; Sodium 1662mg; Carbs: 15.7g; Sugars: 2.43g; Protein 161g

Classic Italian Soup

Prep Time: 30 minutes | Cook Time: 25 minutes |Serves: 8

½ medium yellow onion, peeled and minced
1 large egg, beaten
1 clove garlic, peeled and minced
¼ cup bread crumbs
½ teaspoon Italian seasoning
1 teaspoon salt, divided
¼ teaspoon crushed red pepper flakes
8 ounces ground pork
4 ounces 90% lean ground beef
1 tablespoon vegetable oil

1 medium yellow onion, peeled and roughly chopped
1 medium carrot, peeled and chopped
1 stalk celery, chopped
2 cloves garlic, chopped
½ teaspoon dried thyme
½ teaspoon ground black pepper
⅓cup white wine
4 cups Vegetable Broth
2 cups water
8 ounces baby spinach

1. Combine the ground beef, ground pork, and red pepper flakes in a large bowl along with the chopped onion, minced garlic, bread crumbs, Italian seasoning, and ½ teaspoon salt. Mix gently until well blended. Form the mixture into 1 ½" in diameter meatballs. Place on a tray, then chill until prepared to cook. 2. Press the Sauté button and heat the oil in the Instant Pot. Add the onion, carrot, and celery, and simmer for approximately 5 minutes, or until just soft. Add the pepper, thyme, and minced garlic. For 30 seconds, cook. Keep scraping the pot's bottom, add the wine and simmer for 30 seconds. Click Cancel. 3. Add the remaining ½ teaspoon of salt, water, and vegetable broth. Insert the meatball slowly. Press the Soup button, close the lid, set the steam release to the seal position, and cook the soup for the 20 minutes. 4. When the time beeps, let pressure release naturally on seal position, about 15 minutes. Open lid and stir in spinach. Replace the lid, press the Keep Warm button and simmer for 5 minutes. Serve hot.
Per Serving: Calories 1230; Fat: 134g; Sodium 354mg; Carbs: 3.87g; Sugars: 1.4g; Protein 12g

Healthy Barley Soup with Beans

Prep Time: 10 minutes | Cook Time: 30 minutes |Serves: 8

2 tablespoons vegetable oil
½ medium yellow onion, peeled and chopped
1 medium carrot, peeled and chopped
1 stalk celery, chopped
2 cups sliced mushrooms
2 cloves garlic, peeled and minced
½ teaspoon dried thyme
½ teaspoon ground black pepper
1 large russet potato, peeled and cut into ½" cubes

1 (14-ounce) can fire-roasted diced tomatoes, undrained
½ cup medium pearled barley
4 cups Vegetable Broth
2 cups water
1 (15-ounce) can corn, drained
1 (15-ounce) can cut green beans, drained
1 (15-ounce) can Great Northern beans, drained and rinsed
½ teaspoon salt

1. Press the Sauté button and heat the oil in the Instant Pot. Add the mushrooms, onion, carrot, and celery. Cook for approximately 5 minutes, or until barely tender. Add the pepper, garlic, and thyme. Cook for 30 seconds. Press the Cancel button. 2. Add the barley, potatoes, tomatoes, broth, and water. Press the Soup button, close the lid, set the steam release to seal position, and cook the soup for the preset 20 minutes. 3. After the timer beeps, allow pressure to naturally release for around 15 minutes on the seal position. After lifting the top and stirring the soup, add the corn, green beans, and Great Northern beans. Replace the lid, choose Keep Warm button, and wait for 10 minutes. Remove the lid, then sprinkle with the salt. Serve warm.
Per Serving: Calories 1172; Fat: 113g; Sodium 234mg; Carbs: 42g; Sugars: 4.03g; Protein 8g

Classic Heart Healthy Soup

Prep Time: 20 minutes | Cook Time: 25 minutes |Serves: 8

1 tablespoon vegetable oil
½ pound 90% lean ground beef
½ medium yellow onion, peeled and chopped
1 medium carrot, peeled and chopped
1 stalk celery, chopped
1 medium green bell pepper, seeded and chopped
1 (15-ounce) can diced tomatoes, undrained
1 large russet potato, peeled and cut into ½" cubes

½ cup medium pearled barley
2 cloves garlic, peeled and minced
½ teaspoon dried thyme
½ teaspoon ground black pepper
4 cups Beef Broth
2 cups water
1 (15-ounce) can cut green beans, drained
½ teaspoon salt

1. Press the Sauté button and heat the oil in the Instant Pot. Add the beef and brown it well for 8 minutes. Add the bell pepper, onion, carrot, and celery. Cook for approximately 5 minutes, or until barely tender. Add the tomatoes, potatoes, barley, black pepper, thyme, garlic, broth, and water. Press the Cancel button. 2. Press the Soup button, close the lid, set the steam release to seal position, and cook the soup for the 20 minutes. After the timer beeps, allow pressure to naturally release for around 15 minutes on the seal position. Remove the lid, give the soup a stir, then add the salt and green beans. Replace the lid, press the Keep Warm button, and simmer for 5 minutes. Serve warm.
Per Serving: Calories 321; Fat: 12.17g; Sodium 182mg; Carbs: 24g; Sugars: 3g; Protein 31.39g

Authentic Carrot Potato Soup with Broccoli

Prep Time: 10 minutes | Cook Time: 6 minutes |Serves: 8

3 tablespoons vegetable oil
3 medium carrots, peeled and finely chopped
1 stalk celery, chopped
1 medium yellow onion, peeled and diced
1 medium russet potato, peeled and chopped
2 cloves garlic, peeled and minced
½ teaspoon dried thyme

¼ teaspoon smoked paprika
½ cup nutritional yeast
½ cup whole raw cashews
4 cups Vegetable Broth
1 tablespoon lemon juice
3 cups chopped broccoli
½ teaspoon salt

1. Press the Sauté button and heat the oil in the Instant Pot. Add the onion, celery, and carrots. Cook for approximately 5 minutes, stirring frequently, until softened. 2. Cook the potato, garlic, thyme, and paprika for about 30 seconds, or until the garlic and spices are aromatic. Don't hesitate to click Cancel. Add the lemon juice, cashews, broth, and nutritional yeast. Mix thoroughly. 3. Close the lid, set the steam release to seal position, hit the Pressure Cook button, and select a 5-minute timer. After the timer chimes, allow pressure to naturally relax for around 15 minutes. Open the lid and combine the contents in batches or with an immersion blender. 4. After adding the broccoli to the saucepan, stir thoroughly. Close the lid, set the steam release to seal position, hit the Pressure Cook button, and set the timer to 1 before pressing the Cancel button. When the timer beeps, quick-release the pressure on the vent position. Remove lid, add the salt, and stir well. Serve hot.
Per Serving: Calories 1069; Fat: 111.17g; Sodium 404mg; Carbs: 20.7g; Sugars: 3g; Protein 8.39g

Cheesy Carrot and Broccoli Soup

Prep Time: 20 minutes | Cook Time: 5 minutes |Serves: 8

3 tablespoons unsalted butter
2 medium carrots, peeled and finely chopped
2 stalks celery, finely chopped
1 medium yellow onion, peeled and finely chopped
1 clove garlic, peeled and minced
½ teaspoon dried thyme
3 cups chopped broccoli florets, divided

¼ cup all-purpose flour
3 cups Chicken Broth
1 tablespoon water
½ cup heavy cream
2 cups shredded mild Cheddar cheese
1 cup shredded Gruyère cheese

1. Press the Sauté button and melt the butter in the Instant Pot. Add the onion, celery, and carrots. Cook for approximately 5 minutes, stirring frequently, until softened. After adding the garlic for about 30 seconds, mix in the thyme and 2 cups of the broccoli. 2. After adding the flour and thoroughly combining, cook for 1 minute. Add the broth gradually, scraping the bottom of the pot as you go. Click the Cancel button. 3. Close the lid, set the steam release to seal position, hit the Pressure Cook button, and select a 5-minute timer. When the timer beeps, allow the steam to naturally release on the seal position. Open the lid and use an immersion blender to puree the soup. 4. In a medium bowl that can be microwaved, place in the remaining 1 cup of broccoli and water. When the broccoli is tender, microwave it for 4 minutes with the cover on. Drain, then add the broccoli to the pot. 5. Stir in the cream, then add the cheeses 1 cup at a time, whisking each addition until completely melted before adding another. Serve hot.
Per Serving: Calories 406; Fat: 23g; Sodium 1404mg; Carbs: 18.87g; Sugars: 8.03g; Protein 32.39g

Creamy Tomato Soup with Basil

Prep Time: 5 minutes | Cook Time: 25 minutes |Serves: 4

1 tablespoon unsalted butter
½ small onion, diced
2 (28-ounce) cans crushed tomatoes
2 tablespoons granulated sugar

1 cup low-sodium chicken or vegetable broth
1 teaspoon Worcestershire sauce (optional)
½ cup heavy cream
Chopped fresh basil, for garnish

1. Choose Sauté. Add the butter to the inner pot. After bubbling, add the onion and cook for 5 minutes, or until it starts to brown and caramelize. Stir to remove any onion bits attached to the saucepan and then the tomatoes, sugar, stock, and Worcestershire sauce (if using). 2. Turn the valve to seal position and secure the lid in place. Choose Pressure Cook. Set the pressure to High when cooking. Schedule 7 minutes in the timer. When the timer beeps, quickly release the pressure in the pot on the vent position. 3. Unlock and stir in the cream. Garnish with the basil and serve warm.
Per Serving: Calories 147; Fat: 9g; Sodium 336mg; Carbs: 15g; Sugars: 12g; Protein 3g

Creamy Chicken Rice Soup

Prep Time: 20 minutes | Cook Time: 24 minutes |Serves: 8

3 tablespoons unsalted butter
3 stalks celery, chopped
2 medium carrots, peeled and chopped
1 medium yellow onion, peeled and chopped
2 cloves garlic, peeled and smashed
2 tablespoons all-purpose flour
4 cups Chicken Broth, divided
1 bay leaf

1 teaspoon poultry seasoning
½ teaspoon dried thyme
1 teaspoon salt
¼ teaspoon ground black pepper
1 (3-pound) chicken, cut into pieces
½ cup uncooked white rice
½ cup heavy whipping cream

1. Press the Sauté button and heat the butter in the Instant Pot. Add the onion, carrots, and celery. Cook, often stirring, for approximately 5 minutes or until veggies soften. Add the garlic and cook for 30 seconds, then pour the flour and cook for 1 minute. Add 2 cups of broth and well mix up, being sure to stir bottom. Click the Cancel button. 2. Add the salt, pepper, thyme, poultry seasoning, and bay leaf to the pot. Stir thoroughly, add the chicken, and then pour the remaining liquid up to the Max Fill line. Press the Pressure Cook button, close the lid, set the steam release to seal position, and cook the soup for the 20 minutes. 3. After the timer beeps, allow pressure to naturally relax for 20 to 25 minutes. Open lid and press the Cancel button. 4. Get rid of the bay leaf. Move the chicken to a chopping board using tongs or a slotted spoon. Carefully shred the meat, removing the skin and bones. Stir the chicken back into the pot. Add the rice, close the lid, set the steam release to seal position, select Pressure Cook, and set the timer for 4 minutes. 5. Once the timer beeps, quickly release the steam on the vent position, take off the lid, and thoroughly stir. Add cream and serve hot.
Per Serving: Calories 394; Fat: 16.17g; Sodium 866mg; Carbs: 15.87g; Sugars: 1.63g; Protein 43.19g

Pinto Bean and Tortilla Soup

2 tablespoons vegetable oil
1 medium yellow onion, peeled and chopped
2 cloves garlic, peeled and minced
2 jalapeño peppers, seeded and minced
½ teaspoon ground cumin
¼ teaspoon smoked paprika
1 (15-ounce) can fire-roasted tomatoes, undrained
½ cup roughly chopped cilantro

4 cups Chicken Broth or water
4 cups shredded cooked chicken breast
1 (15-ounce) can pinto beans, drained and rinsed
1 teaspoon salt
¼ teaspoon ground black pepper
¼ cup lime juice
1 cup shredded Cheddar cheese
3 ounces tortilla chips, roughly crushed

1. Press the Sauté button and heat the oil in the Instant Pot. Pour the onion and simmer for 5 minutes or until soft. Cook the garlic, jalapenos, cumin, and paprika for approximately a minute, or until fragrant. Press the Cancel button. 2. Stir in the tomatoes, cilantro, and broth. Stir thoroughly, then cover pot, set the steam release to seal position, push the Pressure Cook button, and choose a 5-minute timer on high. 3. When the timer beeps, allow the steam to naturally release for 15 minutes on the seal position, then quickly remove any leftover pressure. After lifting the lid, Add the chicken, beans, salt, pepper, and lime juice. Press the Keep Warm button and let soup stand. 4. Divide soup among the bowls and garnish with the cheese and tortilla chips. Serve hot.
Per Serving: Calories 429; Fat: 15.7g; Sodium 1004mg; Carbs: 18.87g; Sugars: 3.3g; Protein 51.9g

Lemony Shredded Chicken and Rice Soup

2 tablespoons vegetable oil
2 stalks celery, sliced
1 medium carrot, peeled and chopped
1 medium yellow onion, peeled and chopped
2 cloves garlic, peeled and minced
½ teaspoon dried thyme
1 bay leaf

4 cups Chicken Broth or water
3 cups shredded cooked chicken breast
½ cup uncooked white rice
¼ cup lemon juice
2 tablespoons chopped fresh flat-leaf parsley
1 teaspoon salt
¼ teaspoon ground black pepper

1. Press the Sauté button and heat the oil in the Instant Pot. Cook the celery, carrot, and onion for approximately 5 minutes or until they are soft. Cook the garlic and thyme for about a minute, or until fragrant. Press the Cancel button. 2. Add the rice, chicken, and broth. Stir thoroughly, then cover container, set the steam release to seal position, push the Pressure Cook button, and choose a 5-minute timer on high. 3. When the timer beeps, allow the steam to naturally release for 15 minutes on the seal position, then quickly remove any leftover pressure on the vent position. Remove lid, add the salt, pepper, parsley, and lemon juice. Remove and discard the bay leaf. Serve hot.
Per Serving: Calories 366; Fat: 13.57g; Sodium 834mg; Carbs: 13.87g; Sugars: 1.43g; Protein 43.39g

Fresh Tomato Basil Soup

¼ cup olive oil
1 medium yellow onion, peeled and chopped
4 cloves garlic, minced
3 large tomatoes, peeled and cut into big chunks
1 bay leaf
1 tablespoon sugar
¼ cup chopped basil

1 teaspoon dried oregano
1 teaspoon dried fennel
1 teaspoon salt
½ teaspoon black pepper
2 cups Vegetable Broth or Chicken Broth
2 tablespoons unsalted butter
½ cup heavy cream

1. Press the Sauté button and heat the olive oil in the Instant Pot. After approximately 5 minutes of cooking the onion until it is tender, add the garlic and sauté it for about 30 seconds until it is fragrant. 2. After adding the tomatoes and bay leaf, cook for 4-5 minutes, or until the tomatoes begin to release juice. 3. After pressing the Cancel button, add the honey, basil, oregano, fennel, salt, pepper, and broth. Stir thoroughly, then cover. Press the Pressure Cook button, set the steam release to seal position, then set the timer for 5 minutes on high. 4. When the timer beeps, quickly remove the pressure on the vent, then click Cancel. Open the lid, add the melted butter, and then mix in the cream. Discard the bay leaf. 5. Purée the soup with an immersion blender or transfer to a blender and purée until smooth. If you prefer a slightly chunky soup, only purée half or three-quarters of the soup. Serve hot.
Per Serving: Calories 255; Fat: 17g; Sodium 1101mg; Carbs: 23g; Sugars: 14g; Protein 4.8g

Broccoli and Cheese Soup

Prep Time: 5 minutes | Cook Time: 30 minutes | Serves: 4

2 tablespoons unsalted butter
1 small onion, chopped
1 cup sliced carrots
2 (14-ounce) cans low-sodium chicken or vegetable broth
1 tablespoon all-purpose flour
1 cup milk

1 (16-ounce) package frozen chopped broccoli, thawed
1 cup half-and-half
2 cups shredded Cheddar cheese
1 teaspoon fine sea salt
½ teaspoon ground black pepper

1. Choose Sauté and set the temperature to Medium. Add the butter to the inner cooking kettle. Add the onion and carrots to the foaming butter and cook for 3 minutes. Put the broth in. 2. Turn the valve to seal position and secure the lid in place. Choose Pressure Cook. Set the pressure to High when cooking. Set a 12-minute timer. After cooking is finished, set the valve to the vent position to quickly remove any leftover pressure. After 5 minutes, let the pressure dissipate naturally. 3. Whisk the milk and flour together in a small bowl. Unlock and remove the lid, then add the broccoli to the heated soup. Combine the milk and flour, add the half-and-half, and whisk. Stir in the cheese until melted. Season with the salt and pepper.
Per Serving: Calories 717; Fat: 22g; Sodium 2304mg; Carbs: 95g; Sugars: 38g; Protein 58.39g

Delicious Beef Noodle Soup

Prep Time: 30 minutes | Cook Time: 24 minutes | Serves: 8

2 pounds boneless chuck roast, cut into 1" pieces
¼ cup all-purpose flour
1 teaspoon salt, divided
1 teaspoon ground black pepper, divided
2 tablespoons vegetable oil, divided
2 medium yellow onions, peeled and chopped
2 medium carrots, peeled and chopped
2 stalks celery, chopped

2 cloves garlic, peeled and minced
1 tablespoon tomato paste
¼ teaspoon dried thyme
1 (14-ounce) can diced tomatoes, undrained
4 cups Beef Broth
2 cups water
4 ounces elbow macaroni

1. Fill a big zip-top plastic bag with the beef, flour, and ½ teaspoon of salt and pepper each. Make sure the beef is uniformly covered and shake thoroughly. 2. Press the Sauté button and heat 1 tablespoon of oil in the Instant Pot. Making ensuring there is enough room between each piece, add half the meat to the saucepan. Each side for 2 to 3 minutes. Transfer the hamburger to a dish and repeat with the remaining oil and meat. 3. Add the onions, celery, and carrots to the saucepan. Cook for approximately 5 minutes, or until the vegetables are soft. Cook the garlic, tomato paste, and thyme for about a minute, or until aromatic. Press the Cancel button. 4. Return the beef to the pot. Add the tomatoes, broth, and water. Stir well, being sure to scrape off any food remnants from the pot's bottom. Close lid, set steam release to seal position, press the Pressure Cook button, and cook for 20 minutes on high level. 5. After the timer beeps, allow pressure to naturally release for around 15 minutes on the seal position. Remove lid, then add the final ½ teaspoon of each salt and pepper. Press the Cancel button. 6. Add the macaroni to the pot and stir thoroughly. Close the lid, set the steam release to seal position, hit the Pressure Cook button, and select 4 minutes for the time. Release the pressure immediately once the timer beeps on the vent position. Open lid, then thoroughly stir. Serve hot.
Per Serving: Calories 467; Fat: 19.1g; Sodium 546mg; Carbs: 20.7g; Sugars: 3.9g; Protein 54g

Homemade Tomato Lentil Soup

Prep Time: 5 minutes | Cook Time: 30 minutes | Serves: 4

2 teaspoons cornstarch
6 cups plus 4 teaspoons cold water, divided
1 cup dried lentils
1 (28-ounce) can diced tomatoes, drained
1 chicken or vegetable bouillon cube (optional)

1 tablespoon onion powder
2 teaspoons brown sugar (optional)
1 teaspoon fine sea salt
¼ teaspoon ground black pepper
Chopped fresh basil, for garnish

1. Make a slurry in a small bowl by thoroughly combining the cornstarch with the 4 teaspoons of cold water. Fill the inner cooking pot with the lentils, tomatoes, 6 cups of water, slurry, bouillon (if used), onion powder, brown sugar (if using), salt, and pepper. 2. Turn the valve to seal position and secure the lid in place. Select Pressure Cook and set the pressure to High when cooking. Set a 12-minute timer. After cooking is finished, flip the valve to the vent position to quickly remove any leftover steam. After 10 minutes, let the pressure dissipate naturally. 3. Remove lid. Stir the soup, taste, and make any necessary flavor adjustments. Stir in the basil.
Per Serving: Calories 75; Fat: 1g; Sodium 784mg; Carbs: 16g; Sugars: 7g; Protein 3g

Creamy Baked Potato Soup

4 tablespoons unsalted butter
1 medium yellow onion, peeled and chopped
3 tablespoons all-purpose flour
1 teaspoon salt
½ teaspoon ground black pepper
5 cups Chicken Broth
5 pounds russet potatoes, peeled and cubed

4 ounces cream cheese
1 cup heavy cream
8 slices thick-cut bacon, cooked crisp and chopped
4 scallions, sliced
1 cup shredded Cheddar cheese
1 cup sour cream

1. Press the Sauté button and melt the butter in the Instant Pot. Add the onion and simmer for 3 minutes, or until it is soft. Cook the flour, salt, and pepper for about a minute, or until the flour is moistened. Whisk in the broth gradually and add the potatoes. Press the Cancel button. 2. Close the lid, set the steam release to seal position, push the Pressure Cook button, and select 10 minutes for the time on high. When the timer beeps, allow the steam to naturally release for 15 minutes on the seal position. 3. Lift the lid, then thoroughly stir. Purée the soup using an immersion blender until it is largely smooth with some noticeable potato bits. After adding the cream cheese and well mixing, add the cream. Garnish with the sour cream, bacon, onions, and Cheddar cheese while still hot. Serve.
Per Serving: Calories 795; Fat: 35g; Sodium 1664mg; Carbs: 63g; Sugars: 5.8g; Protein 55g

Kale Tomato Tortellini Soup with Parsley

1 tablespoon vegetable oil
1 medium yellow onion, peeled and chopped
2 stalks celery, chopped
1 medium carrot, peeled and chopped
3 cups chopped kale
2 cloves garlic, chopped
1 teaspoon Italian seasoning

½ teaspoon black pepper
1 (15-ounce) can diced tomatoes, drained
4 cups Vegetable Broth
9 ounces cheese tortellini
½ teaspoon salt
¼ cup chopped fresh flat-leaf parsley

1. Press the Sauté button and heat the oil in the Instant Pot. Add the kale, onion, celery, and carrot. Cook for approximately 5 minutes, or until barely tender. Add the pepper, garlic, and Italian seasoning. Cook for 30 seconds. After adding the tomatoes, cook for 30 seconds again. Press the Cancel button. 2. Add 1 cup of water and broth. Stir well. Close the lid, set the steam release to seal position, select Pressure Cook, and set the timer to 5 minutes on high. 3. When the timer beeps, allow the steam to naturally release for 15 minutes on the seal position. Remove lid, add the salt and pasta. Press the Cancel button, close lid, set steam release to seal position, press the Pressure Cook button, and set time to 10 minutes. When the timer beeps, quick-release the pressure on the vent position. Open lid and stir well. 4. Divide the soup into the bowls. Top each with the parsley and serve hot.
Per Serving: Calories 1029; Fat: 109g; Sodium 797mg; Carbs: 14g; Sugars: 6.55g; Protein 9.45g

Classic Lasagna Soup

1 tablespoon unsalted butter
1 small onion, chopped
1 tablespoon minced garlic
1 green bell pepper, seeded and chopped (optional)
1 pound Italian sausage, casings removed
2 (24-ounce) jars pasta sauce

4 cups low-sodium beef broth
1 tablespoon Italian seasoning
8 ounces lasagna noodles, broken up
1 cup ricotta cheese, for serving (optional)
1 cup shredded mozzarella cheese, for serving

1. Choose Sauté. Add the butter to the inner cooking kettle. When it begins to froth, add the sausage, onion, garlic, bell pepper (if using), and continue to sauté for an additional 5 minutes while breaking up the meat. 2. Add the pasta sauce, stock, and Italian spice at this point. Add the broken lasagna noodles and give them a good toss to coat them. 3. Turn the valve to seal position and secure the lid in place. Choose Pressure Cook. Set the pressure to High when cooking. Set a 4-minute timer. When cooking ends, let the pressure release naturally for 10 minutes, then turn the valve to the vent position to quickly release the remaining pressure. 4. Remove the lid. Stir the soup and add into the bowls. Garnish each bowl with a dollop of ricotta cheese (if using) and a sprinkle of mozzarella.
Per Serving: Calories 740; Fat: 35.17g; Sodium 1800mg; Carbs: 74.87g; Sugars: 4.03g; Protein 59.39g

Wisconsin Brats and Cheddar Chowder

4 tablespoons (½ stick) unsalted butter
1 (28-ounce) bag frozen potatoes O'Brien
1 celery stalk, chopped (optional)
2 carrots, chopped
¼ cup all-purpose flour
2 (14-ounce) cans low-sodium chicken broth

1 tablespoon Dijon mustard
½ small head cabbage, shredded (optional)
1 pound smoked sausage, cut into bite-size pieces
2 cups milk or half-and-half
2 cups shredded sharp Cheddar cheese

1. Choose Sauté. Add the butter to the inner cooking kettle and heat it until it foams. After cooking for 5 minutes, add the potatoes, carrots, and celery (if using). 2. When the veggies are evenly covered, add the flour and stir the mixture constantly. Add the broth gradually while swirling frequently to incorporate the roux into the liquid. Stir the mustard to remove any lumps before adding it. Add the sausage and cabbage, if using. 3. Turn the valve to seal position and secure the lid in place. Choose Pressure Cook. Adjust the heat to High. Set the time for 5 minutes. When cooking ends, carefully turn the valve to the vent position to quick-release. 4. Unlock and remove the lid, and then stir the milk into the soup. Add the cheese and stir until it melts.
Per Serving: Calories 375; Fat: 21g; Sodium 1404mg; Carbs: 26g; Sugars: 9g; Protein 23g

Perfect Chicken Enchilada Soup

2 boneless, skinless chicken breasts
1 (15-ounce) can kidney beans, rinsed and drained
1 (14-ounce) can diced tomatoes, drained
1 (14-ounce) can sweet corn kernels, drained
1 small onion, chopped
1 green bell pepper, seeded, and diced (optional)

1 jalapeño, seeded and diced (optional)
1 (10-ounce) can enchilada sauce
½ cup low-sodium chicken broth
1½ cups milk
3 tablespoons cornstarch
3 tablespoons cold water

1. In the inner cooking pot, combine the chicken, beans, tomatoes, corn, onion, peppers, enchilada sauce, and stock. 2. Turn the valve to the seal position and secure the lid in place. Choose Pressure Cook, then choose High. Set the time for 5 minutes. After 10 minutes, let the steam dissipate naturally. After cooking is finished, flip the valve to vent position to quickly remove any leftover steam. 3. Unlock and remove the lid. Place the chicken on a plate or chopping board. Use two forks to shred, or slice into bite-sized pieces. Add the milk and the chicken back to the saucepan, stirring. In a small bowl, combine the cornstarch and cold water and whisk until the mixture is smooth. When whisk in the slurry, the soup will begin to gently thicken.
Per Serving: Calories 670; Fat: 37g; Sodium 1004mg; Carbs: 35g; Sugars: 13g; Protein 61g

Spicy Red Chili

2 dried Anaheim chilies, halved and seeded
2 dried New Mexico chilies, halved and seeded
1 tablespoon chili powder
1 teaspoon ground cumin
1 (12-ounce) can lager- or bock-style beer, divided
1 tablespoon vegetable oil
2 pounds chili meat made from chuck roast
1 medium onion, peeled and chopped
1 teaspoon hot sauce

2 cloves garlic, peeled and minced
1 tablespoon light brown sugar
½ teaspoon salt
½ teaspoon ground black pepper
2 cups Beef Broth
1½ cups water, divided
¼ cup corn masa
1 tablespoon lime juice

1. Place the chilies on a baking sheet and cook for 8 minutes on Pressure Cook function High. Place the chilies in a large heatproof bowl and cover with the hot water. Let the chilies soak until tender, about 30 minutes. 2. Drain the chilies and blend with the cumin, chili powder, and half the beer. Purée for approximately a minute, or until smooth. Place aside. 3. Press the Sauté button and melt the butter in the Instant Pot. Add the chili meat, and cook it for 8 minutes while stirring often. Add the onion, garlic, brown sugar, salt, and pepper, and then cook for about 10 minutes, or until onions are just soft. Add the remaining beer, broth, 1 cup water, and chili paste. Stir thoroughly, scraping any crumb from the pot's bottom. Click the Cancel button. Cook for 30 minutes, then close the lid, set the steam release to the seal position, and click the Pressure Cook button on high. 5. When the timer beeps, allow the steam to naturally release for 20 minutes on the seal position. Lift the lid, then thoroughly stir. Press the Cancel button and press the Sauté button. 6. In a small bowl, mix the masa with the reserved water. Whisk the mixture into the chili, then add the lime juice and hot sauce. Bring the chili to a boil to thicken, about 5 minutes. Serve hot.
Per Serving: Calories 334; Fat: 10g; Sodium 304mg; Carbs: 8.89g; Sugars: 1.03g; Protein 46.9g

Cheesy Beany Pasta

Prep Time: 20 minutes | Cook Time: 23 minutes |Serves: 8

-pound bulk Italian sausage
medium yellow onion, peeled and chopped
2 stalks celery, chopped
large carrot, peeled and chopped
2 cloves garlic, peeled and chopped
½ teaspoon dried thyme
teaspoon Italian seasoning
½ teaspoon ground black pepper

1 (15-ounce) can diced tomatoes, undrained
4 cups Chicken Broth
1 cup water
1 cup dried cannellini beans, soaked overnight and drained
1 cup ditalini pasta
1 cup grated Parmesan cheese
2 tablespoons chopped fresh flat-leaf parsley
2 tablespoons chopped fresh basil

1. On the Instant Pot, click the Sauté button. Add the sausage and cook it for approximately 8 minutes, breaking it up into bite-sized pieces as it browns. Cook the carrot, celery, and onion for approximately 5 minutes, or until they are barely soft. Add the pepper, Italian spice, garlic, and thyme and cook for 30 seconds. After scraping the pot's bottom, add the tomatoes and heat for 30 seconds. Press the Cancel button. 2. Add the beans, water, and broth. Good stirring. Press the Soup button, close the lid, set the steam release to seal position, and cook the soup for the preset 20 minutes. 3. When the timer beeps, allow the steam to naturally release for 15 minutes on the seal position. Add the pasta and shake off the lid. Close the lid, set the steam release to seal position, hit the Pressure Cook button, and set the timer for 3 minutes before pressing the Cancel button. 4. Divide soup into the bowls. Top each with cheese, parsley, and basil. Serve hot.
Per Serving: Calories 571; Fat: 32g; Sodium 1004mg; Carbs: 26g; Sugars: 4.03g; Protein 4 6.39g

Classic Beef Chili

Prep Time: 25 minutes | Cook Time: 35 minutes |Serves: 8

2 pounds chili meat made from chuck roast
medium onion, peeled and chopped
3 cloves garlic, peeled and minced
¼ cup chili powder
teaspoon ground cumin
2 tablespoons light brown sugar

½ teaspoon salt
½ teaspoon ground black pepper
2 cups Beef Broth
2½ cups water, divided
¼ cup corn masa
1 tablespoon lime juice

1. Use the Instant Pot Sauté function to thoroughly brown the meat for 10 minutes. Cook for about 10 minutes, until the onions are just starting to get soft, adding the onion, garlic, chili powder, cumin, brown sugar, salt, and pepper. 2. Add 2 cups of water and broth, then stir thoroughly. Press the Cancel button, secure the lid, choose the vent position for the steam release, select Pressure Cook, and cook for the 30 minutes on high. 3. Once the timer beeps, quickly remove the pressure on the vent position, open the lid, and stir well when the timer sounds. Press the Sauté button after you've pressed the Cancel button. Whisk tighter the masa and any reserved water, then add the chili. Stirring often, bring to a boil for 5 minutes or until it begins to thicken. Press the Cancel button and add the lime juice. Serve hot.
Per Serving: Calories 299; Fat: 9g; Sodium 385mg; Carbs: 7g; Sugars: 1.03g; Protein 46.9g

Ground Beef Chili with Beans

Prep Time: 20 minutes | Cook Time: 20 minutes |Serves: 8

pound 80% lean ground beef
medium onion, peeled and chopped
2 cloves garlic, peeled and minced
¼ cup chili powder
teaspoon ground cumin
½ teaspoon ground coriander
2 tablespoons brown sugar

½ teaspoon salt
½ teaspoon ground black pepper
1 (14.5-ounce) can diced tomatoes
2 cups dried pinto beans, soaked overnight in water to cover and drained
2 cups Beef Broth
1 tablespoon lime juice

1. Use the Instant Pot Sauté function to brown the meat for 10 minutes or until no pink is visible. Cook for approximately 10 minutes, or until the onions are barely soft, adding the brown sugar, salt, pepper, chili powder, cumin, and coriander. 2. Stir thoroughly before adding tomatoes, soaking beans, and broth. Close the lid, set the steam release to the seal position, click the Pressure Cook button, and set the timer for 20 minutes before pressing the Cancel button. 3. When the timer beeps, allow the steam to naturally release for 20 minutes on the seal position. Open lid and press the Cancel button. Add the lime juice, then thoroughly whisk. Serve hot.
Per Serving: Calories 409; Fat: 11g; Sodium 418mg; Carbs: 38.7g; Sugars: 5.03g; Protein 39g

Traditional Beef and Sweet Potato Chili

Prep Time: 20 minutes | Cook Time: 15 minutes | Serves: 6

2 pounds 80% lean ground beef
1 medium onion, peeled and finely chopped
1 (14.5-ounce) can diced tomatoes, drained
3 cloves garlic, peeled and minced
¼ cup chili powder
½ teaspoon ground cumin
½ teaspoon dried oregano

½ teaspoon smoked paprika
½ teaspoon salt
½ teaspoon ground black pepper
1 (28-ounce) can crushed tomatoes
2 cups Chicken Broth
2 medium sweet potatoes, peeled and diced

1. Choose the Sauté function on the Instant Pot, and brown the meat for 10 minutes while thoroughly crushing it. Pour the onion and simmer for 5 minutes or until soft. Add the tomatoes, garlic, chili powder, cumin, oregano, paprika, salt, and pepper, and cook for 2 minutes or until aromatic. 2. Add the broth, tomatoes, and sweet potatoes and stir thoroughly. Close the lid, set the steam release to the seal position, click the Pressure Cook button, and set the timer to 15 minutes. Then press the Cancel button. 3. When the timer beeps, allow the steam to naturally release for 20 minutes on the seal position. Lift lid and thoroughly stir. Serve hot.
Per Serving: Calories 516; Fat: 20g; Sodium 761mg; Carbs: 21g; Sugars: 9.73g; Protein 60.7g

Savory Chipotle Beer Chili

Prep Time: 25 minutes | Cook Time: 35 minutes | Serves: 8

2 pounds chili meat made from chuck roast
1 medium onion, peeled and chopped
3 cloves garlic, peeled and minced
3 tablespoons minced chipotle in adobo
2 tablespoons chili powder
1 teaspoon ground cumin
½ teaspoon ground coriander
2 tablespoons light brown sugar

½ teaspoon salt
½ teaspoon ground black pepper
2 cups Beef Broth
1 (12-ounce) bottle lager-style beer
½ cup water
¼ cup corn masa
1 tablespoon lime juice

1. Use the Instant Pot Sauté function to thoroughly brown the chili meat for around 10 minutes. Add the onion, garlic, chipotle, chili powder, cumin, coriander, brown sugar, salt, and pepper as needed, and cook for approximately 10 minutes, or until the onions are just soft. 2. Combine the beer and broth. Press the Cancel button, secure the lid, choose vent for the steam release, select Pressure Cook, and cook for the 30 minutes on high. 3. When the timer sounds, quickly remove the steam on the vent position, then open the lid, and thoroughly stir. Press the Cancel button and press the Sauté button. Whisk together the water, masa, and chili. Stirring often, bring to a boil for 5 minutes or until it begins to thicken. Press the Cancel button and add the lime juice. Serve hot.
Per Serving: Calories 294; Fat: 9g; Sodium 374mg; Carbs: 6g; Sugars: 1.03g; Protein 45.39g

Authentic Cincinnati-Style Chili

Prep Time: 15 minutes | Cook Time: 10 minutes | Serves: 8

2 pounds 90% lean ground beef
3 large yellow onions, peeled and diced, divided
3 cloves garlic, peeled and minced
2 (16-ounce) cans kidney beans, rinsed and drained
1 (15-ounce) can tomato sauce
1 cup Beef Broth
2 tablespoons chili powder
2 tablespoons semisweet chocolate chips
2 tablespoons red wine vinegar

2 tablespoons honey
1 tablespoon pumpkin pie spice
1 teaspoon ground cumin
½ teaspoon ground cardamom
¼ teaspoon ground cloves
½ teaspoon salt
½ teaspoon freshly cracked black pepper
1 pound cooked spaghetti
4 cups shredded Cheddar cheese

1. Add the ground beef and ¾ of the diced onion, then press the Sauté button on the Instant Pot. Cook for approximately 8 minutes, turning often or until the meat is browned and the onion is translucent. Drain the extra fat and throw away. Add the garlic and sauté it for 30 seconds. 2. When everything is thoroughly combined, add the beans, tomato sauce, broth, chili powder, chocolate chips, vinegar, honey, pumpkin pie spice, cumin, cardamom, cloves, salt, and pepper. Cook for 1 minute, or until the spices are aromatic. 3. Set the cook time to 10 minutes, click the Pressure Cook button, close the lid, set the steam release to vent, and hit the Cancel button. When the timer sounds, quickly remove the pressure on the vent position and open the lid. Good stirring. Add the cheese and onions that were set aside to serve over pasta.
Per Serving: Calories 645; Fat: 30.17g; Sodium 1704mg; Carbs: 42.87g; Sugars: 17.03g; Protein 53.39g

Mouthwatering Bean Soup

Prep Time: 5 minutes | Cook Time: 50 minutes | Serves: 4

2 tablespoons olive oil
1 cup finely chopped onion
1 cup finely chopped celery (optional)
2 medium carrots, finely chopped
2 garlic cloves, minced

1 pound dried navy beans
8 cups low-sodium chicken broth or water
2 ham hocks (optional)
1 teaspoon fine sea salt

1. Choose Sauté. When the oil is added, heat it until shimmering. After cooking for 5 minutes, add the onion, carrots, garlic, and celery (if using). 2. Wash the beans, then throw away any that float. Stir in the beans, broth, salt, and ham hocks (if using). 3. Turn the valve to seal position and secure the lid in place. Choose Pressure Cook. Set the pressure to High and time for 25 minutes. When cooking is done, let it naturally dissipate for 20 minutes and then switch the valve to the vent position to quickly relieve the pressure. 4. Open the lid, take it off, and check the beans for doneness. To thicken the soup, mash some of the beans against the Instant Pot side with a fork.
Per Serving: Calories 147; Fat: 8g; Sodium 636mg; Carbs: 15g; Sugars: 4g; Protein 6.39g

Yummy Buffalo Chicken Chili

Prep Time: 15 minutes | Cook Time: 32 minutes | Serves: 6

1 tablespoon vegetable oil
1 medium onion, peeled and chopped
1 stalk celery, finely chopped
2 cloves garlic, peeled and minced
½ cup Buffalo-style hot sauce
½ teaspoon salt
½ teaspoon ground black pepper

1 (15-ounce) can fire-roasted tomatoes, drained
2 (15-ounce) cans cannellini beans, drained and rinsed
2 cups Chicken Broth
3 (6-ounce) bone-in chicken breasts, skin removed
8 ounces cream cheese, cubed, at room temperature
1 cup shredded Monterey jack cheese
¼ cup sliced scallions

1. Press the Sauté button and heat the oil in the Instant Pot. Cook the onion, celery, and garlic for approximately 5 minutes, or until the onions are just starting to soften. 2. Stir in the spicy sauce, salt, pepper, tomatoes, and beans. Add the chicken breasts and broth. Close the lid, set the steam release to the seal position, click the Pressure Cook button, and set the timer for 30 minutes on high. 3. When the timer beeps, allow the steam to naturally release for 20 minutes on the seal position. Open the lid and press the Cancel button. With two forks, carefully remove the chicken, pull the flesh from the bones, and shred. Place aside. 4. Select Sauté. Add the cream cheese and properly mix up. Cook the chicken and cheese shreds for approximately 2 minutes, or until the cheese is smooth and melted. Press the Cancel button. Serve hot with the scallions for garnish.
Per Serving: Calories 688; Fat: 42g; Sodium 1002mg; Carbs: 13g; Sugars: 6.2g; Protein 62g

Flavorful Chili Macaroni and Cheese

Prep Time: 25 minutes | Cook Time: 34 minutes | Serves: 8

1-pound chili meat made from chuck roast
1 medium onion, peeled and finely chopped
1 medium red bell pepper, seeded and finely chopped
1 medium carrot, peeled and finely chopped
1 (15-ounce) can fire-roasted tomatoes, drained
3 cloves garlic, peeled and minced
2 tablespoons chili powder
1 teaspoon ground cumin

½ teaspoon dried oregano
½ teaspoon salt
½ teaspoon ground black pepper
2 cups Beef Broth
6 ounces elbow macaroni
4 ounces cream cheese
¼ cup heavy cream
1½ cups shredded mild Cheddar cheese

1. Use the Instant Pot's Sauté function to thoroughly brown the chili meat for around 10 minutes. Add the onion, bell pepper, and carrot once it has browned. Cook for approximately 8 minutes, or until the veggies are soft. Cook the tomatoes, garlic, cumin, oregano, chili powder, salt, and black pepper for approximately 2 minutes, or until aromatic. 2. Add the broth and stir thoroughly. Press the Cancel button, secure the lid, choose vent for the steam release, select Pressure Cook, and cook for the 30 minutes on low. 3. When the timer sounds, quickly remove the steam on the vent position, then open the lid and thoroughly stir. Press the Cancel button and then add the macaroni. Close the lid, set the steam release to the seal position, select Pressure Cook, and set the timer for 4 minutes. When the timer beeps, quick-release the pressure. Open lid and stir well. Add the cream cheese and stir until melted. Add the cream and Cheddar cheese and stir until cheese is completely melted. Serve hot.
Per Serving: Calories 348; Fat: 13g; Sodium 424mg; Carbs: 23g; Sugars: 4.03g; Protein 34.39g

Simple Vegetarian Chili

Prep Time: 10 minutes | Cook Time: 30 minutes |Serves: 8

1 tablespoon olive oil
2 medium white onions, peeled and finely chopped
1 medium red bell pepper, seeded and finely chopped
1 medium carrot, peeled and finely chopped
2 small jalapeño peppers, seeded and finely chopped
2 cloves garlic, minced
1 (28-ounce) can diced tomatoes
1 (15-ounce) can tomato sauce
¼ cup chili powder
¼ cup chopped cilantro

1 tablespoon smoked paprika
1½ teaspoons ground cumin
1 teaspoon ground coriander
½ teaspoon salt
½ teaspoon black pepper
2 cups dried kidney beans, soaked overnight in water to cover and drained
½ cup bulgur wheat
3 cups Vegetable Broth
1 cup water

1. Press the Sauté button and heat the oil in the Instant Pot. Add the onions, bell pepper, and carrot and sauté for about 8 minutes, or until the veggies are soft. Cook the garlic and jalapenos for approximately a minute, or until aromatic. Don't hesitate to click Cancel. 2. In a pot, combine the beans, bulgur, tomatoes, tomato sauce, chili powder, cilantro, paprika, cumin, coriander, salt, and black pepper. Put the cover on, choose vent for the steam release, select Pressure Cook, and cook for the 30 minutes. 3. When the timer sounds, quickly remove the pressure on the vent position, then open the lid and thoroughly stir. If the chili is too thin, click the Cancel and Sauté buttons, then let the chill simmer, covered, until the appropriate thickness is achieved. Serve warm.

Per Serving: Calories 766; Fat: 80g; Sodium 457mg; Carbs: 17g; Sugars: 7.03g; Protein 4.39g

Southwest Chili with Black Beans and Corn

Prep Time: 10 minutes | Cook Time: 30 minutes |Serves: 8

1 tablespoon vegetable oil
1 medium white onion, peeled and chopped
1 medium red bell pepper, seeded and chopped
1 medium carrot, peeled and chopped
½ pound ground turkey
1½ cups dried black beans, soaked overnight in water to cover and drained
1 cup frozen corn kernels
1 (28-ounce) can diced tomatoes

3 tablespoons chili powder
1 tablespoon smoked paprika
2 teaspoons ground cumin
1 teaspoon ground coriander
½ teaspoon salt
½ teaspoon ground black pepper
3 cups Vegetable Broth
1 cup water

1. Press the Sauté button and heat the oil in the Instant Pot. Add the onion, bell pepper, and carrot and simmer until tender for approximately minutes. Add the ground turkey and simmer for about 6 minutes, or until the meat is no longer pink. Don't hesitate to click Cancel. 2. Fill the pot with the remaining ingredients. Put the cover on, choose vent for the steam release, select Pressure Cook, and cook for the predetermined 30 minutes. 3. When the timer sounds, quickly remove the pressure on the vent position, then open the lid and thoroughly stir. If the chili is too thin, click the Cancel and press Sauté buttons, then let the chili simmer, covered, until the appropriate thickness is achieved. Serve warm.

Per Serving: Calories 895; Fat: 80g; Sodium 380mg; Carbs: 36g; Sugars: 6g; Protein 16g

Chapter 4 Poultry Mains Recipes

Spicy Whole Chicken 50

Homemade Chicken Hawaiian 50

Easy Shredded Chicken Breast 50

Nutritious Salsa Chicken Tacos 50

Sour and Sweet Chicken Breast 51

Healthy Chicken Sandwich with Bacon Ranch 51

Coconut Tomato Chicken Curry 51

Potato and Chicken Thigh Casserole 52

Honey Garlic Chicken Thighs.............. 52

Nutritious Congee with Chicken........... 52

Cheesy Rice and Chicken Thighs 53

Basic Chicken Thighs 53

Creamy Chicken Cajun Pasta 53

Classic Chicken Pesto...................... 53

Tasty Chicken Alfredo 54

Savory Chicken Enchiladas 54

Stir-Fried Chicken and Vegetables 54

BBQ Pulled Chicken Sandwiches 55

Best Whole Chicken 55

Chicken Thighs with Carrot and Cherry Tomato 55

Homemade Chicken Wings 56

Spicy Chicken Wings 56

Sticky Asian Sesame Chicken.............. 56

Limey Honey Chicken Wings.............. 57

Flavorful Chicken Fajitas 57

Spicy Worcestershire Chicken Breast 57

Easy Chicken Breast in Sauce.............. 57

Homemade Honey Sriracha Chicken Breast 58

Honey Chicken Thighs with Ketchup...... 58

Simple Thai Chicken 58

Easy Salsa Verde Chicken 58

Curried Coconut Chicken with Potatoes... 59

Spicy Cacciatore Chicken 59

Salsa Chicken Nachos....................... 59

Refreshing Chicken Piccata 60

Authentic Adobo Chicken Drumstick...... 60

Simple Chicken Puttanesca................. 60

Spicy Whole Chicken

Prep Time: 10 minutes | Cook Time: 40 minutes |Serves: 6

1 (6-pound) whole chicken
1 teaspoon salt
½ teaspoon black pepper
½ teaspoon paprika

½ teaspoon garlic powder
1 tablespoon olive oil
1 cup water

1. Remove the giblets from chicken and discard giblets. 2. Combine the salt, pepper, paprika, and garlic powder in a small bowl. Rub the chicken with the spice mixture. 3. After pressing the Sauté button, add the oil to the Instant Pot. 4. In the Instant Pot, add the chicken and cook it for approximately a minute on each side. After removing the chicken, turn off the Instant Pot. 5. Add the water to the Instant Pot and put the steam rack inside. Put the chicken on the rack. 6. Set the pressure release to the seal position and close the lid. 7. Turn the timer to 38 minutes and press the Pressure Cook button on high. 8. When the timer beeps, allow the steam to naturally release on the seal position, then open the lid, and take it off. 9. Serve the chicken hot or cold.
Per Serving: Calories 254; Fat: 8g; Sodium 546mg; Carbs: 1g; Sugars: 0.03g; Protein 42g

Homemade Chicken Hawaiian

Prep Time: 5 minutes | Cook Time: 15 minutes |Serves: 4

1 pound boneless, skinless chicken breasts
1 (20-ounce) can crushed pineapple

1 (18-ounce) bottle barbecue sauce

1. Fill the Instant Pot with the chicken, pineapple (with juice), and barbecue sauce. To blend, stir. 2. Set the pressure release to seal position and close the lid. 3. Set the timer to 15 minutes and press Pressure Cook button on high. 4. When the timer beeps, allow the pressure to naturally release on the seal position, then open the lid, and take it off. 5. Serve.
Per Serving: Calories 721; Fat: 8g; Sodium 1904mg; Carbs: 150g; Sugars: 120g; Protein 14g

Easy Shredded Chicken Breast

Prep Time: 10 minutes | Cook Time: 15 minutes |Serves: 4

1 pound boneless, skinless chicken breasts
1½ cups chicken broth

1 teaspoon salt
¼ teaspoon black pepper

1. In the Instant Pot, combine the chicken, salt, broth, and pepper. 2. Set the pressure release to seal position and close the lid. 3. Set the timer to 15 minutes and press the Pressure Cook button on high. 4. When the timer beeps, allow the pressure to naturally release on the seal position, then open the lid, and take it off. 5. Take the chicken out of the Instant Pot and forked into shreds. Whenever a recipe calls for cooked chicken, use it.
Per Serving: Calories 340; Fat: 13g; Sodium 1200mg; Carbs: 24g; Sugars: 6g; Protein 30g

Nutritious Salsa Chicken Tacos

Prep Time: 5 minutes | Cook Time: 10 minutes |Serves: 4

2 cups chunky salsa
1 cup chicken broth
1 (1-ounce) packet taco seasoning
1 pound boneless, skinless chicken breasts

8 crunchy taco shells
2 cups shredded romaine lettuce
1 cup grated Mexican-blend cheese

1. Combine the chunky salsa, broth, and taco seasoning in a medium basin. Combine by whisking. Place the salsa mixture in the Instant Pot. 2. Stir in the chicken breast with the Instant Pot. 3. Set the pressure release to seal position and close the lid. 4. Press Pressure Cook button and set the timer for 10 minutes on high. 5. When the timer beeps, allow pressure to naturally release on the seal position for 10 minutes, then quickly remove any leftover pressure on the vent position. Remove the lid. 6. To shred chicken, use two forks. 7. Serve the chicken in taco shells with the cheese and lettuce shavings on top.
Per Serving: Calories 570; Fat: 24g; Sodium 1944mg; Carbs: 52g; Sugars: 12g; Protein 34g

Sour and Sweet Chicken Breast

1 cup apple cider vinegar
1 cup granulated sugar
½ cup ketchup
2 tablespoons soy sauce
1½ teaspoons garlic powder
1 teaspoon salt

1 cup cornstarch
2 pounds boneless, skinless chicken breasts, cut into 1" chunks
½ teaspoon salt
¼ teaspoon black pepper
¼ cup vegetable oil
3 large eggs, beaten

1. Mix the vinegar, sugar, ketchup, soy sauce, garlic powder, and salt in a small bowl. Place aside. 2. Fill a gallon-sized zip-top bag with the cornstarch and season with the pepper and salt. 3. Place the chicken into the cornstarch bag. Shake the bag tightly until the chicken is uniformly covered. 4. Press the Instant Pot Sauté button. Add the oil is and heat for 1 minute. 5. Take the chicken pieces out of the bag in batches and dip into beaten eggs. 6. Shake off any extra egg, then equally layer chicken in heated oil at the bottom of the saucepan. Let cook for 30 seconds without moving. 7. Flip and cook for another 30 seconds. 8. Take out of the pot, then proceed with the remaining chicken. 9. Pour the sauce into the pot and deglaze it when the chicken has finished cooking and been taken from the Instant Pot. 10. Turn the chicken in the sauce after adding it. 11. Set the pressure release to seal position and close the lid. 12. Set the timer to 3 minutes and press Pressure Cook button on high. 13. When the timer beeps, allow the pressure to naturally release on the seal position, then open the lid, and take it off. Serve warm.
Per Serving: Calories 562; Fat: 20g; Sodium 1254mg; Carbs: 79g; Sugars: 25g; Protein 16g

Healthy Chicken Sandwich with Bacon Ranch

½ pound bacon, chopped
1 cup chicken broth
1 (1-ounce) ranch seasoning packet
1 pound boneless, skinless chicken breasts
1 (8-ounce) package cream cheese

1 tablespoon cornstarch
½ cup shredded sharp Cheddar cheese
¼ cup sliced green onions
6 hamburger buns

1. Click the Sauté button. 2. In the Instant Pot, add the chopped bacon and cook for 5 minutes, until browned. Remove the bacon and place in between two paper towels. Save some for subsequent garnishing. 3. To deglaze the bottom of the pot, pour the broth into the Instant Pot. 4. Mix the broth with the ranch seasoning package. Add the chicken to the pot and the cream cheese on top. 5. Set the pressure release to seal position and close the lid. 6. Set the timer to 15 minutes and press Pressure Cook button. 7. After the timer beeps, allow pressure to naturally relax for 10 minutes on the seal position, then quickly remove any leftover pressure on the vent position. Remove the lid. 8. With two forks, remove the chicken and shred it. 9. Stir the cornstarch into the sauce while chicken is being removed. 10. Transfer the chicken and bacon to the pot and combine until evenly coated with the sauce. 11. Top with the Cheddar, green onions, and reserved bacon. Serve on the hamburger buns.
Per Serving: Calories 445; Fat: 29g; Sodium 1301mg; Carbs: 22g; Sugars: 5g; Protein 22g

Coconut Tomato Chicken Curry

2 lbs. chicken breast or thighs
16 oz. canned coconut milk
16 oz. canned tomato sauce
6 oz. can tomato paste
2 cloves garlic, minced

1 cup onion, chopped or ¼ cup dry minced onion
2 tbsps. curry powder
3 tbsps. honey
1 tsp salt

1. Stir together all of the ingredients in the Instant Pot, excluding the chicken. 2. Then add the chicken. Lock the lid by closing it. 3. Choose the Pressure Cook mode, and then set the cooking duration to HIGH pressure for 15 minutes. 4. Once cooking is complete, let the pressure release naturally for 15 minutes on the seal position. Release any remaining steam on the vent position. 5. Lift the cover and gently stir. 6. Serve with the cooked rice, potato or peas.
Per Serving: Calories 648; Fat: 38g; Sodium 1043mg; Carbs: 34g; Sugars: 25g; Protein 42g

Potato and Chicken Thigh Casserole

Prep Time: 10 minutes | Cook Time: 15 minutes |Serves: 4

3 medium russet potatoes, peeled and chopped
1 pound boneless, skinless chicken thighs
4 tablespoons unsalted butter
4 tablespoons all-purpose flour
½ teaspoon salt

¼ teaspoon black pepper
1 cup heavy whipping cream
1 cup shredded Cheddar cheese
1 cup water

1. In a 6-cup metal dish, combine the chicken and potatoes and mix. 2. Add the butter in the Instant Pot and select Sauté. 3. Melt the butter, then stir in the flour. After 2 minutes of whisking, the flour should be well mixed and browned. 4. Add the salt and pepper and continue mixing for a further 30 seconds. 5. Whisk the cream in gradually. Whisk for a further 2 minutes, or until the sauce is thickened and lump-free. 6. Pour the sauce over the chicken and potatoes. Add the Cheddar cheese on top. Grease a piece of foil with the cooking spray, then wrap it firmly over the bowl's rim. 7. Add the water to the Instant Pot and put the steam rack inside. To safely drop the bowl into the Instant Pot, make a foil sling. 8. Set the pressure release to the seal position and close the lid. 9. Press Pressure Cook button and adjust time to 10 minutes. 10. Once the timer beeps, allow pressure to naturally release on the seal position, then open the lid and take it off. Using a foil sling, remove the pan from the Instant Pot and remove the foil. Serve.
Per Serving: Calories 618; Fat: 25.17g; Sodium 624mg; Carbs: 80.7g; Sugars: 8.03g; Protein 18.39g

Honey Garlic Chicken Thighs

Prep Time: 5 minutes | Cook Time: 17 minutes |Serves: 4

1 pound boneless, skinless chicken thighs
¼ teaspoon salt
⅛ teaspoon black pepper
1 tablespoon olive oil
1 cup chicken broth
⅓ cup honey

6 cloves garlic, minced
2 tablespoons rice vinegar
1 tablespoon soy sauce
1 tablespoon cornstarch
½ cup cold water

1. Use the salt and pepper to season the chicken. 2. Pour the oil to the Instant Pot and press the Sauté button. 3. Cook the chicken for 30 seconds on each side in the pot. 4. After removing the chicken, deglaze the pan with the stock. Turn off your Instant Pot. 5. Combine the honey, garlic, vinegar, and soy sauce in a small bowl. 6. Remove the chicken to the Instant Pot and cover with the sauce. 7. Set the pressure release to seal position and close the lid. 8. Press Pressure Cook button and adjust time to 10 minutes. 9. After the timer beeps, allow pressure to naturally release on seal position for 10 minutes, then quickly remove any leftover pressure on vent position. Remove the lid by unlocking it. 10. Remove the chicken and set aside. 11. Click the Sauté button. 12. Whip together the cornstarch and water in a small bowl. Bring the sauce in the pot to a boil while incorporating the cornstarch slurry. Let the sauce boil 5 minutes. 13. Serve the sauce over the chicken.
Per Serving: Calories 435; Fat: 14g; Sodium 758mg; Carbs: 51g; Sugars: 29g; Protein 24g

Nutritious Congee with Chicken

Prep Time: 5 minutes | Cook Time: 60 minutes |Serves: 6

6 chicken drumsticks
7 cups water
1 cup Jasmine rice
1 tbsp. fresh ginger

Salt to taste
½ cup scallions, chopped
2 tbsps. sesame oil, optional
Well-rinse the rice.

1. To the Instant Pot, add the chicken, rice, water, and ginger. Good stirring. 2. Lock the lid by closing it. Set the cooking duration to 25 minutes at HIGH pressure and choose the Pressure Cook mode. 3. After cooking is finished, choose CANCEL and wait 10 minutes for the pressure to naturally release on seal position. Release any remaining steam the on vent position. Open the lid. 4. Remove the chicken from the saucepan, shred the flesh, and discard the bones. 5. Refill the pot with the chicken flesh. 6. Choose SAUTÉ and simmer for about 10 minutes, stirring periodically, or until thickened. Top with the scallions and sesame oil. Serve.
Per Serving: Calories 215; Fat: 20g; Sodium 146mg; Carbs: 10g; Sugars: 1.03g; Protein 26g

Cheesy Rice and Chicken Thighs

Prep Time: 5 minutes | Cook Time: 16 minutes | Serves: 4

3 tablespoons olive oil
1 pound boneless, skinless chicken thighs, cut into 1" pieces
1 cup white rice
½ teaspoon salt

¼ teaspoon black pepper
1½ cups chicken broth
1 cup shredded Cheddar cheese

1. Pour the oil to the Instant Pot and press the Sauté button. 2. Add the rice and chicken. Add the salt and pepper to taste. Cook for 5 minutes. 3. Pour in the broth to clean the pot's bottom. 4. Set the pressure release to seal position and close the lid. 5. Press Pressure Cook button and adjust time to 10 minutes. 6. Once the timer beeps, allow pressure to naturally release on seal position, then open the lid, and take it off. 7. Mix in the cheese and serve.
Per Serving: Calories 601; Fat: 23g; Sodium 967mg; Carbs: 62g; Sugars: 6g; Protein 33.39g

Basic Chicken Thighs

Prep Time: 15 minutes | Cook Time: 20 minutes | Serves: 4

5 lbs. chicken thighs
4 cloves garlic, minced
½ cup soy sauce
½ cup white vinegar

1 tsp black peppercorns
3 bay leaves
½ tsp salt
½ tsp ground black pepper

1. Add the garlic, soy sauce, vinegar, peppercorns, salt, bay leaves, and pepper to the Instant Pot, and stir everything together. 2. Add the chicken thighs. Stir to coat the chicken. 3. Lock the lid by closing it. Set the cooking time to 15 minutes and choose the Pressure Cook option on high. 4. After the timer goes off, give the pressure 10 minutes to naturally release on the seal position. Open the lid. 5. Take the bay leaves out before serving.
Per Serving: Calories 1362; Fat: 99g; Sodium 1234mg; Carbs: 11g; Sugars: 6g; Protein 96g

Creamy Chicken Cajun Pasta

Prep Time: 10 minutes | Cook Time: 13 minutes | Serves: 6

2 tablespoons olive oil
1 pound boneless, skinless chicken breasts, sliced
1 tablespoon Cajun seasoning
4 cups chicken broth

1 pound penne pasta
8 tablespoons butter, cubed
1 cup heavy whipping cream
1 cup grated Parmesan cheese

1. Pour the oil to the Instant Pot and press the Sauté button. 2. In the Instant Pot, add the chicken and the Cajun spices. Cook for 7 minutes while periodically stirring. 3. Pour in the broth to clean the pot's bottom. 4. Put the spaghetti in the pot. Add the butter to pasta and chicken. 5. Set the pressure release to seal position and close the lid. 6. Press Pressure Cook button and set time to 5 minutes. 7. When the timer beeps, quickly release the pressure steam on the vent position, then open the lid and take it off. 8. Add the cream and Parmesan, then stir thoroughly. 9. Serve hot.
Per Serving: Calories 799; Fat: 47g; Sodium 1394mg; Carbs: 41g; Sugars: 4g; Protein 49g

Classic Chicken Pesto

Prep Time: 5 minutes | Cook Time: 15 minutes | Serves: 4

1 cup water
1 pound boneless, skinless chicken breasts, cut into strips
½ cup pesto

2 Roma tomatoes, sliced
¼ teaspoon salt
⅛ teaspoon black pepper

1. Add 1 cup of water to the Instant Pot and put the steam rack inside. 2. Combine the chicken, pesto, tomatoes, salt, and pepper in a 6-cup metal bowl. 3. Carefully drop the bowl into the Instant Pot, use a foil sling. 4. Set the pressure release to seal position and close the lid. 5. Set the timer to 15 minutes and press Pressure Cook button on high. 6. When the timer beeps, allow the steam to naturally release on the seal position, open the lid and take it off. Using a foil sling, take the pan out of the Instant Pot. 8. Serve hot.
Per Serving: Calories 365; Fat: 23g; Sodium 729mg; Carbs: 25g; Sugars: 6g; Protein 13.39g

Tasty Chicken Alfredo

Prep Time: 10 minutes | Cook Time: 13 minutes | Serves: 6

2 tablespoons olive oil
1 pound boneless, skinless chicken breasts, sliced
1 teaspoon garlic salt
½ teaspoon black pepper
4 cups chicken broth

1-pound fettuccine
8 tablespoons butter, cubed
1 cup heavy whipping cream
1 cup grated Parmesan cheese

1. On the Instant Pot, choose Sauté and then add the oil. 2. Put the chicken in the pot and season with the salt and pepper and garlic. Cook for minutes while periodically stirring. 3. Pour in the broth to clean the pot's bottom. 4. Put half-broken fettuccine in the pot. Add the butter to the fettuccine. 5. Set the pressure release to seal position and close the lid. 6. Set the timer to 6 minutes and press Pressure Cook button. 7. When the timer beeps, quickly release the pressure steam on the vent position, then open the lid and take it off. 8. Add the cream and Parmesan, then sti thoroughly. 9. Serve hot.
Per Serving: Calories 805; Fat: 52g; Sodium 1581mg; Carbs: 30g; Sugars: 8g; Protein 51g

Savory Chicken Enchiladas

Prep Time: 10 minutes | Cook Time: 12 minutes | Serves: 4

2 tablespoons butter
2 tablespoons all-purpose flour
1 cup chicken broth
1 cup full-fat sour cream
1 (4-ounce) can mild diced green chilies, divided

1 cup water
1½ cups shredded cooked chicken
1½ cups shredded Monterey jack cheese
4 (8") flour tortillas

1. On the Instant Pot, select Sauté and then add the butter. After allowing the butter to melt, mix in the flour. For about 2 minutes, mix the butter and flour continuously until the flour is browned and the sauce is smooth. 2. Whisk in broth gradually. With continual stirring, cook for 2 minutes. 3. Remove the sauce from Instant Pot and let it cool for 5 minutes in a different bowl. 4. Combine the sauce with sour cream and hal of the chopped canned chilies. 5. Add one cup of water after washing the Instant Pot. To the Instant Pot, add a steam rack. 6. Fill four tortilla with the remaining half-can of chopped chilies, chicken, and cheese. 7. In a 7" cake pan, roll up the tortillas and put them side by side. Over the rolled-up tortillas, drizzle the sauce. 8. Set the pressure release to seal position and close the lid. 9. Press Pressure Cook button and set time to ! minutes. 10. When the timer beeps, quickly release the pressure steam on the vent position, then open the lid and take it off. 11. With the help o a foil sling, remove the foil from the pan's top and serve hot.
Per Serving: Calories 719; Fat: 44g; Sodium 1104mg; Carbs: 34g; Sugars: 7g; Protein 39g

Stir-Fried Chicken and Vegetables

Prep Time: 10 minutes | Cook Time: 18 minutes | Serves: 4

2 tablespoons olive oil
1 pound boneless, skinless chicken breasts, cut into 1" pieces
½ teaspoon salt
¼ teaspoon black pepper
1 medium bunch broccoli, cut into small florets
1 medium cucumber, sliced and halved

1 medium red bell pepper, seeded and sliced
1 tablespoon minced ginger
2 cloves garlic, minced
½ cup stir-fry sauce
2 cups cooked brown rice, warmed

1. Press the Instant Pot's Sauté button. Give the oil in the Instant Pot a minute to heat up. 2. To the Instant Pot, add the chicken, salt, and pepper For about 8 minutes, while keeping the lid on, cook until the internal temperature is no longer pink. Remove the chicken and leave aside. 3 To the Instant Pot, add the broccoli, cucumber, bell pepper, and ginger. Stir-fry for about 5 minutes, or until veggies are soft. 4. After adding the garlic, simmer for another 30 seconds. 5. Remove the chicken to the Instant Pot, then add the stir-fry sauce. Mix to evenly distribute sauce Simmer the sauce for 2 minutes before finishing. 6. Remove from heat and serve over the rice after.
Per Serving: Calories 325; Fat: 14g; Sodium 726mg; Carbs: 30g; Sugars: 8g; Protein 17g

BBQ Pulled Chicken Sandwiches

Prep Time: 10 minutes | Cook Time: 15 minutes | Serves: 4

1 pound boneless, skinless chicken breasts
¼ teaspoon salt
⅛ teaspoon black pepper

1½ cups barbecue sauce, divided
1 cup water
4 hamburger buns

1. Put the chicken in a 6-cup metal bowl. Season the chicken with the salt and pepper, then brush with a cup of barbecue sauce. 2. Fill the Instant Pot with the water. Put the steam rack into the Instant Pot. 3. Carefully drop the bowl of chicken into the Instant Pot using a foil sling. 4. Set the pressure release to seal position and close the lid. 5. Set the timer to 15 minutes and press Pressure Cook button. 6. When the timer beeps, allow the pressure to naturally release on the seal position, then quickly remove any leftover pressure on vent position. Remove the lid by unlocking it. 7. To remove the bowl of chicken, use a foil sling. 8. With two forks, shred the chicken after draining any water in the bowl. 9. Add the remaining ½ cup barbecue sauce and stir to combine. 10. Serve the pulled chicken on the warmed hamburger buns.
Per Serving: Calories 682; Fat: 7g; Sodium 1554mg; Carbs: 67g; Sugars: 41.03g; Protein 11g

Best Whole Chicken

Prep Time: 15 minutes | Cook Time: 30 minutes | Serves: 4

1 medium-sized, whole chicken (3 lbs.)
2 tbsps. sugar
2 tsp kosher salt
1 tbsp. onion powder
1 tbsp. garlic powder
1 tbsp. paprika

2 tsp ground black pepper
½ tsp cayenne pepper
1 cup water or chicken broth
1 tbsp. cooking wine
2 tsp soy sauce
1 minced green onion

1. Combine the sugar, salt, onion, garlic, black pepper, paprika, and cayenne pepper in a medium bowl. 2. Add the water to the Instant Pot and put the steam rack inside. 3. Place the wine and soy sauce in the stew. 4. Apply the spice mixture to the chicken's whole surface. 5. Place the chicken on the steam rack and affix the cover. 6. Set the cooking time to 18 minutes at HIGH pressure using the Pressure Cook mode. 7. After the timer goes off, let the pressure 15 minutes to naturally release on the seal position. Take your time to open the lid. Top with the minced green onion and serve.
Per Serving: Calories 168; Fat: 5.17g; Sodium 1404mg; Carbs: 16.87g; Sugars: 9g; Protein 14.39g

Chicken Thighs with Carrot and Cherry Tomato

Prep Time: 5 minutes | Cook Time: 20 minutes | Serves: 4

8 boneless, skinless chicken thighs
1 tsp kosher salt
½ tsp ground black pepper
1 tbsp. olive oil
2 medium-sized, chopped carrots
1 cup stemmed and quartered cremini mushrooms
1 chopped onion
3 cloves garlic, smashed

1 tbsp. tomato paste
2 cups cherry tomatoes
½ cup pitted green olives
½ cup thinly-sliced fresh basil
¼ cup chopped fresh Italian parsley
½ teaspoon salt and pepper should be used to season the chicken thighs.

1. Select SAUTÉ. Add the oil to the pot's bottom after waiting one minute. 2. For about 5 minutes, sauté the carrots, mushrooms, onions, and ½ teaspoon salt until tender. 3. Place in the tomato paste and garlic and cook for a further 30 seconds. 4. Add the chicken thighs, cherry tomatoes, and olives and stir thoroughly. 5. Select the Pressure Cook and cook for 10 minutes at HIGH pressure. 6. Use the Quick Release when the timer runs off. Take your time to open the lid. 7. Add some parsley and fresh basil on top. Serve.
Per Serving: Calories 548; Fat: 18g; Sodium 1292mg; Carbs: 72g; Sugars: 26g; Protein 26g

Homemade Chicken Wings

Prep Time: 5 minutes | Cook Time: 15 minutes |Serves: 4

3 lbs. chicken wings
2 tbsps. olive oil
¼ cup light brown sugar
½ tsp garlic powder
½ tsp cayenne pepper

½ tsp black pepper
½ tsp paprika
½ tsp salt
1½ cups chicken broth or water

1. Rinse the chicken wings and dry with a paper towel. Place inside the big basin. 2. Combine the olive oil, sugar, cayenne pepper, paprika, garlic powder, black pepper, and salt in a medium bowl. Mix thoroughly. 3. Apply the spice mixture to the chicken's whole surface. 4. Add the chicken stock and add the wings to the Instant Pot. 5. Lock the lid by closing it. Choose the Pressure Cook mode, and then set the cooking duration to HIGH pressure for 10 minutes. 6. Use the Quick Release when the Pressure Cooking is finished. Take your time to open the lid. 7. Slide under the broiler for 5–6 minutes if you want a crisp skin. Serve.
Per Serving: Calories 504; Fat: 19g; Sodium 868mg; Carbs: 2.87g; Sugars: 1.03g; Protein 75g

Spicy Chicken Wings

Prep Time: 5 minutes | Cook Time: 20 minutes |Serves: 6

4 lbs. chicken wings, sectioned, frozen or fresh
½ cup cayenne pepper hot sauce
1 tbsp. Worcestershire sauce
½ cup butter

½ tsp kosher salt
1-2 tbsp. sugar, light brown
1½ cups water

For the sauce: Combine the spicy sauce, Worcestershire sauce, butter, salt, and brown sugar in a microwave-safe bowl. Microwave for 2 seconds, or until the butter is melted.
For the wings: 1. Add the water to the Instant Pot and put the steam rack inside. 2. Place the steam rack with the chicken wings on it, then shut the lid. 3. Choose Pressure Cook, then cook for 10 minutes at HIGH pressure. 4. Use a Quick Release when the timer chimes. Take your time to open the lid. 5. Turn on the broiler in the oven. 6. Carefully transfer the chicken wings to a baking sheet. 7. Brush on top of the chicken wings with the sauce. 8. Broil for 4 to 5 minutes, or until browned. 9. Broil for an additional 4-5 minutes while brushing the leftover sauce on the opposite side. Serve.
Per Serving: Calories 796; Fat: 39g; Sodium 892mg; Carbs: 5g; Sugars: 4g; Protein 100g

Sticky Asian Sesame Chicken

Prep Time: 5 minutes | Cook Time: 30 minutes |Serves: 6

6 boneless chicken thigh fillets
5 tbsps. sweet chili sauce
5 tbsps. hoisin sauce
1 chunk peeled, grated fresh ginger
4 peeled and crushed cloves garlic

1 tbsp. rice vinegar
1½ tbsp. sesame seeds
1 tbsp. soy sauce
½ cup chicken stock

1. Stir the chili sauce, hoisin sauce, ginger, garlic, vinegar, sesame seeds, soy sauce, and chicken stock together in a medium bowl until well blended. 2. Pour the sauce mixture over the chicken thigh fillets and add them to the Instant Pot. 3. Lock the lid by closing it. Choose Pressure Cook, then cook for 15 minutes at HIGH pressure. 4. After cooking is finished, allow the pressure to naturally release on seal position for 10 minutes. Release any remaining steam on the vent position. Open the lid. 5. Serve with the mashed potatoes, cooked rice, or another type of garnish.
Per Serving: Calories 782; Fat: 49.17g; Sodium 2304mg; Carbs: 44.87g; Sugars: 9g; Protein 40g

Limey Honey Chicken Wings

Prep Time: 5 minutes | Cook Time: 30 minutes | Serves: 4

2 lbs. chicken wings
3 tbsps. honey
2 tbsps. soy sauce

1 small lime, juiced
½ tsp sea salt
½ cup water

1. Combine the soy sauce, lime juice, honey, and salt in a bowl. 2. Rinse the chicken wings and dry with a paper towel. 3. Add the chicken wings and honey mixture to a Ziploc bag and shake few times. After that, chill for 60 minutes. 4. Add the chicken wings with marinade to the Instant Pot along with the water. 5. Lock the lid by closing it. Choose the Pressure Cook mode, and then set the cooking duration to HIGH pressure for 15 minutes. 6. After the timer goes off, give the pressure 10 minutes to naturally release on the seal position. Open the lid. 7. Choose SAUTÉ and keep cooking until the sauce becomes thick. Serve. If desired, season with some more herbs or spices.
Per Serving: Calories 360; Fat: 9g; Sodium 596mg; Carbs: 16g; Sugars: 14g; Protein 50g

Flavorful Chicken Fajitas

Prep Time: 10 minutes | Cook Time: 12 minutes | Serves: 6

1 pound boneless, skinless chicken thighs, sliced
1 cup chicken broth
1 medium sweet onion, peeled and sliced
1 medium red bell pepper, seeded and sliced
1 medium green bell pepper, seeded and sliced

1 (4-ounce) can mild diced green chilies
1 (1-ounce) packet taco seasoning
2 tablespoons lime juice
6 (10") flour tortillas, warmed

1. In the Instant Pot, mix all the ingredients minus the tortillas. To blend, stir. 2. Set the pressure release to seal position and close the lid. 3. Press Pressure Cook button and adjust time to 12 minutes. 4. Once the timer beeps, allow pressure to naturally release on seal position, then open the lid and take it off. 5. Serve in the warmed flour tortillas.
Per Serving: Calories 372; Fat: 9g; Sodium 957mg; Carbs: 48g; Sugars: 10g; Protein 20g

Spicy Worcestershire Chicken Breast

Prep Time: 10 minutes | Cook Time: 15 minutes | Serves: 4

¾ cup mild hot sauce
3 tablespoons butter, melted
1 tablespoon Worcestershire sauce

½ tablespoon red wine vinegar
½ teaspoon cornstarch
1 pound boneless, skinless chicken breasts

1. Combine the hot sauce, butter, Worcestershire, vinegar, and cornstarch in the Instant Pot. 2. Turn the chicken in the Instant Pot to coat it with the sauce. 3. Set the pressure release to seal position and close the lid. 4. Set the timer to 15 minutes and press the Pressure Cook button on high. 5. When the timer beeps, allow the pressure to naturally release on the seal position, then open the lid, and take it off. 6. Serve.
Per Serving: Calories 293; Fat: 15g; Sodium 757mg; Carbs: 28.7g; Sugars: 8.03g; Protein 11.39g

Easy Chicken Breast in Sauce

Prep Time: 5 minutes | Cook Time: 15 minutes | Serves: 4

½ cup soy sauce
½ cup rice vinegar
½ cup packed light brown sugar
1 tablespoon cornstarch

1 teaspoon minced ginger
¼ teaspoon garlic powder
1 pound boneless, skinless chicken breasts

1. Combine the soy sauce, rice vinegar, brown sugar, ginger, cornstarch, and garlic powder in a small basin. 2. Place the chicken and sauce into Instant Pot. To blend, stir. 3. Set the pressure release to seal position and close the lid. 4. Set the timer to 15 minutes and press Pressure Cook button. 5. Once the timer beeps, allow pressure to naturally release on the seal position, then open the lid and take it off. 6. Serve.
Per Serving: Calories 319; Fat: 12g; Sodium 794mg; Carbs: 35g; Sugars: 12g; Protein 13g

Homemade Honey Sriracha Chicken Breast

Prep Time: 5 minutes | Cook Time: 15 minutes |Serves: 4

4 diced chicken breasts
5 tbsps. soy sauce
2-3 tbsps. honey
¼ cup sugar

4 tbsps. cold water
1 tbsp. minced garlic
2-3 tbsps. sriracha
2 tbsps. cornstarch

1. Stir the soy sauce, honey, sugar, 2 tablespoons of water, garlic, and sriracha together in the Instant Pot. 2. Toss the chicken breasts in the mixture. Lock the lid by closing it. 3. Select Pressure Cook, and then cook for 9 minutes at HIGH pressure. 4. In the meantime, mix cornstarch and 2 tablespoons of water in a small dish. 5. Use a Quick Release once the timer goes off. Carefully unlock the lid. 6. Add the cornstarch mixture to the saucepan. 7. Use the SAUTÉ button. Simmer the sauce while sometimes stirring until it starts to thicken. Serve.
Per Serving: Calories 639; Fat: 30g; Sodium 484mg; Carbs: 26.87g; Sugars: 20.03g; Protein 62.39g

Honey Chicken Thighs with Ketchup

Prep Time: 10 minutes | Cook Time: 35 minutes |Serves: 4

2 lbs. boneless chicken thighs
¼ cup soy sauce
3 tbsps. organic ketchup
¼ cup coconut oil

¼ cup honey
2 tsp garlic powder
½ tsp black pepper
1½ tsp sea salt

1. In the Instant Pot, mix the soy sauce, ketchup, coconut oil, honey, garlic powder, pepper, and salt. 2. Toss the mixture with the chicken thighs. Lock the lid by closing it. 3. Set the cooking time to 18 minutes at HIGH pressure using the Pressure Cook mode. 4. Use a Quick Release when the timer chimes. Take your time to open the lid. 5. Choose the SAUTÉ option, then cook the sauce for 5 minutes, or until it starts to thicken. Serve with the vegetables.
Per Serving: Calories 738; Fat: 54g; Sodium 1381mg; Carbs: 24g; Sugars: 21.03g; Protein 39g

Simple Thai Chicken

Prep Time: 5 minutes | Cook Time: 20 minutes |Serves: 4

2 lbs. chicken thighs, boneless and skinless
1 cup lime juice
½ cup fish sauce
¼ cup extra virgin olive oil

2 tbsps. coconut nectar
1 tsp ginger, grated
1 tsp mint, chopped
2 tsp cilantro, finely chopped

1. Mix the coconut nectar, ginger, mint, lime juice, fish sauce, olive oil, and cilantro in a medium bowl. 2. To the instant pot, add the chicken thighs. 3. On top, pour the marinade. 4. Close the lid. Choose Pressure Cook, then 10 minutes of HIGH Pressure Cooking. 5. Use a Quick Release when the timer beeps. Open the lid. Serve.
Per Serving: Calories 665; Fat: 48g; Sodium 3157mg; Carbs: 7g; Sugars: 2g; Protein 49g

Easy Salsa Verde Chicken

Prep Time: 5 minutes | Cook Time: 20 minutes |Serves: 6

2½ lbs. boneless chicken breasts
1 tsp smoked paprika
1 tsp cumin

1 tsp salt
2 cup (16 oz.) salsa verde

1. Add the salt, paprika, cumin, and chicken breasts to the Instant Pot. 2. Add the green salsa on top. 3. Lock the lid by closing it. Choose the Pressure Cook mode, and then set the cooking duration to HIGH pressure for 20 minutes. 4. Use a Quick Release when the Pressure Cooking is finished. Open the lid. Shred the meat. Serve.
Per Serving: Calories 419; Fat: 8g; Sodium 2534mg; Carbs: 17g; Sugars: 10g; Protein 68g

Curried Coconut Chicken with Potatoes

Prep Time: 5 minutes | Cook Time: 30 minutes | Serves: 4

1 lb. chicken breast, chopped
1 tbsps. extra virgin olive oil
1 yellow onion, thinly sliced
1 bag (1 oz.) chicken curry base

5 oz. canned coconut cream
6 potatoes, cut into halves
½ bunch coriander, chopped

1. Heat the oil in the Instant Pot on the SAUTÉ mode. 2. Add the chicken and sauté for 2 minutes, or until it begins to brown. 3. Stir in the onion and heat for a further minute. 4. Thoroughly mix the coconut cream and chicken curry base in a medium bowl. 5. Pour into the pot, then whisk in the potatoes. Lock the lid by closing it. 6. Select the Pressure Cook and cook for 15 minutes at HIGH pressure. 7. Use the Quick Release when the timer runs off. Open the lid slowly. Top with the coriander and serve.
Per Serving: Calories 652; Fat: 13.17g; Sodium 176mg; Carbs: 98.7g; Sugars: 5g; Protein 36g

Spicy Cacciatore Chicken

Prep Time: 10 minutes | Cook Time: 35 minutes | Serves: 4

4 chicken thighs, with the bone, skin removed
2 tbsps. olive oil
1 tsp kosher salt
1 tsp ground black pepper
½ cup diced green bell pepper
¼ cup diced red bell pepper

½ cup diced onion
½ (14 oz.) can crushed tomatoes
2 tbsps. chopped parsley or basil
½ tsp dried oregano
1 bay leaf

1. Select SAUTÉ. Add 1 tablespoon of oil to the bottom of the pot after waiting 1 minute. 2. Add the pepper and salt to the meat to season it. 3. For a few minutes on each side, brown the meat. Take the chicken out of the pot and placed aside. 4. Add the bell peppers and onion to the saucepan with another tablespoon of oil, and cook for about 5 minutes, or until soft and golden. 5. In the Instant Pot, place the chicken thighs. Give the tomatoes a pour. 6. Add the oregano and bay leaf and stir thoroughly. Put the lid on. 7. To halt the SAUTE feature, use the CANCEL button. Set the cooking duration to 25 minutes at HIGH pressure and choose the Pressure Cook mode. 8. Once cooking is complete, select CANCEL and let Naturally Release for 5 minutes on the seal position, then use a Quick Release on the vent position. Carefully unlock the lid. 9. Serve.
Per Serving: Calories 502; Fat: 39g; Sodium 768mg; Carbs: 4.87g; Sugars: 2.03g; Protein 32g

Salsa Chicken Nachos

Prep Time: 10 minutes | Cook Time: 35 minutes | Serves: 6

2 lbs. chicken thighs, boneless, skinless
1 tbsps. olive oil
1 package (1 oz.) taco seasoning mix

⅔ cup mild red salsa
⅓ cup mild Herdez salsa verde

1. Heat the oil in the Instant Pot using the SAUTÉ mode. 2. Add the chicken thighs, and brown the meat well for a few minutes on each side. 3. Mix the salsa and taco seasoning in a medium basin. 4. Add the ingredients to the saucepan and stir thoroughly. Lock the lid by closing it. 5. Before selecting the Pressure Cook and setting the cooking duration for 15 minutes at HIGH pressure, hit the CANCEL button to reset the cooking procedure. 6. Once the food has finished cooking, utilize a Natural Release for ten minutes before y releasing any leftover pressure the on vent position. Open the pot's lid. Shred the meat. Serve with the tortilla chips.
Per Serving: Calories 374; Fat: 28g; Sodium 317mg; Carbs: 2.87g; Sugars: 1.03g; Protein 2 5.39g

Refreshing Chicken Piccata

4 chicken breasts skinless, boneless, 1½ to 1¾ lbs.
1 tbsp. olive oil
¼ tsp black pepper
½ tsp salt
1 cup chicken broth

¼ cup fresh lemon juice
2 tbsps. butter
2 tbsps. brined capers, drained
2 tbsps. flat-leaf fresh parsley, chopped
Cooked rice or pasta

1. Choose SAUTÉ. Add the oil to the Instant Pot's bottom after waiting two minutes. 2. Add the chicken to the saucepan, season with the pepper and salt, and cook for 3 minutes on each side. 3. Put the broth in. Lock the lid by closing it. 4. Press the Cancel button. Set the cooking time to ? minutes at HIGH pressure on the Pressure Cook mode. 5. Once pressure cooking is complete, use a Quick Release on vent position. Open the lid 6. Transfer the cooked chicken to a serving dish. 7. To decrease the sauce, use the SAUTÉ setting and cook for 5 minutes. 8. Add the juice of fresh lemon. 9. Add the butter. Stir in the parsley and capers when the butter has melted. Press the CANCEL button to stop the cooking program 10. Pour the sauce over the chicken breasts. Serve with the rice or pasta.
Per Serving: Calories 182; Fat: 13.17g; Sodium 686mg; Carbs: 2.8g; Sugars: 0.53g; Protein 13.9g

Authentic Adobo Chicken Drumstick

4 chicken drumsticks
½ tsp kosher salt
1 tsp ground black pepper
2 tbsps. olive oil
¼ cup white vinegar

⅓ cup soy sauce
¼ cup sugar
1 onion, chopped
5 cloves garlic, crushed
2 bay leaves

1. Heat SAUTÉ on a high setting. Add the oil to the pot's bottom after waiting one minute. 2. Add ½ teaspoon pepper and salt to the legs seasoning. 3. In the Instant Pot, add the chicken drumsticks and cook for 4 minutes on each side. 4. Add the bay leaves, vinegar, soy sauce, sugar onion, garlic, and ½ teaspoon of pepper. 5. Lock the lid by closing it. Choose Pressure Cook, then cook for 10 minutes at HIGH pressure. 6. Use the Quick Release when the timer runs off. Open the lid slowly. 7. To reduce the sauce, use the SAUTÉ setting and simmer for 10 minutes. Press the CANCEL button to stop the cooking program. 8. Remove the bay leaves. Serve.
Per Serving: Calories 376; Fat: 22.17g; Sodium 754mg; Carbs: 16.87g; Sugars: 11.03g; Protein 25.39g

Simple Chicken Puttanesca

6 chicken thighs, skin on
2 tbsps. olive oil
1 cup water
14 oz. canned chopped tomatoes
2 cloves garlic, crushed
½ tsp red chili flakes or to taste

6 oz. pitted black olives
1 tbsp. capers, rinsed and drained
1 tbsp. fresh basil, chopped
1 tsp kosher salt
1 tsp ground black pepper

1. Heat the oil in the Instant Pot using the SAUTÉ mode. 2. Cook the chicken thighs for 4-6 minutes with the skin side down. 3. Transfer the chicken to a bowl. 4. Fill the Instant Pot with the water, tomatoes, garlic, chili flakes, black olives, capers, fresh basil, salt, and pepper. Simmer and stir. 5. Put the chicken back in the pot. Lock the lid by closing it. 6. Selecting the Pressure Cook option and setting the cooking duration fo 16 minutes at HIGH pressure. 7. After the timer goes off, wait for 10 minutes for the pressure to naturally dissipate on the seal position, then quickly releasing any leftover pressure on the vent position. Open the lid and serve.
Per Serving: Calories 522; Fat: 41g; Sodium 1104mg; Carbs: 4.87g; Sugars: 1g; Protein 33g

Chapter 5 Fish and Seafood Recipes

Chickpea Curry with Patota 62

Steamed Mussels with Pepper 62

Delicious Manchester Stew................. 62

Spice Trade Beans and Bulgur 63

Herbed Poached Salmon with Carrots ... 63

Lentil Stew with Rice 63

Perfect Clam Sauce.......................... 64

Classic Tomato-Poached Halibut 64

Hearty Fish Stew............................ 64

Easy Stuffed Peppers 65

Authentic Alaskan Wild Cod 65

Steamed Fish with Cherry Tomatoes and Olives 65

Simple Steamed Tilapia 65

Asian Fish and Vegetables 66

Fresh Salmon Fillets with Dill 66

Lemony Garlic Squid 66

Lemon-Dill Fish 67

Lemony Butter Cod Fillets 67

Gingered Orange Cod Fillets 67

Mustard Tilapia with Almond 67

Parmesan Haddock Fillets 68

Easy Oysters with Butter 68

Lemony Butter Crab Legs 68

Coconut Milk Crabs 68

Buttered Lobster Claws 69

Simple Lemon Octopus 69

Delicious Mediterranean Squid 69

Maple Sea Scallops.......................... 69

Healthy Seafood Gumbo.................... 70

Seafood Plov with Cranberries 70

Nutritious Seafood Gumbo 70

Mussels in White Wine 71

Tender Mixed Seafood with Rice 71

Simple Shrimp and Grits.................... 71

Traditional Shrimp Scampi 72

Delicious Shrimp Paella 72

Cajun Shrimp Boil 72

Chickpea Curry with Patota

Prep Time: 25 minutes | Cook Time: 5 minutes | Serves: 6

1 Tbsp. canola oil
1 medium onion, chopped
2 garlic cloves, minced
2 tsp. minced fresh gingerroot
2 tsp. ground coriander
1 tsp. garam masala
1 tsp. chili powder
½ tsp. salt
½ tsp. ground cumin
Optional: Sliced red onion and lime wedges

¼ tsp. ground turmeric
2½ cups vegetable stock
2 cans (15 oz. each) chickpeas or garbanzo beans, rinsed and drained
1 can (15 oz.) crushed tomatoes
1 large baking potato, peeled and cut into ¾-in. cubes
1 Tbsp. lime juice
Chopped fresh cilantro
Hot cooked rice

1. Set the Instant pot to the sauté setting. Add the oil and adjust for medium heat. Once the oil is heated, cook the onion and stir for 2-4 minutes. Add the dry spices, ginger, and garlic; simmer and stir for 1 minute. Add the stock to the Instant pot. Stir to release browned parts from the pan and cook for 30 seconds. Select Cancel. Toss in the potatoes, tomatoes, and chickpeas. 2. Close the pressure-release valve and lock the lid. Adjust to Pressure Cook on high for 3 minutes. When the timer beeps, allow any leftover pressure to naturally relax for 10 minutes on the seal position and quickly release it the on vent position. 3. Add the lime juice and cilantro, often stirring. Serve with the lime wedges, red onion, and rice, if preferred.
Per Serving: Calories 989; Fat: 95.17g; Sodium 554mg; Carbs: 34g; Sugars: 6.88g; Protein 8g

Steamed Mussels with Pepper

Prep Time: 30 minutes | Cook Time: 5 minutes | Serves: 4

2 lbs. fresh mussels, scrubbed and beards removed
2 Tbsp. olive oil
1 jalapeno pepper, seeded and chopped
3 garlic cloves, minced
1 bottle (8 oz.) clam juice
½ cup white wine or additional clam juice
⅓ cup chopped sweet red pepper

3 green onions, sliced
½ tsp. dried oregano
1 bay leaf
2 Tbsp. minced fresh parsley
¼ tsp. salt
¼ tsp. pepper
French bread baguette, sliced, optional

1. Tap the mussels and throw away those that don't shut. Place aside. Set the Instant pot to the sauté setting. Add the oil and adjust for medium heat. Cook and stir the chopped jalapeño for 2 to 3 minutes, or until it is crisp-tender. Add the garlic and simmer for another minute. Select Cancel. After stirring, add the mussels, wine, clam juice, red pepper, green onions, oregano, and bay leaf. Close the pressure-release valve and lock the lid. Adjust to Pressure Cook on high 2 minutes. Rapidly release pressure on the vent position. 2. Throw away the bay leaf and any closed mussels. Add the parsley, salt, and pepper to taste. Serve with pieces of baguette, if preferred.
Per Serving: Calories 265; Fat: 12g; Sodium 804mg; Carbs: 10g; Sugars: 1g; Protein 27g

Delicious Manchester Stew

Prep Time: 25 minutes | Cook Time: 5 minutes | Serves: 6

2 tbsp. olive oil
2 medium onions, chopped
2 garlic cloves, minced
1 tsp. dried oregano
1 cup dry red wine
1 lb. small red potatoes, quartered
1 can (16 oz.) kidney beans, rinsed and drained
½ lb. sliced fresh mushrooms

2 medium leeks (white portion only), sliced
1 cup fresh baby carrots
2 ½ cups water
1 can (14½ oz.) no-salt-added diced tomatoes
1 tsp. dried thyme
½ tsp. salt
¼ tsp. pepper
Fresh basil leaves

1. Choose the Instant Pot's sauté setting. Add the oil. After the oil is heated, cook and stir the onions for 2 to 3 minutes. After adding the garlic and oregano, cook and stir for another minute. Stir in the wine. Bring to a boil and simmer for 3 to 4 minutes, or until liquid is reduced by half. Select Cancel. 2. Add the carrots, potatoes, beans, mushrooms, leeks, and beans. Add the salt, pepper, tomatoes, water, and thyme while stirring. Close the pressure-release valve and lock the lid. Set to Pressure Cook for 3 minutes on high. When the timer beeps, allow any leftover pressure to naturally relax on the seal position for 10 minutes and quick-releasing it on the vent position. Add the basil leaves on top and serve.
Per Serving: Calories 201; Fat: 8g; Sodium 244mg; Carbs: 28.7g; Sugars: 8g; Protein 6g

Spice Trade Beans and Bulgur

Prep Time: 30 minutes | Cook Time: 15 minutes | Serves: 10

3 Tbsp. canola oil, divided
1½ cups bulgur
2 medium onions, chopped
1 medium sweet red pepper, chopped
5 garlic cloves, minced
1 Tbsp. ground cumin
1 Tbsp. paprika
2 tsp. ground ginger
1 tsp. pepper
½ tsp. ground cinnamon

½ tsp. cayenne pepper
1 carton (32 oz.) vegetable broth
2 Tbsp. soy sauce
1 can (28 oz.) crushed tomatoes
1 can (14½ oz.) diced tomatoes, undrained
1 can (15 oz.) garbanzo beans or chickpeas, rinsed and drained
½ cup golden raisins
2 Tbsp. brown sugar
Minced fresh cilantro, optional

1. Set the Instant pot to the sauté setting. Add 1 Tbsp. oil and adjust for medium heat. Once the oil is heated, cook and stir bulgur for 2 to 3 minutes. Remove from the pot. 2. In the Instant pot, heat the final 2 tablespoons of oil. Cook and stir red pepper and onions for 2 to 3 minutes, or until they are crisp-tender. After adding the spices, simmer for another minute. Select Cancel. Add the broth, soy sauce, and bulgur to the pot. 3. Close the pressure-release valve and lock the lid. Make adjustments for 12 minutes of low Pressure Cook. Rapidly release pressure on the vent position. Select Cancel. Choose the sauté option and lower the heat. Add the tomatoes, beans, raisins, and brown sugar. Cook, stirring periodically, for about 10 minutes, until the sauce is slightly thickened and well cooked. If desired, sprinkle with the minced cilantro.
Per Serving: Calories 178; Fat: 6g; Sodium 263mg; Carbs: 28.7g; Sugars: 13g; Protein 5g

Herbed Poached Salmon with Carrots

Prep Time: 10 minutes | Cook Time: 5 minutes | Serves: 4

2 cups water
1 cup white wine
1 medium onion, sliced
1 celery rib, sliced
1 medium carrot, sliced
2 Tbsp. lemon juice
3 fresh thyme sprigs

1 fresh rosemary sprig
1 bay leaf
½ tsp. salt
¼ tsp. pepper
4 salmon fillets (1¼ in. thick and 6 oz. each)
Lemon wedges

1. Add the first 11 ingredients in the Instant pot, then add the salmon. Close the pressure-release valve and lock the lid. Select Pressure Cook on high for 3 minutes. Rapidly release pressure on the vent position. When implanted the fish, a thermometer should register at least 290°F/145°C. 2. Take the fish out of the pot. Serve warm or cold with the lemon wedges.
Per Serving: Calories 390; Fat: 18g; Sodium 1303mg; Carbs: 2.87g; Sugars: 1.03g; Protein 52g

Lentil Stew with Rice

Prep Time: 45 minutes | Cook Time: 20 minutes | Serves: 8

2 Tbsp. canola oil
2 large onions, thinly sliced, divided
8 plum tomatoes, chopped
2 Tbsp. minced fresh gingerroot
3 garlic cloves, minced
2 tsp. ground coriander
1½ tsp. ground cumin
¼ tsp. cayenne pepper
Optional: Sliced green onions or minced fresh cilantro

3 cups vegetable broth
2 cups dried lentils, rinsed
2 cups water
1 can (4 oz.) chopped green chilies
¾ cup heavy whipping cream
2 Tbsp. butter
1 tsp. cumin seeds
6 cups hot cooked basmati or jasmine rice

1. Choose the Instant Pot's sauté setting. Add the oil. After the oil is heated, cook and stir the half of the onions for 2 to 3 minutes, or until crisp-tender. After adding the tomatoes, ginger, garlic, coriander, cumin, and cayenne, cook and stir for a further minute. Select Cancel. Stir in the remaining onion, green chilies, lentils, broth, and water. 2. Close the pressure-release valve and lock the lid. Adjust to Pressure Cook on high for 15 minutes. Allow the pressure to drop naturally on the seal position. Add the cream right before serving. Melt the butter in a small pan over a medium heat. Cook and swirl the cumin seeds for 1-2 minutes, or until they turn golden brown. To the lentil mixture, add. 3. Serve with the rice. Add the chopped cilantro or green onion slices as desired.
Per Serving: Calories 1162; Fat: 111.7g; Sodium 83mg; Carbs: 63g; Sugars: 13g; Protein 15g

Perfect Clam Sauce

4 Tbsp. butter
2 Tbsp. olive oil
½ cup finely chopped onion
8 oz. fresh mushrooms, chopped
2 garlic cloves, minced
2 cans (10 oz. each) whole baby clams
½ cup water
¼ cup sherry
2 tsp. lemon juice
1 bay leaf

¾ tsp. dried oregano
½ tsp. garlic salt
¼ tsp. white pepper
¼ tsp. Italian seasoning
¼ tsp. black pepper
2 Tbsp. chopped fresh parsley
Hot cooked pasta
Grated Parmesan cheese, additional lemon juice, minced parsley
optional

1. Select sauté setting on the Instant pot and adjust for medium heat. Add the butter and oil. When heated, sauté the onion for 2 minutes while stirring. After adding the garlic and mushrooms, cook for another minute. Select Cancel. 2. Drain the liquid from clams and chop them coarsely. To the Instant Pot, add the clams, conserved clam liquid, and remaining 9 ingredients. Close the pressure-release valve and lock the lid. Adjust to Pressure Cook on high 2 minutes. Rapidly releasing pressure on the vent position. 3. Discard the bay leaf and add the parsley and spaghetti. Serve with more lemon juice, parsley, and grated Parmesan cheese, if preferred.
Per Serving: Calories 425; Fat: 19g; Sodium 685mg; Carbs: 63g; Sugars: 7g; Protein 7g

Classic Tomato-Poached Halibut

1 Tbsp. olive oil
2 poblano peppers, finely chopped
1 small onion, finely chopped
1 can (14½ oz.) fire-roasted diced tomatoes, undrained
1 can (14½ oz.) no-salt-added diced tomatoes, undrained
½ cup water
¼ cup chopped pitted green olives

3 garlic cloves, minced
¼ tsp. pepper
⅛ tsp. salt
4 halibut fillets (4 oz. each)
⅓ cup chopped fresh cilantro
4 lemon wedges
Crusty whole grain bread, optional

1. Select sauté setting on the Instant pot and adjust for medium heat. Add the oil. After the oil is heated, cook and stir the Poblano peppers and onion for 2 to 3 minutes, or until crisp-tender. Select Cancel. After stirring, add the salt, pepper, olives, garlic, and tomatoes stirring. Put fillets on top. 2. Close the pressure-release valve and lock the lid. Adjust to Pressure Cook on high for 3 minutes. Rapidly release pressure on the vent position. When inserted the fish, a thermometer should read at least 290°F/145°C. 3. Put some cilantro on top. Serve with the bread, if preferred and lemon wedges.
Per Serving: Calories 343; Fat: 20g; Sodium 637mg; Carbs: 23g; Sugars: 9g; Protein 22g

Hearty Fish Stew

1 lb. potatoes (about 2 medium), peeled and finely chopped
1 can (14½ oz.) diced tomatoes, undrained
1 can (10½ oz.) condensed cream of celery soup, undiluted
1 pkg. (10 oz.) frozen corn, thawed
1½ cups frozen lima beans, thawed
1½ cups vegetable or chicken broth
1 large onion, finely chopped
1 celery rib, finely chopped
1 medium carrot, finely chopped

½ cup white wine or additional vegetable broth
4 garlic cloves, minced
1 bay leaf
1 tsp. lemon-pepper seasoning
1 tsp. dried parsley flakes
1 tsp. dried rosemary, crushed
½ tsp. salt
1 lb. cod fillets, cut into 1-in. pieces
1 can (12 oz.) fat-free evaporated milk

1. In the Instant Pot, combine the first 16 ingredients and add the cod on top. Close the pressure-release valve and lock the lid. Adjust to pressure-cook on high for 2 minutes. 2. Allow the pressure to drop naturally on seal position. Remove the bay leaf. Thoroughly stir in the milk to heat. 3. Serve.
Per Serving: Calories 360; Fat: 13g; Sodium 744mg; Carbs: 40g; Sugars: 60g; Protein 21g

Easy Stuffed Peppers

Prep Time: 15 minutes | Cook Time: 5 minutes | Serves: 4

4 medium sweet red peppers
1 can (15 oz.) black beans, rinsed and drained
1 cup shredded pepper jack cheese
¾ cup salsa
1 small onion, chopped

½ cup frozen corn
⅓ cup uncooked converted long grain rice
1¼ tsp. chili powder
½ tsp. ground cumin
Reduced-fat sour cream, optional

1. Pour 1 cup of water into the Instant Pot and put the steam rack inside. 2. Remove the peppers' tops and throw them away. Fill the peppers with a mixture of beans, cheese, salsa, onion, corn, rice, chili powder, and cumin. Put the peppers on the rack. 3. Close the pressure-release valve and lock the lid. Adjust to pressure-cook on high for 5 minutes. Allow the pressure to drop naturally on the seal position. Serve with the sour cream, if preferred.
Per Serving: Calories 265; Fat: 10g; Sodium 547mg; Carbs: 32g; Sugars: 9g; Protein 11g

Authentic Alaskan Wild Cod

Prep Time: 5 minutes | Cook Time: 10 minutes | Serves:2

1 large fillet wild Alaskan Cod
1 cup cherry tomatoes, chopped

Salt and ground black pepper to taste
2 tbsps. butter

1. Place the tomatoes in the Instant Pot. 2. Then add the fish. 3. Add the salt and pepper to taste. 4. Lock the lid by closing it. Choose Pressure Cook, then cook for 8 minutes at HIGH pressure. 5. Use a Quick Release on the vent position when the timer chimes. Take your time to open the lid. 6. Cover the fish fillet with the butter. After covering it, leave the dish alone for 1 minute. Serve.
Per Serving: Calories 782; Fat: 23g; Sodium 884mg; Carbs: 23.87g; Sugars: 11.03g; Protein 18.39g

Steamed Fish with Cherry Tomatoes and Olives

Prep Time: 5 minutes | Cook Time: 25 minutes | Serves: 4

4 white fish fillet
1 cup water
1 lb. cherry tomatoes cut into halves
1 cup olives, pitted and chopped

1 tbsp. olive oil
1 clove garlic, minced
½ tsp thyme, dried
Salt and ground black pepper to taste

1. Pour the water into the Instant Pot and put the steam rack inside. 2. Place the fish fillets on the rack. 3. Then add the tomatoes and olives on top. Add the olive oil, garlic, thyme, salt, and pepper. 4. Lock the lid by closing it. Choose Pressure Cook, then cook for 10 minutes at LOW pressure. 5. When the cooking is, choose Cancel and let the pressure naturally release for 10 minutes on the seal position. Open the lid. Serve the fish with the tomatoes mix.
Per Serving: Calories 287; Fat: 10g; Sodium 312mg; Carbs: 20g; Sugars: 14g; Protein 28g

Simple Steamed Tilapia

Prep Time: 5 minutes | Cook Time: 15 minutes | Serves: 4

1 lb. tilapia fillets
1 cup water

½ cup green commercial chutney

1. Pour the water into the Instant Pot and put the steam rack inside. 2. Place the fish in the center of a huge parchment paper square. 3. Season all of the fillets with the green chutney. 4. To create a package, tightly roll the paper's edges together. Put inside of steamer basket. 5. Lock the lid by closing it. Choose Pressure Cook, then cook for 10 minutes at HIGH pressure. 6. Use a Quick Release when the timer beeps on the vent position. Open the lid. Serve.
Per Serving: Calories 112; Fat: 2g; Sodium 68mg; Carbs: 1.87g; Sugars: 1.03g; Protein 23g

Asian Fish and Vegetables

Prep Time: 10 minutes | Cook Time: 30 minutes |Serves: 4

2 fillets white fish
1 cup water
½ lb. frozen vegetables of your choice
1 clove garlic, minced
2 tsp grated ginger

¼ long red chili, sliced
1 tbsp. honey
2 tbsps. soy sauce
Salt and ground black pepper to taste

1. Pour the water into the Instant Pot and put the steam rack inside. 2. In the pan, place the veggies. Put the pan on the steam rack. 3. Combine the garlic, ginger, red chili, honey, salt, soy sauce, and pepper in a bowl. Good stirring. 4. Add the fillets and thoroughly coat them with the mixture in the basin. 5. Arrange the fish fillets on top of the veggies. Lock the lid by closing it. 6. Set the cooking time to 15 minutes by pressing the STEAM button. 7. After cooking is finished, choose Cancel and wait 10 minutes for the pressure to naturally release on the seal position. Quickly expel any lingering steam on the vent position. Open the pot's lid. Serve.
Per Serving: Calories 603; Fat: 60g; Sodium 154mg; Carbs: 6g; Sugars: 5g; Protein 14g

Fresh Salmon Fillets with Dill

Prep Time: 10 minutes | Cook Time: 30 minutes |Serves: 4

4 salmon fillets
12 oz. squid
5 cups water
¼ cup soy sauce
¼ tsp thyme
½ cup fresh dill

½ tbsp. coriander
1 tbsp. kosher salt
1 tsp ground black pepper
1 tsp chili flakes
1 clove garlic, sliced

1. Choose Sauté in the Instant Pot. 2. Add the water, soy sauce, thyme, fresh dill, coriander, salt, black pepper, and chili flakes to the Instant Pot. Mix thoroughly. 3. Sauté the mixture for 15 minutes with the lid on. 4. Slice the squid and fish into 1 to 2 inch chunks. 5. When the time is up, remove all of the ingredients from the pot, excluding the liquid. 6. Add the fish, squid, and garlic. Continue light stirring. 7. Lock the lid by closing it. Choose Pressure Cook, then cook for 10 minutes at HIGH pressure. 8. Use the Quick Release on the vent position when the timer runs off. Open the lid slowly. 9. Serve with the cooked rice noodles.
Per Serving: Calories 512; Fat: 22g; Sodium 3131mg; Carbs: 7g; Sugars: 3g; Protein 66g

Lemony Garlic Squid

Prep Time: 10 minutes | Cook Time: 25 minutes |Serves: 4

1 lb. squid
1 tsp onion powder
2 tbsps. starch
1 tbsp. garlic, minced
1 tbsp. chives
¼ tsp chili pepper, chopped

1 tsp salt
1 tsp white pepper
1 tbsp. lemon juice
3 tbsps. fish sauce
2 tbsps. butter

1. Cut up the squid. 2. Mix the onion powder, starch, garlic, chives, chili pepper, salt, and white pepper in a large bowl. Mix thoroughly. 3. Add the squid to the spice mixture. Gently stir. 4. Stir in the fish sauce and lemon juice to season the mixture. For 10 minutes, set the mixture aside. 5. By choosing SAUTÉ, the Instant Pot will be preheated. Add the butter to melt. 6. Add the squid mixture to the pot and secure the lid. 7. Select the Pressure Cook setting and cook for 13 minutes. Allow the pressure to release naturally on the seal position. 8. Uncover the pot and serve when the cooking is finished.
Per Serving: Calories 170; Fat: 7g; Sodium 733mg; Carbs: 6g; Sugars: 1g; Protein 18.39g

Lemon-Dill Fish

Prep Time: 5 minutes | Cook Time: 10 minutes | Serves: 2

2 cod fillets
1 cup water
Salt and ground black pepper to taste
¼ tsp garlic powder

2 sprigs fresh dill
4 slices lemon
2 tbsps. butter

1. Put the steam rack in the Instant Pot and fill it with water. 2. Place the cod fillets on the steam rack. Add some garlic powder, salt, and pepper. 3. Put one dill sprig, two lemon slices, and one tablespoon of butter in that order on each fillet. 4. Lock the lid by closing it. Choose Pressure Cook, then cook for 5 minutes at HIGH pressure. 5. Use a Quick Release on the vent position when the cooking is finished. Open the lid by slowly unlocking it. Serve.
Per Serving: Calories 382; Fat: 27g; Sodium 513mg; Carbs: 16g; Sugars: 4g; Protein 20g

Lemony Butter Cod Fillets

Prep Time: 5 minutes | Cook Time: 20 minutes | Serves: 4

1½ lbs. fresh (or frozen) cod fillets
3 tbsps. butter
1 onion, sliced

1 can diced tomatoes
1 lemon juice, freshly squeezed
Salt and ground black pepper to taste

1. Choose SAUTÉ on the Instant Pot. 2. Add the butter to melt once it is heated. 3. Add the salt, pepper, onion, tomatoes, and lemon juice. Stir well and cook for 9 minutes. 4. Place the fish fillets in the pot and well cover in the sauce. 5. To stop the SAUTE feature, hit the CANCEL button. Then choose the Pressure Cook setting, and set the cooking time to 3 minutes (or 5 minutes for frozen), at HIGH pressure. 6. Use a Quick Release on the vent position when the cooking is finished. Open the lid by slowly unlocking it. Serve the fish with the sauce.
Per Serving: Calories 304; Fat: 15.17g; Sodium 234mg; Carbs: 40.87g; Sugars: 35g; Protein 5g

Gingered Orange Cod Fillets

Prep Time: 5 minutes | Cook Time: 10 minutes | Serves: 4

4 cod fillets, boneless
A small ginger piece, grated
1 cup white wine

Juice from 1 orange
Salt and ground black pepper to taste.
4 spring onions, chopped

1. Mix thoroughly the ginger, wine, and orange juice and add to the Instant Pot. 2. On top, put a steam rack. 3. Place the cod fillets in the basket. Add the salt and pepper to taste. 4. Lock the lid by closing it. Choose Pressure Cook, then cook for 7 minutes at HIGH pressure. 5. Use the Quick Release on the vent position when the timer runs off. Open the lid slowly. 6. Add the green onions and sauce to the fish before serving.
Per Serving: Calories 260; Fat: 15g; Sodium 434mg; Carbs: 10g; Sugars: 2g; Protein 20g

Mustard Tilapia with Almond

Prep Time: 5 minutes | Cook Time: 10 minutes | Serves: 4

4 tilapia fillets
1 cup water
1 tsp olive oil

¼ tsp lemon pepper
2 tbsps. Dijon mustard
⅔ cup sliced almonds

1. Pour the water into the Instant Pot and put the steam rack inside. 2. Mix the oil, lemon pepper, and Dijon mustard together in a bowl. 3. Apply the mixture like a brush to the fish fillets. 4. To coat all sides, add the fillets to the almond. 5. Suspend from the steam rack. Lock the lid by closing it. 6. Choose Pressure Cook, then cook for 5 minutes at HIGH pressure. 7. Use the Quick Release on the vent position when the timer runs off. Open the lid slowly. Serve.
Per Serving: Calories 127; Fat: 3.17g; Sodium 147mg; Carbs: 0.87g; Sugars: 0.03g; Protein 23g

Parmesan Haddock Fillets

Prep Time: 5 minutes | Cook Time: 10 minutes |Serves: 2

1 lb. fresh or frozen haddock fillets
1 tbsp. butter
1 tbsp. flour
¼ tsp salt

Ground black pepper to taste
½ cup milk
1 cup parmesan cheese, grated
1 cup water

1. Choose SAUTÉ to start the Instant Pot heating up. Melt the butter before adding it. 2. Add the salt, flour, and pepper and stir thoroughly. Sauté for 1 minute. 3. Pour the milk in slowly and whisk occasionally for 3 to 5 minutes, or until the sauce is thick and smooth. 4. When adding the cheese, whisk the mixture. 5. To stop the SAUTÉ button, use the CANCEL button. 6. Combine the sauce and fish fillets in a pan. Use foil to securely enclose. 7. With the water, clean the inside pot. 8. Pour 1 cup of water into the Instant Pot and put the steam rack inside. 9. Place the pan on the steam rack. 10. Choose Pressure Cook for 5 minutes at HIGH pressure. 11. Use a Quick Release on the vent position when the cooking is finished. Open the lid by slowly unlocking it. Serve.
Per Serving: Calories 496; Fat: 27g; Sodium 1829mg; Carbs: 24g; Sugars: 9g; Protein 38g

Easy Oysters with Butter

Prep Time: 5 minutes | Cook Time: 10 minutes |Serves: 6

36 in-shell oysters
1 cup water

Salt and ground black pepper to taste
6 tbsps. butter, melted

1. Clearly clean the oysters.2. Add the oysters, water, salt, and pepper to the Instant Pot. 3. Close the lid. Set the cooking time to 3 minutes at HIGH pressure on the Pressure Cook setting. 4. Use a Quick Release on the vent position when the timer beeps. Carefully unlock the lid. 5. Serve with the melted butter.
Per Serving: Calories 137; Fat: 12g; Sodium 146mg; Carbs: 3g; Sugars: 1g; Protein 3g

Lemony Butter Crab Legs

Prep Time: 5 minutes | Cook Time: 10 minutes |Serves: 4

4 lbs. king crab legs, broken in half
1 cup water

¼ cup butter
3 lemon wedges

1. Pour the water into Instant Pot and put the steam rack inside. 2. Place the crab legs on the rack. 3. Lock the lid by closing it. Choose Pressure Cook, then cook for 3 minutes at HIGH pressure. 4. Use the Quick Release on the vent position when the timer runs off. Open the lid slowly. 5. Place the legs in a serving basin together with the lemon wedges and melted butter. Serve.
Per Serving: Calories 482; Fat: 14.17g; Sodium 3998mg; Carbs: 0.87g; Sugars: 0.03g; Protein 83.9g

Coconut Milk Crabs

Prep Time: 5 minutes | Cook Time: 10 minutes |Serves: 4

1 lb. crabs, halved
1 tbsp. olive oil
1 onion, chopped
3 cloves garlic, minced

1 can coconut milk
1 thumb-size ginger, sliced
1 lemongrass stalk
Salt and ground black pepper to taste

1. By choosing SAUTÉ, the Instant Pot will be preheated. Oil is added, then heated. 2. Sauté for two minutes after adding the onion. 3. Add the garlic and cook for a further minute. 4. Crabs, coconut milk, ginger, lemongrass stem, salt, and pepper should also be added. 5. To stop the SAUTÉ feature, use the CANCEL key. 6. Lock the lid by closing it. Choose Pressure Cook, and then cook for 6 minutes at HIGH pressure. 7. Use the Quick Release on vent position when the timer runs off. Open the lid slowly. Serve.
Per Serving: Calories 238; Fat: 12g; Sodium 438mg; Carbs: 7g; Sugars: 2g; Protein 24g

Buttered Lobster Claws

Prep Time: 5 minutes | Cook Time: 20 minutes |Serves: 4

4 lobster tails, cut in half
1 cup water

½ cup white wine
½ cup butter, melted

1. Add the water and wine to the Instant Pot and put the steam rack inside. 2. Put the basket with the lobster tails inside. 3. Select the Pressure Cook setting and set the cooking time for 5 minutes at LOW pressure. 4. Once cooking is finished cooking, utilize a Natural Release for 10 minutes on the seal position and then quickly release any leftover pressure on the vent position. Open the lid. 5. Place the serving bowl with the legs in it. Add the melted butter and serve.
Per Serving: Calories 321; Fat: 24g; Sodium 820mg; Carbs: 0.8g; Sugars: 0.06g; Protein 25g

Simple Lemon Octopus

Prep Time: 5 minutes | Cook Time: 25 minutes |Serves:6

2½ lbs. whole octopus, cleaned and sliced
1 cup water

3 tbsps. lemon juice, freshly squeezed
Salt and ground black pepper to taste

1. Add the water and lemon juice to the Instant Pot. 2. Season with the salt and pepper, then add the octopus. 3. Lock the lid by closing it. Choose Pressure Cook, and then cook for 15 minutes at HIGH pressure. 4. Use the Quick Release on the vent position when the timer runs off. Open the lid slowly. 5. Return the food to the pot and simmer for an additional 5 minutes if necessary. Serve.
Per Serving: Calories 208; Fat: 6g; Sodium 1692mg; Carbs: 2.87g; Sugars: 2.03g; Protein 36g

Delicious Mediterranean Squid

Prep Time: 5 minutes | Cook Time: 20 minutes |Serves: 4

2 lbs. squid, chopped
2 tbsps. olive oil
Salt and ground black pepper to taste
1 cup red wine
3 stalks of celery, chopped

1 can (28 oz.) crushed tomatoes
1 red onion, sliced
3 cloves garlic, chopped
3 sprigs fresh rosemary
½ cup Italian parsley, chopped

1. Combine the squid, olive oil, salt, and pepper in a bowl. 2. To the cooking pot, add the wine, tomatoes, onion, garlic, rosemary, and celery. 3. In the pot, place the steam rack. 4. Place the squid on the steam rack. 5. Lock the lid by closing it. Choose Pressure Cook for 4 minutes at HIGH pressure. 6. After the timer goes off, wait 10 minutes for the pressure to drop naturally on the seal position and then quickly release any leftover steam on the vent position. Open the lid. Top with the fresh parsley and serve.
Per Serving: Calories 319; Fat: 10g; Sodium 318mg; Carbs: 18g; Sugars: 6g; Protein 38g

Maple Sea Scallops

Prep Time: 5 minutes | Cook Time: 10 minutes |Serves:2

1 lb. sea scallops, shells removed
1 cup water
1 tbsp. olive oil
3 tbsps. maple syrup

½ cup soy sauce
½ tsp ground ginger
½ tsp garlic powder
½ tsp salt

1. Pour the water into the Instant Pot and put the steam rack inside. 2. Place the scallops, olive oil, maple syrup, soy sauce, ginger, garlic powder, and salt in a baking dish that is 6-7 inches in diameter. 3. Place the pan on the steam rack. 4. Set the cooking time to 6 minutes using the STEAM setting. 5. Use a Quick Release on the vent position when the timer chimes. Carefully unlock the lid. Serve.
Per Serving: Calories 319; Fat: 14g; Sodium 534mg; Carbs: 18g; Sugars: 15g; Protein 28g

Healthy Seafood Gumbo

Prep Time: 5 minutes | Cook Time: 20 minutes |Serves: 4

12 oz. sea bass filets cut into 2" chunks
1 lb. medium to large raw shrimp, deveined
Salt and ground black pepper to taste
1½ tbsp. Cajun or creole seasoning
1½ tbsp. ghee or avocado oil
1 yellow onion, diced

2 celery ribs, diced
¾ cups bone broth
14 oz. diced tomatoes
⅛ cup tomato paste
2 bay leaves
1 bell pepper, diced

1. Apply the salt, pepper, and half of the Cajun or Creole spice to the both sides of fillets. 2. By choosing SAUTÉ, the Instant Pot will be preheated. Heat the oil or ghee before adding it. 3. Cook the fish for 2 minutes on each side in the pot. 4. From the saucepan, remove the fillets. Add the celery, onions, and any extra Cajun or Creole flavor. 5. For 2 minutes, sauté until aromatic. 6. Add the cooked fish, the shrimp, the bell pepper, the tomato paste, and the broth. 7. Once the cooking has been reset by pressing the CANCEL button, click the Pressure Cook button to set the cooking time to 5 minutes at HIGH pressure. 8. Use a Quick Release on the vent position when the cooking is finished. Open the lid by slowly unlocking it. Serve.
Per Serving: Calories 407; Fat: 20g; Sodium 1275mg; Carbs: 21g; Sugars: 7g; Protein 35g

Seafood Plov with Cranberries

Prep Time: 10 minutes | Cook Time: 20 minutes |Serves: 4

1 package (16 oz.) frozen seafood blend
2-3 tbsps. butter
1 onion, large-sized, chopped
1 bell pepper, red or yellow, sliced
3 big carrots, shredded

1½ cups basmati rice, organic
½ cup dried cranberries
Salt and ground black pepper to taste
3 cups water
1 lemon, sliced (optional)

1. Choose SAUTÉ to start the Instant Pot heating up. 2. Add the butter to melt once it is heated. 3. Add the carrots, bell pepper, and onion. Sauté while occasionally stirring for 5-7 minutes. 4. Add the fish mixture, rice, and cranberries and stir thoroughly. 5. To taste, add salt and pepper to the food. 6. Add some water. Lock the lid by closing it. 7. Choose Pressure Cook and set time for 10 minutes. 8. Naturally release the pressure on the vent position for 10 minutes after the timer beeps. Open the lid. 9. You may drizzle the meal with the fresh lemon juice if you'd like. Serve.
Per Serving: Calories 403; Fat: 20g; Sodium 165mg; Carbs: 60g; Sugars: 31g; Protein 10g

Nutritious Seafood Gumbo

Prep Time: 30 minutes | Cook Time: 30 minutes |Serves: 2

3 tablespoons oil, divided
½ pound andouille sausage, cut into ½-inch slices
1 small onion, diced
1 celery stalk, diced
1 cup diced green bell pepper
3 garlic cloves, minced
2 tablespoons butter
3 tablespoons all-purpose flour
3 cups Chicken Stock (here)
1 cup sliced okra

2 tablespoons tomato paste
1 tablespoon Creole seasoning, plus more for seasoning (optional)
¼ teaspoon cayenne pepper, plus more for seasoning (optional)
Kosher salt
Freshly ground black pepper
1 medium tomato, diced
½ pound raw medium shrimp, tail-on, peeled and deveined
¼ pound lump crabmeat, picked over
Gumbo filé powder (optional)

1. Set the Instant pot to the sauté setting. Add two teaspoons of oil. Add the sausage, onion, celery, bell pepper, and sauté for 6 to 8 minutes, or until browned. Add the garlic and stir for 1 minute. Put the mixture on a dish and reserve. 2. Melt the butter in the pot with the remaining tablespoon of oil. Add the flour and whisk in. Cook the roux until it reaches a medium to dark brown color for 12 to 15 minutes, continually whisking to prevent burning. 3. Stir and add the liquid, tomato paste, okra, sausage combination, creole spice, and cayenne pepper. To taste, add salt and black pepper to the food. Add the tomato. 4. Secure the lid and cook on Pressure Cook and high pressure for 4 minutes, then quickly release the pressure in the pot on the vent position and remove the lid. choose sauté. If necessary, Taste the dish and adjust the flavors and add extra cayenne pepper or Creole spice. 5. Stir in the shrimp and add the crabmeat on top, and simmer for 4 to 5 minutes, or until the shrimp are pink. Mix in the gumbo filé powder (if using). 6. Serve with the white rice and a sprinkle of scallions.
Per Serving: Calories 1020; Fat: 67g; Sodium 1404mg; Carbs: 34g; Sugars: 9.9g; Protein 70g

Mussels in White Wine

3 lbs. mussels, cleaned and debearded
5 tbsps. butter
4 shallots, chopped

1 cup white wine
1½ cups chicken stock

1. Select SAUTÉ and add the butter to the Instant Pot. 2. After the butter has melted and sauté the shallots for 2 minutes. 3. Add the wine, stir, and simmer for an additional 30 seconds. 4. Add the stock and mussels and stir thoroughly. Lock the lid by closing it. 5. After selecting the Pressure Cook option and setting the cooking time to 3 minutes at HIGH pressure. 6. Once cooking is complete, use a Quick Release on the vent position. Open the lid. Remove unopened mussels and serve.
Per Serving: Calories 488; Fat: 26g; Sodium 1404mg; Carbs: 18g; Sugars: 2g; Protein 43g

Tender Mixed Seafood with Rice

2 cups chopped white fish and scallops
2 cups mussels and shrimp
4 tbsps. olive oil
1 onion, diced
1 red bell pepper, diced

1 green bell pepper, diced
2 cups rice
A few saffron threads
2 cups fish stock
Salt and ground black pepper to taste

1. Heat up the oil in the instant pot while it is in SAUTÉ mode. 2. For 4 minutes, add the onion and bell peppers and sauté. 3. Stir in the rice, fish, and saffron. Cook for a further 2 minutes. 4. Add the fish stock and stir while adding the salt and pepper. 5. Then add the shellfish. 6. To stop the SAUTÉ button, use the CANCEL button. 7. Lock the lid by closing it. Choose Pressure Cook, and then cook for 6 minutes at HIGH pressure. 8. After cooking is finished, choose CANCEL and wait 10 minutes for the pressure to naturally release the on seal position. Release any remaining steam quickly on the vent position. Open the lid. Stir the dish and let sit for 5 minutes. Serve.
Per Serving: Calories 906; Fat: 85g; Sodium 211mg; Carbs: 12g; Sugars: 6g; Protein 20g

Simple Shrimp and Grits

3 uncooked bacon slices, chopped
2 shallots, chopped
¼ green bell pepper, chopped
¼ cup chopped celery
1 garlic clove, minced
Splash dry white wine or stock
½ cup fresh or canned diced tomatoes
⅓ cup Chicken Stock
1 tablespoon freshly squeezed lemon juice

Kosher salt
Freshly ground black pepper
½ cup dry grits
1 cup milk
1 cup water
½ pound uncooked shrimp, tails removed, peeled and deveined
1 tablespoon butter
¾ cup shredded Cheddar cheese
2 tablespoons heavy cream

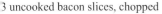

1. Set the Instant pot to the sauté setting. Add the bacon to the pot when the unit indicates "hot" and cook for 5 to 6 minutes, or until crispy. Transfer to a plate covered with paper towels to drain. Don't drain the pot. In the bacon fat in the pot, add the shallots, bell pepper, and celery. Sauté for 2 to 3 minutes, stirring regularly. 2. Add the garlic and then press the Cancel button. For 1 minute, sauté. 3. Pouring the wine into the pot while scraping off the browned pieces from the bottom will deglaze it. Allow the liquid to reduce for 1 to 2 minutes while stirring regularly, and then add the chopped tomatoes, stock, and lemon juice. Add the salt and pepper and stir. Pour the tomato sauce into a big basin, cover, and put aside. Clean the cooking pot, pat it dry, and put it back in the pot. 4. Combine the grits, milk, and water in a medium glass or metal heatproof bowl along with the salt and pepper. Place the grits dish on top of a steam rack or egg rack in the pot. 5. Select Pressure Cook, cook the food for 10 minutes on high pressure, then let the pressure naturally drop for around 10 minutes on the seal position. Then use a Quick Release on the vent position. After taking off the cover, carefully take the grits bowl from the cooking pot and set it aside. 6. Place the shrimp in the pot, then whisk in the tomato sauce. Replace the lid and cook the shrimp for 7 to 8 minutes in the residual heat, tossing once or twice to ensure equal cooking on both sides. 7. While waiting, use a fork to fluff the grits and whisk in the butter and cheese. To keep the bowl warm, cover it with the plastic wrap. 8. Stir in the cream and let it warm through when the shrimp is almost done cooking. 9. Add the shrimp and tomato sauce on top of the divided grits in two dishes. Add the chopped bacon on top, garnish with the scallions, and serve with the spicy sauce.
Per Serving: Calories 538; Fat: 32g; Sodium 1375mg; Carbs: 27g; Sugars: 22g; Protein 34g

Traditional Shrimp Scampi

6 ounces linguine
1 tablespoon oil
1 tablespoon butter
1 shallot, chopped
1 tablespoon minced garlic
Pinch red pepper flakes, plus more for seasoning (optional)
¼ cup white wine

¼ cup Chicken Stock
1 tablespoon freshly squeezed lemon juice
¾ pound thawed frozen raw jumbo shrimp, tails removed, peeled and deveined
Kosher salt
Freshly ground black pepper

1. While the other ingredients are cooking in the Instant Pot, prepare the pasta according to the package's instructions. Drain and rinse the pasta then transfer to a serving bowl, cover it, and put aside. 2. Set the Instant pot to the sauté setting. Add the oil and butter and stir until they melt Add the garlic, shallot, and red pepper flakes and sauté for 2 minutes. 3. Pour the wine into the pot to deglaze it, scraping off any browned pieces with a wooden spoon and adding them to the liquid as you go. Cook for 1 minute, then cut in half. Select Cancel. 4. Add the shrimp, lemon juice and stock. Close the lid. Select Pressure Cook on high for 5 minutes. Remove the lid after quickly release the pressure in the pot. Select Cancel. Season with the salt, pepper, and more red pepper flakes (if preferred) and add the parsley. Pour into the pasta serving bowl and stir. Serve with pieces of stale bread.
Per Serving: Calories 596; Fat: 14g; Sodium 1404mg; Carbs: 46g; Sugars: 15g; Protein 68.39g

Delicious Shrimp Paella

2 tablespoons oil
½ onion, chopped
2 garlic cloves, minced
Kosher salt
Freshly ground black pepper
1 teaspoon paprika
¼ teaspoon red pepper flakes

Pinch saffron threads
¼ cup white wine
½ cup basmati rice
1 (14-ounce) can diced tomatoes and chilies, with their juices
½ cup Chicken Stock
½ pound peel-on large raw shrimp, deveined

1. Set the Instant pot to the sauté setting. Add the oil when the display reads "hot." Add the onion and cook for 3 minutes, or until tender. For 1 minute, stir regularly while cooking the garlic. Season with the salt and pepper, mix to incorporate, and add the paprika, red pepper flakes and saffron. 2. Pour the wine into the pot to deglaze it while scraping the browned pieces from the bottom. Stir the rice in and add the stock tomatoes, chilies, and their juices. Make sure the rice is well coated by stirring. 3. Secure the lid and cook on high pressure for 5 minutes o Pressure Cook button, then quickly release the pressure in the pot on the vent position and remove the lid. After pressing Cancel, choose sauté 4. Stir the shrimp into the rice, cover the pot with the lid loosely, and cook for 3 to 5 minutes, or until pink. Serve with the chopped fresh cilantr and lime wedges.
Per Serving: Calories 439; Fat: 12g; Sodium 704mg; Carbs: 50g; Sugars: 17g; Protein 28.9g

Cajun Shrimp Boil

1 cup water
½ pound red potatoes, halved
1 medium sweet onion, chopped
2 ears of corn, shucked and broken in half
½ pound fully cooked kielbasa sausage, cut into 2-inch slices

2 tablespoons Old Bay seasoning, plus more for seasoning
2 tablespoons crab boil seasoning (optional)
½ teaspoon kosher salt
1-pound peel-on large raw shrimp, deveined

1. Combine the water, potatoes, onion, corn, kielbasa, 2 tablespoons of Old Bay, salt, and crab boil spice (if using) in the Instant pot. 2. Secur the lid and cook on Pressure Cook and high pressure for 4 minutes, then quickly release the pressure in the pot on the vent position and remov the lid. Select Cancel. 3. Add the shrimp, cover loosely, and simmer for 3 to 4 minutes in the residual heat. Season with the Old Bay an additional salt. Drain the water into a big colander. 4. Serve in sizable, shallow dishes along with some lemon wedges, melted butter, and crust bread for dipping.
Per Serving: Calories 982; Fat: 40.17g; Sodium 799mg; Carbs: 46g; Sugars: 11g; Protein 11g

Chapter 6 Meat Mains

Mustard Pork Chops 74

Apple and Pork Curry 74

Healthy Carnitas Lettuce Wraps 74

Tasty Pork and Squash Ragu 75

Mushroom Pork Ragout 75

Beef and Mushroom Stew with Egg Noodle 75

Tasty Satay Pork with Rice Noodles 76

Simple and Quick Meatloaf 76

Yummy Pork Tacos with Mango Salsa ... 76

Red Beans and Ham Hocks with Rice ... 77

Pork Roast with Apples and Plums......... 77

Hawaiian Pulled Pork 77

Chuck Roast with Vegetables 78

Delicious Flank Steak Taco................. 78

Flavorful Pork Chops and Sauerkraut...... 78

Coconut Beef Fajitas 79

Spiced Baby Back Pork Ribs 79

Asian Short Ribs with Sesame 79

Balsamic Pork Chops with Pears and Figs 80

Teriyaki Pork Roast........................... 80

Spiced Hoisin Short Ribs 80

Italian Sausage and Peppers Hoagies 81

Tasty Barbecued Ribs 81

Tasty Marinara Meatballs 81

Simple Mongolian beef 82

Cubano Sloppy Joe Wraps 82

Cheesy Italian Sausage and Peppers 82

Classic Beef Biryani 83

Mexican Stuffed Peppers 83

Swiss Steak with Potato and Carrot 83

Best Pot Roast 84

Pork Chops and Acorn Squash 84

Homemade Pork Chops with Cherry 84

Rosemary Pork Tenderloin 85

Spicy Barbecued Pork....................... 85

Homemade Meat Pie 85

Mustard Pork Chops

½ cup all-purpose flour, divided
½ tsp. ground mustard
½ tsp. garlic-pepper blend
¼ tsp. seasoned salt

4 boneless pork loin chops (4 oz. each)
2 Tbsp. canola oil
1 can (14½ oz.) chicken broth, divided

1. Combine the ¼ cup flour, mustard, garlic pepper, and seasoned salt in a small bowl. Add each addition of 1 pork chop, shake off excess, and toss to coat. 2. Use the sauté or browning mode. Add the canola oil. Once the oil is heated, brown the pork in batches. Add the 1½ cups of broth to pot. Cook for 30 seconds, stirring to loosen browned bits from pan. 3. Secure the lid and close the pressure-release valve. Adjust to Pressure Cook on high for 3 minutes. Rapidly release pressure on the vent position. Pork should register a temperature of at least 145°F/60°C on a thermometer. Select Cancel. Remove the pork to serving plate and keep warm. 4. Thoroughly combine the remaining ¼ cup flour and ¼ cup broth in a small bowl and stir into Instant Pot. Choose the sauté button. Simmer for 1 to 2 minutes, stirring often to achieve thickening. Serve with the pork.
Per Serving: Calories 257; Fat: 14g; Sodium 774mg; Carbs: 8g; Sugars: 3.03g; Protein 23g

Apple and Pork Curry

2 lbs. boneless pork loin roast, cut into 1-in. cubes
1 small onion, chopped
½ cup orange juice
1 Tbsp. curry powder
1 tsp. chicken bouillon granules
1 garlic clove, minced
½ tsp. salt
½ tsp. ground ginger

¼ tsp. ground cinnamon
1 medium apple, peeled and chopped
2 tbsp. cornstarch
2 tbsp. cold water
Hot cooked rice, optional
¼ cup raisins
¼ cup sweetened shredded coconut, toasted

1. Combine the first nine ingredients in the instant pot. Close the pressure-release valve and lock the lid. Set to Pressure Cook for 3 minutes on high. Release the pressure quickly on the vent position. Pork should register a temperature of at least 145°F/60°C on a thermometer. Select Cancel. 2. Add the apple to the Instant Pot. Blend the cornstarch and water in a small bowl and add to the Instant Pot. Choose the sauté button and lower the heat. Cook for 3 to 5 minutes, stirring often, until thickened and apple is soft. 3. You can add the rice if you'd like. Add some coconut and raisins as garnish. Serve.
Per Serving: Calories 174; Fat: 6g; Sodium 404mg; Carbs: 8g; Sugars: 4g; Protein 22g

Healthy Carnitas Lettuce Wraps

1 tablespoon unsweetened cocoa powder
2 teaspoons salt
1 teaspoon cayenne pepper
2 teaspoons ground oregano
1 teaspoon white pepper
1 teaspoon garlic powder
1 teaspoon onion salt
1 teaspoon ground cumin
½ teaspoon ground coriander

1 (3-pound) pork shoulder
2 tablespoons olive oil
2–3 cups water
1 head butter lettuce, washed and dried
1 small jalapeño, sliced
¼ cup julienned radishes
1 medium avocado, diced
2 small Roma tomatoes, diced
2 limes, cut into wedges

1. Combine the cocoa powder, salt, cayenne pepper, oregano, white pepper, garlic powder, onion salt, cumin, and coriander in a small basin. Rub spice into the pork shoulder and place in the refrigerator overnight. 2. On the Instant Pot, click the Sauté button. Add 2 teaspoons of oil. About 8 to 10 minutes, sear the roast on all sides, making sure that they are completely browned. Pour 2 to 3 cups of water, or enough to almost cover the meat. Lock the lid. 3. Set the time to 45 minutes and press the Pressure Cook button. When the timer beeps, allow pressure to naturally relax for 10 minutes on the seal position. Release any further pressure quickly on the vent position until the float valve lowers, and then open the lid. 4. Place the meat on a plate. Shred the meat with the two forks. Save for ½ cup, discard the entire cooking liquid. Remove the meat to the Instant Pot. Press the Sauté button and stir-fry meat for 4–5 minutes creating some crispy edges. 5. Serve with the lettuce leaves, jalapeño slices, radishes, avocado, tomatoes, and lime wedges.
Per Serving: Calories 717; Fat: 50g; Sodium 916mg; Carbs: 8.7g; Sugars: 2.03g; Protein 59g

Tasty Pork and Squash Ragu

Prep Time: 20 minutes | Cook Time: 15 minutes | Serves: 10

2 cans (14½ oz. each) stewed tomatoes, undrained
1 pkg. (12 oz.) frozen cooked winter squash, thawed
1 large sweet onion, cut into ½-in. pieces
1 medium sweet red pepper, cut into ½-in. pieces
¼ cup reduced-sodium chicken broth
1 ½ tsp. crushed red pepper flakes

2 lbs. boneless country-style pork ribs
1 tsp. salt
¼ tsp. garlic powder
¼ tsp. pepper
Hot cooked pasta
Shaved Parmesan cheese, optional

1. In Instant pot, combine the first six ingredients. Season the ribs with the pepper, salt, and garlic powder and place in the Instant Pot. Close the pressure-release valve and lock the lid. Adjust to Pressure Cook on high for 15 minutes. Allow any leftover pressure to naturally relax for 10 minutes on the seal position before quick-release it on the vent position. 2. Take off the lid and stir the meat to break it up, accompanied by spaghetti. Add the Parmesan cheese on top.
Per Serving: Calories 196; Fat: 8g; Sodium 804mg; Carbs: 13g; Sugars: 6g; Protein 18.39g

Mushroom Pork Ragout

Prep Time: 20 minutes | Cook Time: 10 minutes | Serves: 2

1 pork tenderloin (¾ lb.)
⅛ tsp. salt
⅛ tsp. pepper
1½ cups sliced fresh mushrooms
¼ cup canned crushed tomatoes
¾ cup reduced-sodium chicken broth, divided

⅓ cup sliced onion
1 Tbsp. chopped sun-dried tomatoes (not packed in oil)
1¼ tsp. dried savory
1 Tbsp. cornstarch
1½ cups hot cooked egg noodles

1. Season the pork with the pepper and salt, then chop it in half. Put the ingredients in the pot. Add the savory, onion, sun-dried tomatoes, mushrooms, tomatoes, and ½ cup broth to the top. 2. Close the pressure-release valve and lock the lid. Set to Pressure Cook for 6 minutes on high. Rapidly release pressure on the vent position. Pork should register a temperature of at least 145°F/60°C on a thermometer. Select Cancel. 3. To keep warm, remove the meat. Thoroughly blend the cornstarch and remaining broth in a small dish and stir into the Instant Pot. Choose the sauté button. Simmer for 1-2 minutes while stirring often to achieve thickening. Sever the sliced pork with the noodles and sauce.
Per Serving: Calories 387; Fat: 8g; Sodium 404mg; Carbs: 37g; Sugars: 8g; Protein 43g

Beef and Mushroom Stew with Egg Noodle

Prep Time: 5 minutes | Cook Time: 60 minutes | Serves: 4

3 pounds beef stew meat or chuck cubes
Kosher salt and black pepper, to season beef (1–2 teaspoons of each)
3 tablespoons extra-virgin olive oil
5 tablespoons salted butter, divided
1 large yellow onion, diced
1-pound baby bella mushrooms, sliced
3 cloves garlic, minced or pressed
¼ cup dry white wine (like a sauvignon blanc)
1 tablespoon Dijon mustard
1 teaspoon seasoned salt

1½ cups beef broth
1 teaspoon dried thyme
4 tablespoons cornstarch
1 packet dry onion soup/dip mix
1 cup sour cream
1 (5.2-ounce) package Boursin spread (any flavor) or 4 ounces cream cheese, cut into chunky cubes
1 (12-ounce) package wide egg noodles, prepared separately according to package directions

1. Thoroughly rub the black pepper and kosher salt into the meat. 2. Add 2 tablespoons of butter and olive oil to the Instant Pot and hit Sauté. After adding butter to melt, sauté the beef for 2 to 3 minutes in the melted butter, until it is gently browned on both sides. With a slotted spoon, remove the meat and set it aside. 3. The onion should start to soften after 2 minutes of cooking in the saucepan with the remaining 3 tablespoons of butter and the onion. For three more minutes, add the mushrooms. After one more minute, add the garlic. After adding the white wine and scraping off any browned pieces from the pan's bottom, add the Dijon mustard and seasoned salt and mix thoroughly. 4. Place the meat chunks in the sauce, then add the beef broth and thyme. 5. Put the lid on tightly, turn the valve to the seal position, and then press Pressure Cook. Cook for 20 minutes at high pressure. After finishing, let a fast release on the vent position after a 10-minute natural release on the seal position. 6. Construct a slurry by mixing 4 tablespoons of cold water with the cornstarch in the meantime. Place aside. 7. Press Sauté. Bring the saucepan to a simmer and stir the cornstarch slurry in. Before switching the pot to the Keep Warm setting, add the package of onion soup and allow it to boil for 30 seconds. 8. Stir in the sour cream and Boursin (or cream cheese) until combined after the bubbles have mostly disappeared. 9. Serve over the egg noodles.
Per Serving: Calories 1397; Fat: 41g; Sodium 2589mg; Carbs: 170g; Sugars: 4g; Protein 99g

Tasty Satay Pork with Rice Noodles

Prep Time: 20 minutes | Cook Time: 5 minutes |Serves: 6

1½ lbs. boneless pork loin chops, cut into 2-in. pieces
¼ tsp. pepper
1 medium onion, halved and sliced
⅓ cup creamy peanut butter
¼ cup reduced-sodium soy sauce
½ tsp. onion powder

½ tsp. garlic powder
½ tsp. hot pepper sauce
1 can (14½ oz.) reduced-sodium chicken broth, divided
3 tbsp. cornstarch
9 oz. uncooked thick rice noodles
Optional: Minced fresh cilantro and chopped peanuts

1. Add the pepper to the meat. Place in the Instant pot and add the onion. Combine the peanut butter, soy sauce, onion, garlic, and pepper sauce in a small bowl. Add 1½ cups broth gradually. Add over the onion. 2. Close the pressure-release valve and lock the lid. Set to Pressure Cook for 3 minutes on high. Rapidly release pressure on the vent position. Pork should register a temperature of at least 145°F/60°C on a thermometer Select Cancel. Take the pork chops out of the Instant Pot and keep warm. 3. Stir the remaining ¼ cup of the broth and cornstarch together in a small dish and add to the pot. Choose the sauté button and lower the heat. Simmer for 1-2 minutes while stirring often to achieve thickening. Sauté the meat until done. 4. Rice noodles should be prepared as directed on the box while waiting. With the pork combination, serve.
Per Serving: Calories 427; Fat: 14g; Sodium 444mg; Carbs: 44g; Sugars: 3g; Protein 29g

Simple and Quick Meatloaf

Prep Time: 10 minutes | Cook Time: 35 minutes |Serves: 6

1-pound ground beef
1-pound ground pork
4 large eggs
1 cup panko bread crumbs
1 large shallot, finely diced
¼ cup seeded and finely diced red bell pepper
½ cup tomato sauce

1 tablespoon Italian seasoning
½ teaspoon smoked paprika
½ teaspoon garlic powder
½ teaspoon celery seed
1 teaspoon sea salt
½ teaspoon ground black pepper
1 cup beef broth

1. With the exception of the broth, mix all the ingredients in a big basin using your hands. 2. Place the meatloaf onto a 7-cup glass dish by shaping the mixture into a ball and flattening the top. 3. Fill the Instant Pot with the beef broth. Place the steam rack. Put a glass dish on top of the rack. Lock the lid. 4. Press the Pressure Cook button and cook for the 35 minutes on high. When the timer beeps, allow pressure to naturally relax for 10 minutes on the seal position. Release any further pressure quickly on the vent position until the float valve lowers, and then open the lid. 5. Take the meatloaf out of the pot and let it cool for 10 minutes at room temperature. Pour any liquid or rendered fat into a glass bowl that has been tilted over a sink. Slice and serve.
Per Serving: Calories 525; Fat: 30g; Sodium 967mg; Carbs: 9g; Sugars: 3g; Protein 51g

Yummy Pork Tacos with Mango Salsa

Prep Time: 25 minutes | Cook Time: 5 minutes |Serves: 12

2 tbsp. white vinegar
2 tbsp. lime juice
3 cups cubed fresh pineapple
1 small red onion, coarsely chopped
3 tbsp. chili powder
2 chipotle peppers in adobo sauce
2 tsp. ground cumin
Optional toppings: Cubed fresh pineapple, cubed avocado and queso fresco

1½ tsp. salt
½ tsp. pepper
1 bottle (12 oz.) dark Mexican beer
3 lbs. pork tenderloin, cut into 1-in. cubes
¼ cup chopped fresh cilantro
1 jar (16 oz.) mango salsa
24 corn tortillas (6 in.), warmed

1. Blend the first nine ingredients until smooth and then add the beer. Combine the pork and pineapple combination in the pot. Close the pressure-release valve and lock the lid. Set to Pressure Cook for 3 minutes on high. Rapidly release pressure on the vent position. Pork should register a temperature of at least 145°F/60°C on a thermometer. Stir to disperse the pork. 2. Add the cilantro to the salsa. Serve the pork mixture in the tortillas using a slotted spoon and top with the salsa and other ingredients as desired.
Per Serving: Calories 282; Fat: 6g; Sodium 695mg; Carbs: 30g; Sugars: 5.03g; Protein 26.39g

Red Beans and Ham Hocks with Rice

Prep Time: 20 minutes | Cook Time: 45 minutes |Serves: 6

3 cups water
2 smoked ham hocks (about 1 lb.)
1 cup dried red beans
1 medium onion, chopped
1½ tsp. minced garlic

1 tsp. ground cumin
1 medium tomato, chopped
1 medium green pepper, chopped
1 tsp. salt
4 cups hot cooked rice

1. In Instant Pot, combine the first six ingredients. Close the pressure-release valve and lock the lid. Adapt to Pressure Cook for 35 minutes on high. 2. Allow the pressure to drop naturally. Select Cancel. Remove the ham hocks and allow them to cool. Take the flesh off the bones. Remove the meat from Instant Pot, cut finely, and add back in bones. Add the salt, green pepper, and tomato to the mixture. Choose the sauté button and lower the heat. For 8 to 10 minutes, simmer while stirring often until the pepper is soft. Serve with the rice.
Per Serving: Calories 216; Fat: 2g; Sodium 404mg; Carbs: 49g; Sugars: 3g; Protein 12g

Pork Roast with Apples and Plums

Prep Time: 20 minutes | Cook Time: 35 minutes |Serves: 10

1 boneless pork loin roast (3 to 4 lbs.)
2 tbsp. all-purpose flour
1 tbsp. herbes de Provence
1½ tsp. salt
¼ tsp. pepper
2 tbsp. olive oil

1 cup apple cider or unsweetened apple juice
2 medium onions, halved and thinly sliced
1 cup beef stock
2 bay leaves
2 large tart apples, peeled and chopped
1 cup pitted dried plums

1. Halve the roast. Rub the pork with a mixture of flour, herbes de Provence, salt, and pepper. Use the sauté option. Add 1 tbsp. oil and adjust for medium heat. Cook a roast half on all sides in the heated oil. After removing the roast, repeat with the remaining pork and oil. 2. To the Pot, add the cider. Stirring to release browned parts from the pan, cook for 1 minute. Select Cancel. Add the onions, stock, and bay leaves and roast. 3. Close the pressure-release valve and lock the lid. Set to Pressure Cook for 25 minutes on high. Allow any leftover pressure to naturally relax for 10 minutes on the seal position before quick-release it on the vent position. Pork should register a temperature of at least 145°F/60°C on a thermometer. Select Cancel. Discard the bay leaves and transfer the roast and onions to a serving plate while covering with foil. 4. Select sauté setting and adjust for low heat. Add the apples and plums and simmer, uncovered, until the apples are tender, 6-8 minutes, stirring occasionally. Serve with the roast.
Per Serving: Calories 286; Fat: 9.17g; Sodium 554mg; Carbs: 22g; Sugars: 13g; Protein 28.39g

Hawaiian Pulled Pork

Prep Time: 15 minutes | Cook Time: 95 minutes |Serves: 10

1 (5-pound) bone-in pork butt or shoulder
Dry Rub
½ teaspoon ground ginger
½ teaspoon celery seed
½ teaspoon cayenne pepper
1 teaspoon garlic powder
1 teaspoon sea salt
1 teaspoon onion powder
1 teaspoon ground cumin

Sauce
1 (8-ounce) can crushed pineapple
¼ cup soy sauce
¼ cup tomato sauce
¼ cup pure maple syrup
1 tablespoon rice wine
3 cloves garlic, peeled and halved
1 tablespoon grated fresh ginger

1. Dry the pork butt with paper towels and set it aside. 2. Mix the ingredients for the dry rub in a small dish. Rub the pork on all sides with the rub. Covered refrigeration is recommended for up to overnight. 3. In a small saucepan, combine the ingredients for the sauce. Up to a boil. Once the sauce has reduced by a quarter and begun to thicken, turn the heat down and let it simmer for 10 minutes. Allow to cool for 5 minutes. Add and pulse till smooth in a food processor. 4. Put the pork butt in the Instant Pot and cover it with the sauce. Lock the lid. 5. Set the timer to 85 minutes and press the Pressure Cook button. When the timer sounds, the pressure to release naturally until the float valve lowers and open the lid allow. Make sure the pork can be easily pulled apart. If not, select Sauté and cook without a lid for an extra 10 minutes. 6. Pull the pork apart with two forks while the meat is still in the Instant Pot. Get rid of the bone. In the Instant Pot, stir the sauce and the meat. Use a slotted spoon for serving.
Per Serving: Calories 872; Fat: 36.17g; Sodium 504mg; Carbs: 85g; Sugars: 83g; Protein 48.39g

Chuck Roast with Vegetables

Prep Time: 15 minutes | Cook Time: 65 minutes | Serves: 8

2 tablespoons Dijon mustard
1 teaspoon sea salt
½ teaspoon ground black pepper
1 teaspoon smoked paprika
1 (3-pound) boneless chuck roast
1 tablespoon olive oil
1 (12-ounce) bottle dark lager

2 tablespoons tomato paste
1 cup beef broth
2 teaspoons Worcestershire sauce
1 medium yellow onion, peeled and diced
2 large carrots, peeled and diced
1 small stalk celery, diced
2 cups sliced mushrooms

1. Combine the mustard, paprika, salt, and pepper in a small bowl. Apply the mustard mixture to the meat on both sides. 2. Select Sauté. Heat the oil. Meat needs roughly 5 minutes to be seared on both sides. Remove and keep the meat. 3. Pour in the beer and use the Instant Pot to deglaze it by swirling and scraping any browned pieces from the bottom and sides. 4. Whisk in the tomato paste. Refill the saucepan with the stock, Worcestershire sauce, onion, carrots, celery, and mushrooms and the meat back in. Lock the lid. 5. Set the timer to 60 minutes by pressing the Pressure Cook button. When the timer sounds, allow the pressure to naturally dissipate on the seal position until the float valve lowers, and then open the lid. 6. Remove the meat and put on a serving dish. Allow to rest for 5 minutes. Slice. If desired, use an immersion blender to purée the juices in the Instant Pot. Pour the juices over the sliced meat. Serve warm.
Per Serving: Calories 264; Fat: 12g; Sodium 824mg; Carbs: 2.87g; Sugars: 2g; Protein 33g

Delicious Flank Steak Taco

Prep Time: 10 minutes | Cook Time: 45 minutes | Serves: 4

¼ cup ketchup
¼ cup apricot preserves
⅛ cup honey
⅛ cup apple cider vinegar
¼ cup soy sauce
⅛ teaspoon cayenne pepper

1 teaspoon ground mustard
¼ teaspoon ground black pepper
1 (2-pound) flank steak
2 tablespoons avocado oil, divided
1 large sweet onion, peeled and sliced
1½ cups beef broth

1. In a small bowl, combine the preserves, ketchup, honey, vinegar, soy sauce, cayenne pepper, mustard, and pepper. Spread the mixture on all sides of the flank steak. 2. Press the Sauté button on Instant Pot. Heat 1 tablespoon oil. Sear the meat on each side for approximately 5 minutes. Remove the meat and set aside. Add remaining 1 tablespoon oil and onions. Sauté the onions for 3–5 minutes until translucent. 3. Add the beef broth. Set meat and all of the sauce on the layer of onions. Lock the lid. 4. Press the Pressure Cook button and adjust time to 35 minutes. When timer beeps, let pressure release naturally on the seal position until float valve drops and then unlock lid. 5. Transfer the meat to a serving platter. Thinly slice against the grain and serve immediately.
Per Serving: Calories 267; Fat: 12g; Sodium 408mg; Carbs: 28.7g; Sugars: 23g; Protein 11g

Flavorful Pork Chops and Sauerkraut

Prep Time: 15 minutes | Cook Time: 30 minutes | Serves: 4

2 tablespoons olive oil
4 (1"-thick) bone-in pork loin chops
1 teaspoon sea salt
½ teaspoon ground black pepper
4 slices bacon, diced
1 stalk celery, finely chopped
3 large carrots, peeled and sliced

1 large onion, peeled and diced
1 clove garlic, peeled and minced
1 (12-ounce) bottle lager
4 medium red potatoes, peeled and quartered
2 medium red apples, peeled, cored, and quartered
1 (1-pound) bag high-quality sauerkraut, rinsed and drained
1 tablespoon caraway seeds

1. On the Instant Pot, click the Sauté button. Warm the olive oil. Season the pork chops with the salt and pepper. Sear the pork chops in batches for 1–2 minutes each side. Set aside the pork. 2. To the Instant Pot, add the bacon, celery, carrots, and onion. Stir-fry the onions for 3 to 5 minutes, or until they are transparent. Place in the garlic and cook for another minute. Pour in the beer and whisk continuously while you deglaze the Instant Pot. Cook without a lid for 5 minutes. 3. Add the sauerkraut, apples, and potatoes. Add some caraway seeds. To avoid crowding the meat, slightly lean the pork chops against the pot's sides. Lock the lid. 4. Set the timer to 15 minutes and press the Pressure Cook button. When the timer beeps, allow pressure to naturally relax for 5 minutes on the seal position. Release any further pressure quickly on the vent position until the float valve lowers, and then open the lid. 5. Put the apples, potatoes, sauerkraut, and pork chops on a serving platter.
Per Serving: Calories 823; Fat: 35.17g; Sodium 866mg; Carbs: 76g; Sugars: 16g; Protein 51g

Coconut Beef Fajitas

Prep Time: 15 minutes | Cook Time: 45 minutes |Serves: 6

⅛ cup avocado oil
¼ cup coconut aminos
1 tablespoon fish sauce
1 teaspoon ground cumin
1 teaspoon chili powder
2 tablespoons tomato paste

½ teaspoon sea salt
1 (2-pound) skirt steak
1 small onion, peeled and diced
1 medium green bell pepper, seeded and diced
1 medium red bell pepper, seeded and diced
1 cup beef broth

1. Combine the oil, coconut aminos, fish sauce, cumin, chili powder, tomato paste, and salt in a small dish. On the beef's four sides, evenly distribute ¾ of the mixture. Set aside more sauce. 2. On the Instant Pot, click the Sauté button. Add the skirt steak and sear for about 5 minutes on each side. Remove and save the meat. Add the onion, peppers, and saved sauce to the Instant Pot. Sauté for 3–5 minutes until onions are translucent. 3. Add beef broth. Place the meat over the onion and pepper layer. Lock the lid. 4. Press the Pressure Cook button and set the cook time for the 35 minutes. When the timer sounds, allow the pressure to gradually subside until the float valve lowers, and open the lid. 5. Using a slotted spoon, remove the meat and vegetables to a serving platter. Thinly slice the skirt steak against the grain. Serve.
Per Serving: Calories 402; Fat: 10.17g; Sodium 704mg; Carbs: 9g; Sugars: 6.03g; Protein 23.39g

Spiced Baby Back Pork Ribs

Prep Time: 40 minutes | Cook Time: 30 minutes |Serves:6

2 racks (about 3 pounds) baby back pork ribs
1 teaspoon instant coffee crystals
1 teaspoon sea salt
½ teaspoon chili powder
½ teaspoon ground cumin
½ teaspoon cayenne pepper
½ teaspoon ground mustard
½ teaspoon garlic powder

½ teaspoon onion powder
¼ teaspoon ground coriander
¼ cup pure maple syrup
¼ cup soy sauce
1 tablespoon apple cider vinegar
2 tablespoons tomato paste
1 tablespoon olive oil
1 medium onion, peeled and large diced

1. Section the ribs into two pieces. Combine the coffee, salt, chili powder, cumin, cayenne pepper, mustard, garlic powder, onion powder, and coriander in a small bowl. Rub this mixture into the rib regions with your palms. Covered refrigeration is recommended for up to 24 hours. 2. Combine the tomato paste, soy sauce, apple cider vinegar, and maple syrup in a small mixing bowl. 3. On the Instant Pot, click the Sauté button. Warm the olive oil. When the onions are transparent, add them and sauté for 3 to 5 minutes. Add the mixture of maple syrup. Add a couple ribs at a time, coating them with sauce carefully with the tongs. The meaty side should be facing outside when you arrange the ribs standing erect. Lock lid. 4. Set the timer to 25 minutes and press the Pressure Cook button on high. When the timer beeps, let pressure release naturally on the seal position until float valve drops and then unlock the lid. Serve warm.
Per Serving: Calories 197; Fat: 8g; Sodium 605mg; Carbs: 16g; Sugars: 12g; Protein 15g

Asian Short Ribs with Sesame

Prep Time: 10 minutes | Cook Time: 25 minutes |Serves: 6

½ cup soy sauce
½ cup pure maple syrup
½ cup rice wine
1 tablespoon sesame oil
1 teaspoon white pepper
½ teaspoon ground ginger

½ teaspoon garlic powder
½ teaspoon gochujang
3 pounds beef short ribs
1 cup beef broth
2 green onions, sliced
1 tablespoon toasted sesame seeds

1. Combine the soy sauce, maple syrup, rice wine, sesame oil, white pepper, ground ginger, garlic powder, and gochujang in a small bowl. Rub this mixture into the rib regions with your palms. Place covered in the refrigerator for up to overnight. 2. Fill the Instant Pot with the beef broth. Place the steam rack. The meaty side should be facing outside when you arrange the ribs standing erect. Lock the lid. 3. Set the timer to 25 minutes and press the Pressure Cook button. When the timer beeps, allow pressure to naturally release on the seal position until the float valve lowers, and then open the lid. 4. Transfer the ribs on a serving plate and top with the green onions and sesame seeds.
Per Serving: Calories 526; Fat: 27g; Sodium 545mg; Carbs: 24g; Sugars: 20g; Protein 47g

Balsamic Pork Chops with Pears and Figs

Prep Time: 10 minutes | Cook Time: 15 minutes | Serves: 2

2 (1"-thick) bone-in pork chops
1 teaspoon sea salt
1 teaspoon ground black pepper
¼ cup balsamic vinegar
¼ cup chicken broth

1 tablespoon dried mint
2 tablespoons avocado oil
1 medium sweet onion, peeled and sliced
3 pears, peeled, cored, and diced large
5 dried figs, stems removed and halved

1. With a paper towel, pat the pork chops dry. Then, liberally sprinkle the pepper and salt on both sides. Place aside. 2. Mix the vinegar, broth, and mint in a small bowl. Place aside. 3. On the Instant Pot, click the Sauté button. Heat the oil and cook the pork chops on both sides for minutes. Remove and save the chops. 4. By adding vinegar mixture and scraping the brown particles from the Instant Pot's sides and bottom you may deglaze the appliance. The pears and figs are arranged on top of the layered onions in the saucepan. Put the pork chops there. Lock th lid. 5. To set the time to 3 minutes, press the Steam button. When the timer beeps, allow the pressure to naturally relax for 10 minutes on the sea position. Quick-release any additional pressure on the vent position until the float valve drops and then unlock lid. 6. By using a slotted spoon transfer the pork, onions, figs, and pears to a serving platter. Serve warm.
Per Serving: Calories 835; Fat: 34g; Sodium 1404mg; Carbs: 85g; Sugars: 67g; Protein 50g

Teriyaki Pork Roast

Prep Time: 10 minutes | Cook Time: 30 minutes | Serves: 10

¾ cup unsweetened apple juice
2 Tbsp. sugar
2 Tbsp. reduced-sodium soy sauce
1 Tbsp. white vinegar
1 tsp. ground ginger

¼ tsp. garlic powder
⅛ tsp. pepper
1 boneless pork loin roast (about 3 lbs.), halved
8 tsp. cornstarch
3 Tbsp. cold water

1. In the Instant Pot, combine the first 7 ingredients. Add the roast and turn to coat. Close the pressure-release valve and lock the lid. Adapt t pressure-cook for 25 minutes on high. Allow any leftover pressure to naturally relax for 10 minutes on the seal position before quick-releasing on the vent position. Pork should register a temperature of at least 145°F/60°C on a thermometer. Select Cancel. 2. Transfer the pork to a serving dish and keep warm. Whisk the cornstarch and water together until thoroughly combined and add to the Instant pot. Choose the sauté button and lower the heat. Simmer for 1-2 minutes while stirring often to achieve thickening. With the meat, serve.
Per Serving: Calories 198; Fat: 6g; Sodium 999mg; Carbs: 7g; Sugars: 4g; Protein 27g

Spiced Hoisin Short Ribs

Prep Time: 5 minutes | Cook Time: 90 minutes | Serves: 4

1 cup beef broth
¾ cup dry red wine (like a cabernet)
½ cup hoisin sauce
3 cloves garlic, minced or pressed
1 teaspoon ground allspice
1 teaspoon cinnamon
1 teaspoon Chinese five spice powder (optional)

5–6 pounds bone-in short ribs
Kosher salt and black pepper, to season ribs (about 1½ teaspoons o each)
1 large Spanish (or yellow) onion, quartered
¼ cup cornstarch
½ cup honey

1. Mix the beef broth, red wine, hoisin sauce, garlic, allspice, cinnamon, and five spice powder in a bowl to make the sauce (if using). Plac aside. 2. Sprinkle the kosher salt and black pepper all over the short ribs in a light coating. 3. Hit Sauté and then adjust it such that More or Hig is selected. Working in batches, cook the short ribs for 2 minutes and sear them for 1 minute on each side. 4. Add about a half cup of the sauc to the saucepan. Stir while doing so to scrape out any browned pieces. To turn the pot off after the bottom is clean, press Keep Warm/Cancel. 5 Place all of the short ribs on top of the onion wedges with the rounded side up. Pour the remaining sauce on top. 6. Put the lid on tightly, turn th valve to the seal position, choose Keep Warm/Cancel, then select Pressure Cook on high. 45 minutes of high pressure cooking. When finished let a rapid release on the vent position after a 15-minute natural release on the seal position. 7. In the meantime, create a slurry by mixing th cornstarch with ¼ cup cold water. 8. After remove the ribs from the saucepan (they will be delicate and likely to come apart) and place in serving plate. Hit Sauté and adjust the temperature to High then bring the sauce to a bubble. Add the honey and the cornstarch slurry and sti thoroughly. Before clicking Keep Warm/Cancel to turn the pot off, let it boil for 30 seconds. Wait for 5 minutes. 9. Pour the sauce over the shor ribs and serve with some bread to sop up the extra sauce.
Per Serving: Calories 1260; Fat: 55.17g; Sodium 1174mg; Carbs: 62.87g; Sugars: 45.03g; Protein 129g

Italian Sausage and Peppers Hoagies

Prep Time: 15 minutes | Cook Time: 20 minutes |Serves: 6

2 tablespoons olive oil, divided
1 pound sweet Italian sausage links, uncooked, divided
1 large onion, peeled and sliced
1 small red bell pepper, seeded and sliced
1 small green bell pepper, seeded and sliced
1 small yellow bell pepper, seeded and sliced
4 cloves garlic, minced
½ cup chicken broth

1 (15-ounce) can diced stewed tomatoes, including juice
¼ cup chopped fresh basil
2 tablespoons fresh oregano leaves
1 teaspoon cayenne pepper
1 teaspoon sea salt
½ teaspoon ground black pepper
6 hoagie rolls

1. On the Instant Pot, click the Sauté button. Heat 1 tablespoon olive oil. For about 4-5 minutes, add half of the sausage links and brown them on both sides. Take out and place aside. Add the remaining sausages and 1 tablespoon of olive oil. For a further 4-5 minutes, brown all sides. Take out of the Instant Pot, then leave it aside. 2. Stir-fry the bell peppers and onions in the Instant Pot for 3 to 5 minutes, or until the onions are transparent. Add the garlic cook for 1 more minute. By adding the broth and scraping the Instant Pot's sides and bottom, you may deglaze it. Add the tomatoes, basil, oregano, cayenne, salt, and pepper. Lock lid. 3. Set the timer to 5 minutes and press the Pressure Cook button. When the timer beeps, quickly release the pressure on vent position. Then unlock the lid. 4. Using a slotted spoon, transfer the pot ingredients to a serving platter. Slice the sausages. Serve on the hoagie rolls.
Per Serving: Calories 344; Fat: 14g; Sodium 1200mg; Carbs: 32g; Sugars: 7g; Protein 22g

Tasty Barbecued Ribs

Prep Time: 5 minutes | Cook Time: 80 minutes |Serves: 4

2–6 pounds (up to 3 full racks) of St. Louis or baby back ribs (pork loin back ribs), unseasoned
1 (64-ounce) bottle of apple juice 1 cup apple cider vinegar

¼ cup liquid smoke (either hickory or mesquite is fine)
Barbecue sauce (a few cups' worth)

1. Take the ribs and coil them so they fit in the Instant Pot lined against the edge of the pot. Add into the pot. 2. Add the liquid smoke, vinegar, and apple juice. 3. Set valve to the seal position, close the lid, and press Pressure Cook for 5-6 pounds/1.5-2 racks of ribs, cook under high pressure for 30 minutes (25 minutes for 2-4 pounds/1 rack). 4. When finished, quickly release the pressure on the vent position after a 5-minute natural release on the seal position. 5. Carefully remove the ribs from the saucepan since they will be quite tender (bone side down) and then delicately transfer to a baking sheet covered with nonstick foil. After the ribs are taken out of the saucepan, discard the fluids. 6. Apply plenty of barbecue sauce to the ribs' tops using a basting brush. Put a lot of it on to make them attractive and saucy. 7. Remove the ribs from the pot, grab lots of napkins, chop up the ribs, and enjoy!
Per Serving: Calories 567; Fat: 10g; Sodium 191mg; Carbs: 51g; Sugars: 43g; Protein 63g

Tasty Marinara Meatballs

Prep Time: 15 minutes | Cook Time: 30 minutes |Serves: 4

½-pound ground beef
½-pound ground pork
2 large eggs
1 tablespoon Italian seasoning
1 teaspoon garlic powder
1 teaspoon celery seed

½ teaspoon onion powder
½ teaspoon smoked paprika
½ cup old-fashioned oats
2 tablespoons plus 2 cups marinara sauce, divided
3 tablespoons avocado oil, divided
2 cups water

1. Combine the beef, pork, eggs, Italian seasoning, celery seed, onion powder, smoked paprika, oats, and 2 tablespoons marinara sauce in a medium bowl. Form into 20 meatballs. Place aside. 2. Heat 2 tablespoons of oil in the Instant Pot by pressing the Sauté button. Place 10 meatballs around the pot's edge. The meatballs need around 4 minutes to be seared on both sides. Remove and reserve the first batch. Add a further tablespoon of oil and sear the remaining meatballs. Delete the meatballs. 3. Discard the extra juice and oil from the Instant Pot. In a 7-cup glass dish, put the seared meatballs. Add the last 2 cups of marinara sauce on top. 4. Fill the Instant Pot with the water. Add the steam rack. Place the glass dish on the rack. Lock the lid. 5. Set the time to 20 minutes and press the Pressure Cook button. When the timer beeps, allow the pressure to naturally relax for 10 minutes on the seal position. Release any further pressure quickly on the vent position until the float valve lowers, and then open the lid. 6. Transfer the meatballs to a serving dish.
Per Serving: Calories 518; Fat: 33g; Sodium 278mg; Carbs: 20g; Sugars: 8g; Protein 35g

Simple Mongolian beef

Prep Time: 10 minutes | Cook Time: 15 minutes | Serves: 4

1 tablespoon sesame oil
1 (2-pound) skirt steak, sliced into thin strips
¼ cup coconut aminos
½ cup pure maple syrup

1" knob of fresh gingerroot, peeled and grated
4 cloves garlic, minced
½ cup plus 2 tablespoons water, divided
2 tablespoons arrowroot powder

1. On the Instant Pot, click the Sauté button. Cook the steak strips in the hot oil for 2 to 3 minutes, or until just barely browned on all sides. 2. Mix the coconut aminos, maple syrup, garlic, ginger, and ½ cup water in a medium bowl. Pour over the meat and swirl to remove any browned particles from the Instant Pot's bottom and sides. Lock the lid. 3. Select Pressure Cook and set the timer to 10 minutes. When the timer beeps, quickly release pressure on the vent position until the float valve lowers, and then open the lid. 4. To make a slurry, combine the arrowroot and 2 tablespoons water in a small bowl and whisk until combined. Add this to the meat mixture and stir. Press the Sauté and Adjust buttons to lower the temperature to Less, then boil the dish without a lid for 5 minutes to thicken the sauce. 5. Ladle the mixture into the bowls and serve.
Per Serving: Calories 612; Fat: 26g; Sodium 947mg; Carbs: 32.87g; Sugars: 24g; Protein 63g

Cubano Sloppy Joe Wraps

Prep Time: 10 minutes | Cook Time: 10 minutes | Serves: 8

1-pound ground pork
½ medium onion, peeled and diced
¼ cup chicken broth
1 tablespoon fresh lime juice
1 tablespoon fresh orange juice
1 teaspoon garlic powder
1 teaspoon dried oregano
1 teaspoon cayenne pepper

2 teaspoons ground cumin
1 teaspoon sea salt
1 teaspoon ground black pepper
8 slices Swiss cheese
8 (8") flour tortillas
8 slices ham
24 dill pickle slices
8 teaspoons yellow mustard

1. On the Instant Pot, click the Sauté button. Stir the pork with onions for 5 minutes and pork should no longer be pink. 2. Deglaze the Instant Pot by adding chicken stock and scraping any browned residue from the sides and bottom. Stir and add the lime juice, orange juice, cayenne pepper, cumin, oregano, garlic powder, and salt and pepper. Lock the lid. 3. Set the timer to 5 minutes and press the Pressure Cook button. When the timer sounds, allow the pressure to naturally dissipate on the seal position until the float valve lowers and open the lid. 4. Place a Swiss cheese slice on a flour tortilla and then assemble the tortillas. Each tortilla should have a piece of ham and three slices of pickles. Place one teaspoon of yellow mustard down the middle. Add ⅛ of the Instant Pot's ground pork mixture down the center using a slotted spoon. Fold the bottom 2-3" of the tortilla upward and flip the tortilla's edges toward the center. For the remaining tortillas, repeat. Serve right away.
Per Serving: Calories 463; Fat: 24g; Sodium 1237mg; Carbs: 28.7g; Sugars: 2g; Protein 32g

Cheesy Italian Sausage and Peppers

Prep Time: 5 minutes | Cook Time: 45 minutes | Serves: 4

3 tablespoons extra-virgin olive oil
2 tablespoons (¼ stick) salted butter
2 Vidalia (sweet) onions, cut into strands
2 green bell peppers, cut lengthwise into slices
2 red bell peppers, cut lengthwise into slices
6 cloves garlic, minced or pressed
2 pounds Italian sausage links (sweet and/or hot), sliced into disks ½

inch thick
½ cup dry white wine (like a chardonnay)
1 teaspoon oregano
1 teaspoon Italian seasoning
1 cup grated Parmesan cheese
1 (5.2-ounce) package Boursin spread (any flavor) or 4 ounces cream cheese, cut into chunky cubes

1. Add the butter and olive oil to the Instant Pot and hit Sauté. Add the onion and peppers when the butter has melted. Sauté the onion for 10 minutes, or until tender and starting to brown. Place the garlic and cook for another minute. 2. Sausage will cook for 2 to 3 minutes, until it begins to faintly brown. If the insides are still raw, don't worry; pressure cooking will fix that. 3. Sauté for a further 1 to 2 minutes, until simmering and aromatic, before adding the wine, oregano, and Italian seasoning. 4. Select Pressure Cook on high and secure the lid. Cook for 5 minutes at high pressure. Quickly let pressure go on the vent position once finished. 5. Once melted and creamy, stir in the Parmesan and Boursin (or cream cheese). 6. Serve the dish as a hero, over white or brown rice, pasta, or with crusty bread to sop up the sauce.
Per Serving: Calories 658; Fat: 40g; Sodium 2186mg; Carbs: 27g; Sugars: 11g; Protein 49g

Classic Beef Biryani

Prep Time: 10 minutes | Cook Time: 25 minutes |Serves: 6

1 tablespoon ghee
1 small onion, peeled and sliced
1-pound top round, cut into strips
1 tablespoon minced fresh gingerroot
2 cloves garlic, peeled and minced
½ teaspoon ground cloves
½ teaspoon ground cardamom
½ teaspoon ground coriander

½ teaspoon ground black pepper
½ teaspoon ground cinnamon
½ teaspoon ground cumin
1 teaspoon salt
1 cup plain yogurt
1 (28-ounce) can whole stewed tomatoes, including juice
2 cups cooked basmati rice

1. On the Instant Pot, click the Sauté button. Burn ghee. Sauté the onion for 3 to 5 minutes, or until transparent. Add the rice to the Instant Pot. Lid closed. 2. Select Pressure Cook and set the timer to 10 minutes. When the timer beeps, quickly release the pressure on the vent position until the float valve lowers, and then open the lid. 3. Press the Sauté, adjust, and less temperature, then simmer the food, covered, for about 10 minutes, or until most of the liquid has evaporated. Serve over the cooked basmati rice.
Per Serving: Calories 303; Fat: 12.17g; Sodium 628mg; Carbs: 28.7g; Sugars: 6g; Protein 30g

Mexican Stuffed Peppers

Prep Time: 10 minutes | Cook Time: 20 minutes |Serves: 4

4 large red bell peppers
¼-pound chorizo, loose or cut from casings
½-pound ground pork
1 medium onion, peeled and diced
1 small Roma tomato, diced
1 tablespoon tomato paste
½ cup corn kernels (cut from the cob is preferred)

1 large egg
1 teaspoon ground cumin
1 teaspoon sea salt
1 teaspoon garlic powder
½ cup vegetable broth
½ cup shredded Cheddar cheese

1. Remove the bell pepper tops as near to the tops as feasible. Hollow out the seeds and discard them. Make a few tiny holes in the peppers' bottoms to let the fat leak out. 2. Combine the other ingredients in a medium bowl, leaving out the cheese and broth. Put the same quantity of the mixture into each bell pepper. 3. Place the steam rack inside the Instant Pot, then add the broth. On the rack, arrange the peppers upright. Lock the lid. 4. Set the time to 15 minutes and press the Pressure Cook button. When the timer beeps, allow the pressure to naturally release on the seal position until the float valve lowers, and then open the lid. Press the Sauté button and melt the cheese after 3 minutes of simmering in the Instant Pot. 5. Place the peppers on a dish and served warm.
Per Serving: Calories 601; Fat: 52.17g; Sodium 1022mg; Carbs: 14g; Sugars: 5g; Protein 24g

Swiss Steak with Potato and Carrot

Prep Time: 10 minutes | Cook Time: 35 minutes |Serves: 6

2½ (1"-thick) pounds beef round steak
1 teaspoon sea salt
½ teaspoon ground black pepper
2 tablespoons olive oil, divided
1 medium yellow onion, peeled and diced
2 stalks celery, diced

1 large green bell pepper, seeded and diced
1 cup tomato juice
1 cup beef broth
6 large carrots, peeled and cut into 1" pieces
6 medium Yukon gold potatoes, diced large
4 teaspoons butter

1. Season the round steak with the salt and peppered on both sides and then divide into six serving-sized pieces. 2. On the Instant Pot, click the Sauté button. Heat 1 tablespoon oil. 3 Add the pieces of beef and sear each for 3 minutes. Repeat with the remaining 1 tablespoon oil and the remaining 3 pieces of pork, then transfer to a dish. 3. Add the onion, celery, and green pepper on top of the final three pieces of browned beef in the Instant Pot. Place the remaining 3 pieces of beef on top and cover with the tomato juice and broth. On top of the meat, arrange the potatoes and carrots. Lock the lid. 4. Set the time to 20 minutes and press the Pressure Cook button. When the timer beeps, quickly release pressure on the vent position until the float valve lowers, and then open the lid. 5. Place the meat, potatoes, and carrots on a serving plate. Cover up to stay warm. 6. Remove any fatty particles from the juices still in the Instant Pot. To simmer the juices without a cover for 5 minutes, press the Sauté button, adjust button, and reduce temperature to Low. 7. One spoonful of butter at a time, whisk in. Serve the finished gravy beside the meat at the table. Serve immediately.
Per Serving: Calories 1415; Fat: 38g; Sodium 1023mg; Carbs: 74g; Sugars: 8g; Protein 184g

Best Pot Roast

Prep Time: 15 minutes | Cook Time: 20 minutes | Serves: 4

2 teaspoons black pepper
1½ teaspoons kosher salt
1½ teaspoons seasoned salt
1½ teaspoons dried parsley
1 teaspoon dried thyme
1 teaspoon dried rosemary
1 teaspoon onion powder
1 teaspoon garlic powder
1 (3-pound) chuck roast
3 tablespoons extra-virgin olive oil
1 tablespoon salted butter

2 medium yellow onions, sliced into thick wedges
3 cloves garlic, sliced
2 tablespoons Worcestershire sauce
1 cup dry red wine (like a cabernet)
6–8 ounces portobello mushrooms, sliced
2 cups beef broth
8 ounces fresh baby carrots
1-pound baby white potatoes
3 tablespoons cornstarch
1 packet beef gravy mix

1. Rub the roast with the mixture of pepper, kosher salt, seasoned salt, parsley, thyme, rosemary, onion powder, and garlic powder. 2. Press Sauté on the Instant Pot and change the setting to High. Pour the oil into the pan and heat it for 3 minutes. Then, without moving the roast, sear each side for around 1 to 2 minutes. Take the roast out of the saucepan and place aside. 3. Put the butter in the Instant Pot without removing the inner pot, and as it melts, use a wooden spoon to scrape up any spices fallen to the bottom. While continuing to stir and scrape off any browned parts, add the onions and simmer for 2 minutes. Rub the roast with the mixture of pepper, kosher salt, seasoned salt, parsley, thyme, rosemary, onion powder, and garlic powder. 4. Press Sauté on the Instant Pot and change the setting to High. Pour the oil into the pan and heat it for 3 minutes. Then, without moving the roast, sear each side for around 1 to 2 minutes. Take the roast out of the saucepan and place aside. 5. Put the butter in the Instant Pot, and as it melts, use a wooden spoon to scrape up any spices that may have fallen to the bottom. While continuing to stir and scrape off any browned parts, add the onion and simmer for 2 minutes. When done, use a natural release for 15 minutes on the seal position, and then quickly release on the vent position. 6. In the meanwhile, combine the cornstarch with 3 tablespoons of cold water to produce a slurry, and put it aside. 7. After the vegetables in the foil-wrapped pot have completed cooking, remove them and set them aside. Carefully remove the steam rack and the roast, then set the meat aside on a chopping board. 8. Press Keep Warm/Cancel and then Sauté and adjust to High level, bring the sauce to simmer. Unwrap the vegetables, add the cornstarch slurry, and gravy package to the sauce. After 30 seconds of simmering, switch the pot to the Keep Warm position. 9. Slice the pot roast into strips that are around ¼-inch-thick, cutting against the grain (or make thicker or bite-size cuts if you wish). Add them to the sauce after that (still on the Keep Warm setting). Don't forget to add any last strands of meat off the cutting board, give everything one more swirl, and then serve.
Per Serving: Calories 809; Fat: 26g; Sodium 4449mg; Carbs: 43g; Sugars: 6g; Protein 93g

Pork Chops and Acorn Squash

Prep Time: 15 minutes | Cook Time: 5 minutes | Serves: 6

6 boneless pork loin chops (4 oz. each)
2 medium acorn squash, halved lengthwise, seeded and sliced
½ cup packed brown sugar
½ cup reduced-sodium chicken broth
2 Tbsp. butter, melted

1 Tbsp. orange juice
¾ tsp. salt
¾ tsp. browning sauce, optional
½ tsp. grated orange zest

1. Place the squash and pork chops in the pot. Mix the remaining ingredients in a small dish and pour over the squash. 2. Close the pressure release valve and lock the lid. Set to Pressure Cook for 4 minutes on high. 3. Rapidly release pressure on the vent position. Pork should register a temperature of at least 145°F/60°C on a thermometer. Serve.
Per Serving: Calories 350; Fat: 11g; Sodium 777mg; Carbs: 42.87g; Sugars: 23g; Protein 824g

Homemade Pork Chops with Cherry

Prep Time: 15 minutes | Cook Time: 5 minutes | Serves: 4

1 cup fresh or frozen pitted tart cherries, thawed
1 cup reduced-sodium chicken broth
¼ cup chopped sweet onion
2 Tbsp. honey
1 tsp. seasoned salt

½ tsp. pepper
4 boneless pork loin chops (5 oz. each)
1 tbsp. cornstarch
1 tbsp. cold water

1. Combine the first six ingredients in the Instant Pot, then add the pork chops. Close the pressure-release valve and lock the lid. Set to Pressure Cook for 3 minutes on high. Rapidly release pressure on the vent position. Pork should register a temperature of at least 145°F/60°C on a thermometer. Select Cancel. 2. Transfer the pork to a serving dish and keep it heated. Smoothly combined the cornstarch and water in a small bowl and add to the Instant Pot. Choose the sauté option and lower the heat. Simmer for 1-2 minutes while stirring often to achieve thickening. Serve alongside pork.
Per Serving: Calories 260; Fat: 8g; Sodium 664mg; Carbs: 17g; Sugars: 14g; Protein 29g

Rosemary Pork Tenderloin

Prep Time: 5 minutes | Cook Time: 30 minutes | Serves: 6

2 tablespoons avocado oil
2 (3-pound) pork tenderloins, halved
½ cup balsamic vinegar
¼ cup olive oil
¼ cup cherry preserves

½ teaspoon sea salt
¼ teaspoon ground black pepper
¼ cup finely chopped fresh rosemary
4 garlic cloves, minced

1. On the Instant Pot, click the Sauté button. Heat the oil and brown the pork for 2 minutes on each side (4 sides total). 2. Mix the other ingredients in a small bowl and pour over the meat. Lid locked. 3. Set the time to 20 minutes and press the Pressure Cook button. After the timer chimes, allow the pressure to naturally relax for 5 minutes on the seal position. Release any further pressure quickly on vent position until the float valve lowers, and then open the lid. 4. Move the tenderloin to a chopping board. Allow to rest for 5 minutes. Slice into the medallions and serve.

Per Serving: Calories 624; Fat: 25.17g; Sodium 390mg; Carbs: 5.87g; Sugars: 4.03g; Protein 87g

Spicy Barbecued Pork

Prep Time: 5 minutes | Cook Time: 90 minutes | Serves: 4

1 tablespoon light- or dark-brown sugar
1 tablespoon onion powder
1 tablespoon garlic powder
1½ teaspoons paprika
1½ teaspoons ground cumin
1 teaspoon salt
1 teaspoon black pepper

3–4-pound boneless pork shoulder or butt, cut into 1-pound segments (you can also use country-style ribs)
1 tablespoon liquid smoke
1 large Spanish (or yellow) onion, quartered
2 cups Coca-Cola or Dr Pepper
1 cup barbecue sauce (use your favorite)
Potato rolls or hamburger buns, for serving

1. Combine the sugar, paprika, cumin, garlic powder, salt, onion powder, and pepper in a large bowl. 2. Apply the liquid smoke on the pork, then roll it in the spice bowl to coat. Place aside. 3. Round sides down, add the onion wedges to the Instant Pot. Place the pig slices on top of the onion, then add the soda. 4. Put the lid on tightly, turn the valve to the seal position, and press Pressure Cook for 60 minutes at High Pressure. When the timer beeps, allow a 10-minute natural release on the seal position, then a rapid release on the vent position. 5. Add the onion and pork to a mixing bowl. Out of the pot's juices, set aside ¼ cup and throw away the remainder. 6. Shred the pork and onion using a pair of forks or a hand mixer, and mix in the reserved juices and barbecue sauce before serving with some slaw in rolls or buns.

Per Serving: Calories 1106; Fat: 61g; Sodium 1577mg; Carbs: 44g; Sugars: 28g; Protein 88g

Homemade Meat Pie

Prep Time: 5 minutes | Cook Time: 45 minutes | Serves: 4

The Meat
¼ cup extra-virgin olive oil
1 large yellow onion, diced
3 cloves garlic, minced
1½ pounds ground meat (I like ground lamb or a veal, pork, and beef mix)
½ cup dry red wine (like a cabernet)
1 teaspoon seasoned salt
1 teaspoon Italian seasoning
¼ teaspoon nutmeg

1 (10-ounce) box frozen mixed peas and carrots
4 tablespoons tomato paste, divided
The potatoes
1½ pounds baby potatoes (any color you like), skin on
3 tablespoons salted butter
¼ cup heavy cream or half-and-half
Half package (3 ounces) of Boursin spread (any flavor) or 2 ounces cream cheese, cut into chunky cubes
½ teaspoon garlic salt
1 teaspoon black pepper

1. Press Sauté on the Instant Pot and change the setting to High. Add the oil and heat for 3 minutes. Add the onion and cook for an additional 3 minutes, or until the onion is tender. Add the garlic and cook for a further minute. 2. Then add the wine, seasoned salt, Italian seasoning, and nutmeg and bring to a boil, scraping up any browned pieces from the bottom of the pot as you go. Add the beef and sauté for 2 minutes, until starting to brown. Stir in 2 tablespoons of tomato paste and add the peas and carrots and then cook for a further minute. 3. Scoop the beef mixture with a mixing spoon into a round 112-quart oven-safe casserole dish that will fit inside your Instant Pot. 4. Scrape the bottom of the Instant Pot after adding 1 cup of water to let any meat scraps rise to the surface. Keep the water in; it's necessary to create pressure. The casserole dish should be set on the rack, which is in the pot. Add the entire baby potatoes on top of the meat. 5. To cook for 12 minutes under high pressure, secure the lid, select Pressure Cook. Quickly let go on the vent position once finished. 6. Carefully move the potatoes to a basin, then mash them until the appropriate consistency is achieved. Combine the black pepper, garlic salt, Boursin (or cream cheese), and butter. 7. Carefully remove the casserole dish from the rack and Instant Pot using oven mitts. Skim off excess juices by pressing the back of a mixing spoon against the top of the meat and letting the spoon fill; discard. About 5 spoonsful should do the trick. Stir in the remaining 2 tablespoons of tomato paste, layer the mashed potatoes on top, and serve.

Per Serving: Calories 734; Fat: 37g; Sodium 1030mg; Carbs: 57g; Sugars: 5g; Protein 43.9g

Chapter 7 Dessert Recipes

Chocolate Cookies Cheesecake 87

Pumpkin Cheesecake with Granola 87

Cinnamon Raisin-Filled Apples 87

Mini Monkey Breads with Cereal 88

Sweet Bread Pudding with Pomegranates 88

Simple Chai Spice Rice Pudding 88

Vanilla Pudding Cups 89

Coconut Banana Bread with Chocolate Chips 89

Apple Sauce with Pear and Sweet Potato 89

Perfect Chocolate Cake 90

Yummy Coconut Brownies.................. 90

Sweet Apple Crisp Doughnut 90

Easy Cranberry-Pear Crisp 91

Lemony Raspberry Curd.................... 91

Simple Honey Lemon Curd 91

Hot Spiced Apple-Cranberry Cider 92

Delicious Dulce De Leche 92

Banana Cake with Almonds 92

Creamy Brownie Pudding 93

Savory Butterscotch Pudding 93

Sugar Tapioca Pudding 93

Vanilla Rice Pudding 94

Sweet Coconut Rice with Fresh Mango ... 94

Classic Sugar Flan 94

Buttery Caramel Pears 95

Traditional Noodle Kugel 95

Quick Vanilla Custard 95

Fluffy Eggnog Cheesecake 96

Soft Lemon Sponge Cake 96

Sugar Chocolate Cakes 97

Tasty Orange Pecan Cake 97

Vanilla Date Nuts Cakes 98

Maple Apple Cake 98

Pumpkin Spice Cheese 99

Yummy Key Lime Cake Soufflé 99

Chocolate Cookies Cheesecake

Prep Time: 5 minutes | Cook Time: 25 minutes | Serves: 4

Crust
2 cups (180g) finely ground chocolate sandwich cookies, preferably Oreos
Pinch of salt
3 tbsps. (43g) unsalted butter, melted
Cheesecake
16 oz. (455g) cream cheese, softened
1⅓ cups (268g) sugar
1 tbsp. (5.6g) finely ground chocolate sandwich cookies, preferably Oreos
1 tsp pure vanilla extract

1 tbsp. (13g) sugar

2 large eggs
½ cup (120ml) heavy cream
1 cup (237ml) water

1. Prepare the crust. Combine the cookie crumbs, sugar, salt, and butter in a medium bowl. In a round, leak-proof springform pan measuring 7 inches (18.5 cm), press the mixture into the bottom. 2. Prepare the cheesecake. Place the cream cheese and sugar in the paddle-equipped bowl of an electric stand mixer until it is light and fluffy. Scrape the sides clean. 3. Add the vanilla and cookie crumbs. Assemble by combining. Once mixed, add each egg one at a time, scraping the bowl as necessary. Incorporate the heavy cream. 4. Over the springform pan's shell, pour the cheese mixture. 5. Add the water to the Instant Pot and put the steam rack inside. Put the springform pan on the rack. 6. Secure the lid with the steam vent in the seal position. Select Pressure Cook. Adjust the time to 25 minutes. 7. Allow the pressure to naturally release on the seal position as the timer goes off. 8. Remove the springform pan from the pot when the float valve opens. Before cutting, place the cake in the refrigerator to cool for the night.
Per Serving: Calories 448; Fat: 60g; Sodium 834mg; Carbs: 62.87g; Sugars: 43g; Protein 13g

Pumpkin Cheesecake with Granola

Prep Time: 5 minutes | Cook Time: 35 minutes | Serves: 4

1 cup (237ml) water
Nonstick cooking spray, for pan
1½ cups (183g) granola
4 tbsps. (55g) unsalted butter, melted
2 (8-oz [225-g]) packages cream cheese, softened

½ cup (100g) sugar
2 large eggs
½ cup (123g) pure pumpkin puree
1½ tsp (3g) pumpkin pie spice
½ tsp pure vanilla extract

1. Add the water to the Instant Pot and insert the steam rack. 2. Coat a 7-inch (18.5-cm) cheesecake pan with a removable bottom using nonstick cooking spray. Grind the granola into big crumbs in a food processor or strong blender. Combine the granola crumbs and melted butter, and then firmly press the mixture into the pan's bottom. 3. Combine the cream cheese and sugar in a medium basin and beaten until smooth. Add the eggs one at a time, whisking well after each addition. Add the pumpkin pie spice, vanilla, and pumpkin puree and blend them well. 4. After adding the batter to the cheesecake pan, wrap it with aluminum foil. Sling some foil. Carefully set the pan on the rack using the sling. 5. Put the steam vent in the seal position and fasten the lid. As soon as you press manual, set the timer to 30 minutes. Verify that high pressure is beneath the display light. 6. When the timer beeps, allow the pressure to naturally drop on the seal position for 15 minutes, then quickly release the pressure on the vent position and gently remove the lid. Use the sling to carefully remove the cheesecake, and then allow it to cool completely on a wire rack (gently dab any condensation from the top of cheesecake before cooling). At least four hours to chill.
Per Serving: Calories 491; Fat: 32g; Sodium 153mg; Carbs: 40g; Sugars: 23g; Protein 10g

Cinnamon Raisin-Filled Apples

Prep Time: 5 minutes | Cook Time: 5 minutes | Serves: 4

4 medium Honeycrisp apples
⅓ cup (37g) crushed pecans
⅓ cup (75g) coconut sugar or dark brown sugar
½ cup (75g) raisins
2 tsp (5g) ground cinnamon

Pinch of sea salt
4 tbsp. (55g) butter, cut into 4 equal pieces
¾ cup (160ml) water
2 cups (280g) vanilla ice cream (optional)

1. Remove the core of each apple from the top, leaving approximately ¼ inch (6 mm) of the apple around the edges and at the bottom. 2. Mix the nuts, coconut sugar, raisins, cinnamon, and salt in a medium bowl. Fill each apple's cavity with the mixture. Add a piece of butter on top. 3. Fill the Instant Pot with the water. Alongside one another, add enough apples to fill the pot's cavity. 4. Put the steam valve in the seal position and fasten the lid. Choose Pressure Cook, then cook for 3 minutes at high pressure. 5. Use a fast release on the vent position, then use tongs to remove the apples. 6. With the vanilla ice cream, serve warm (if using).
Per Serving: Calories 288; Fat: 17g; Sodium 94mg; Carbs: 35g; Sugars: 27g; Protein 1g

Mini Monkey Breads with Cereal

1 (1-lb [455-g]) can buttermilk biscuits
⅓ cup (68g) granulated sugar
Pinch of salt
½ cup (20g) crushed cinnamon crunch cereal, divided, plus more for sprinkling

¼ cup (60ml) melted unsalted butter
1 cup (237ml) water
1 cup (120g) confectioners' sugar
2 tbsps. (30ml) milk

1. Cut each biscuit into 6 pieces. 2. Add the salt, sugar, and half of the crushed cereal to a bowl. To the bowl, add the chopped biscuit pieces. Toss to coat completely. 3. Place a spoonful of the cereal mixture and around 2 heaping teaspoons (35g) of the coated biscuits into each well of a silicone egg bite mold. Add the melted butter to the top of each pile of dough covered. 4. Add the water to the Instant Pot and put the steam rack inside. Place the full mold on the rack. 5. Put the steam valve in the seal position and fasten the lid. When the display light is below high pressure, push Pressure Cook. Adjust the time with the plus and minus buttons until the display says "20 minutes." 6. Once the timer beeps, release the pressure immediately on the vent position. Take the top off and the silicone mold will come out. In the mold, let the monkey cake cool. 7. In the meantime, blend the milk and confectioners' sugar in a medium bowl. 8. Take the monkey breads out of the mold. Each monkey bread should be icing-drizzled. Sprinkle some crumbled cereal on top.
Per Serving: Calories 223; Fat: 8g; Sodium 30mg; Carbs: 37g; Sugars: 34g; Protein 1g

Sweet Bread Pudding with Pomegranates

1 cup (237ml) whole milk
1 cup (237ml) heavy cream
2 tbsps. (30g) unsalted butter, melted, plus more for pan
1 tsp pure vanilla extract
⅓ cup (67g) plus 1 tsp granulated sugar, plus more for sprinkling
Pinch of salt

2 large eggs, beaten
½ loaf challah bread, cut into 2" (5-cm) cubes
½ cup (87g) pomegranate arils, divided
1 cup (237ml) water
Confectioners' sugar

1. Combine the milk, cream, melted butter, vanilla, sugar, salt, and eggs in a large basin until smooth, and whisk. Add the challah cubes to the basin. Mix until the bread is well covered. Let the bread soak in the liquid for a few minutes and add three-quarters of the pomegranate arils. 2. Butter a 7" (18.5 cm) heatproof dish. To the prepared bowl, add the challah mixture. Top the challah mixture with the rest of the pomegranate seeds. Add little sugar granules. 3. Add the water to the Instant Pot and put the steam rack inside. Put the pudding bowl on the rack's middle. 4. Put the steam valve in the seal position and fasten the lid. Push Pressure Cook on high. Adjust the time until the display reads "15 minutes." 5. When the timer sounds, quickly release the pressure on the vent position. Remove the lid and carefully remove the bowl. Lightly dust with the confectioners' sugar.
Per Serving: Calories 265; Fat: 19g; Sodium 70mg; Carbs: 18g; Sugars: 14g; Protein 5g

Simple Chai Spice Rice Pudding

1 cup (195g) uncooked arborio rice
1½ cups (355ml) water
Pinch of salt
2 cups (475ml) whole milk or almond milk, divided
½ cup (100g) sugar
2 large eggs
½ tsp pure vanilla extract

½ tsp ground cardamom
½ tsp ground allspice
2 tsp (5g) ground cinnamon
¼ tsp ground cloves
1 tbsp. (6g) ground ginger
½ cup (75g) golden raisins

1. Put the rice, water, and salt in the Instant Pot. Good stirring. 2. Ensure that the lid is closed. Press high pressure and Pressure Cook. Adjust the time with the plus and minus buttons until the display says "3 minutes." 3. When the timer beeps, allow the steam to naturally release for 10 minutes on the seal position, then quickly relieve any pressure that remains on vent position. 4. Take off the lid. Add the sugar and ½ cup of milk. To blend, stir. 5. Mix the raisins, vanilla, cardamom, allspice, cinnamon, cloves, and the remaining 1 ½ cups (355ml) of milk with the eggs in a small dish. 6. Choose sauté. Through a mesh strainer, add the egg to the Instant Pot. To blend, stir. 7. Once the pudding starts to simmer, press Cancel. Stir in the raisins. 8. Serve the pudding warm or cool completely in the refrigerator.
Per Serving: Calories 352; Fat: 12g; Sodium 65mg; Carbs: 62.87g; Sugars: 40g; Protein 9g

Vanilla Pudding Cups

1½ cups (355ml) heavy cream
½ cup (120ml) milk
¾ cup (131g) chocolate chips or chopped chocolate
2 large eggs
¼ cup (60ml) pure maple syrup or honey
1½ tbsp. (11g) unsweetened cocoa powder
2 tbsps. (28g) grass-fed butter, ghee or coconut oil, melted, divided
1 tbsp. (15ml) pure vanilla extract
½ tsp organic orange extract

½ tsp ground cinnamon
⅛ tsp ground cayenne
⅛ tsp sea salt
1 tsp grass-fed bovine gelatin
1 cup (237ml) water
Homemade whipped cream, for garnish (optional)
Shaved or chopped organic stone-ground Mexican chocolate, for garnish (optional)

1. Warm the cream, chocolate, and milk in a small saucepan over low heat while stirring until smooth. Turn off the heat and leave the pot alone. 2. Put the eggs, your preferred sweetener, cocoa powder, melted fat of your choice, vanilla, orange essence, cinnamon, cayenne, and salt in a blender. Process slowly for 30 seconds to completely combine. Remove the vent cap from the blender while it's running, add the chocolate mixture, followed by the gelatin, and blend for an additional 30 seconds to integrate completely. 3. Fill 5 half-pints (250ml) glass jars with the custard mixture evenly, allowing at least a 12-inch (1.3-cm) headroom at the top. Cover the jars and seal with lids. 4. Add the water to the Instant Pot and put the steam rack inside. 5. Put the rack on top of the five jars. They ought should fit the Instant Pot just right. Fix the cover in the sealed position. Press Pressure Cook, then set the timer for 5 minutes on LOW pressure. 6. When the timer beeps, select Cancel or keep warm. Perform a fast release on the vent position while holding an oven mitt. Carefully open the lid after the steam valve stops and the float valve drops. 7. Carefully take out the jars and take off their lids using an oven mitt or tongs. After thoroughly stirring the ingredients to make it smooth, let each pudding cup cool to room temperature. Transfer them to the refrigerator to set after they have cooled. For the most realistic solid texture, refrigerate them for at least 6 hours, preferably overnight. 8. Serve chilled as is or garnished, if desired, with the homemade whipped cream and/or shaved or chopped organic stone-ground Mexican chocolate.
Per Serving: Calories 250; Fat: 17g; Sodium 99mg; Carbs: 16g; Sugars: 12g; Protein 3g

Coconut Banana Bread with Chocolate Chips

1½ cups (150g) blanched almond flour
2 tbsps. (14g) coconut flour
2 tsp (5g) ground cinnamon
Pinch of ground nutmeg
¾ tsp baking soda
½ tsp sea salt
¼ cup (60ml) melted coconut oil

2 medium very ripe bananas, mashed
2 large eggs
2 tbsps. (30ml) pure maple syrup
1 tsp pure vanilla extract
½ cup (88g) chocolate chips
Nonstick cooking spray, for dish or pan

1. Combine the almond flour, coconut flour, cinnamon, nutmeg, baking soda, and salt in a small basin. 2. Combine the bananas, eggs, maple syrup, coconut oil, and vanilla in a large bowl with an electric mixer on low speed until largely smooth. When all dry pockets have been eliminated, fold in the flour mixture and continue beating. Add the chocolate chunks and stir. 3. Use the nonstick cooking spray to coat a 6- to 7-inch (15- to 18.5-cm) springform pan or a 7-inch (18.5-cm) heatproof round glass dish. Once the batter has been added to the dish, it should be covered with foil. 4. Add the water to the Instant Pot and put the steam rack inside. Put the dish on the rack. 5. Ensure that the lid is sealed. Select Pressure Cook and high pressure for 35 minutes. 6. Use a Quick Release on the seal position. Carefully take the dish out of the Instant Pot, using pot holders. Let the banana bread completely cool before slicing.
Per Serving: Calories 418; Fat: 31g; Sodium 400mg; Carbs: 30g; Sugars: 18g; Protein 9g

Apple Sauce with Pear and Sweet Potato

5 Honeycrisp apples, cored and chopped
1 sweet potato, peeled and chopped
1 Bartlett pear, cored and chopped
Pinch of salt

1 cup (237ml) water
½ tsp cinnamon
1 tbsp. (15ml) pure maple syrup

1. Mix all the ingredients thoroughly and add them to the Instant Pot. 2. Put the steam valve in the seal position and fasten the lid. Choose Pressure Cook on high. Adjust the time with the plus and minus buttons until the display says "10 minutes." 3. Once the timer beeps, release the pressure immediately on the vent position. Then, using an immersion blender, purée the mixture until it is smooth. Serve.
Per Serving: Calories 109; Fat: 1g; Sodium 3mg; Carbs: 28.7g; Sugars: 20g; Protein 1g

Perfect Chocolate Cake

Prep Time: 5 minutes | Cook Time: 35 minutes |Serves: 6

5 oz. (140g) high-quality unsweetened chocolate
6 tbsps. (85g) unsalted butter
1 tbsp. (15ml) pure vanilla or chocolate extract
1 cup (200g) sugar
4 large eggs, whisked

½ cup (55g) unsweetened cocoa powder
Nonstick cooking spray, for pan
1 cup (237ml) water
½ cup (65g) raspberries, for serving (optional)

1. Melt the butter and chocolate together in a microwave or double boiler, then allow to cool. 2. Once the chocolate liquid is smooth, add the vanilla, sugar, eggs, and cocoa powder. 3. Spray some nonstick cooking spray in a 6-inch (15-cm) springform pan lightly. Use a 6- to 7-inch (15 to 18.5-cm) round cake pan as an alternative, but make a sling out of foil to make removing the cake easier. After pouring the batter into the pan, wrap it with foil. 4. Add the water to the Instant Pot and put the steam rack inside. Then place the cake pan on the steam rack. 5. Put the steam valve in the seal position and fasten the lid. Set the cooking time to 35 minutes on high pressure with the Pressure Cook button. 6. Use a Quick Release on the vent position. Remove the lid, then use potholders to remove the cake pan. 7. Chill for 1 to 2 hours before removing from the pan and slicing. Serve chilled or at room temperature with berries (if using).
Per Serving: Calories 422; Fat: 35.17g; Sodium 15mg; Carbs: 26.87g; Sugars: 21g; Protein 3g

Yummy Coconut Brownies

Prep Time: 5 minutes | Cook Time: 35 minutes |Serves: 6

1 cup (245g) pure pumpkin puree
¼ cup (65g) almond butter
2 large eggs
1 tbsp. (30ml) pure vanilla extract
1 cup (225g) coconut sugar
½ cup (50g) almond flour

½ cup (55g) unsweetened cocoa powder
½ tsp baking powder
½ tsp sea salt
½ cup (88g) chocolate chips
Nonstick cooking spray, for pan
2 cups (475ml) water

1. Using an electric mixer, thoroughly combine the pumpkin, almond butter, eggs, vanilla, and coconut sugar in a medium bowl. 2. Mix the almond flour, baking powder, salt, and cocoa powder in a separate basin. When there are no dry pockets left, add the dry ingredients to the wet components and continue beating. Add the chocolate chunks and stir. 3. Apply the nonstick cooking spray to a 7-inch (18.5-cm) round springform or cake pan to prepare it. Pour the batter into the pan (it should be thick) and smooth it. After wrapping the pan in foil, cover it with a paper towel. This will aid in preventing moisture buildup. 4. Add the water to the Instant Pot and put the steam rack inside. On the rack, put the pan. Affix the lid. Set the cooking time to 35 minutes on high pressure with the Pressure Cook option. 5. For at least 15 minutes, use a natural release on the seal position, and then let out any leftover steam on the vent position. Remove the cover and lift the pan with pot holders. 6. Cool the brownies for at least 15 minutes before being taken out of the pan. Serve.
Per Serving: Calories 282; Fat: 18g; Sodium 276mg; Carbs: 26g; Sugars: 17g; Protein 10g

Sweet Apple Crisp Doughnut

Prep Time: 5 minutes | Cook Time: 10 minutes |Serves: 6

6 Honeycrisp apples, partially peeled
½ cup (115g) brown sugar, divided
1 tsp ground cinnamon
½ tsp pure vanilla extract
1 cup (237ml) water

½ cup (40g) old-fashioned rolled oats
3 tbsps. (43g) unsalted butter
¼ cup (30g) all-purpose flour
3 leftover glazed doughnuts, cut into 1" (2.5-cm) pieces
Vanilla ice cream, for topping

1. To avoid the seeds, cut each apple into four wedges (discard the seeds). You should have 8 pieces if you cut those wedges in half. In the Instant Pot, add the apples, ¼ cup (58g) of the brown sugar, the cinnamon, vanilla, and water. 2. Put the steam valve in the seal position and fasten the lid. Choose Pressure Cook on high. Adjust the time with the plus and minus buttons until the display says "1 minute." 3. Once the timer beeps, release the pressure immediately on the vent position. Take off the lid. 4. Combine the remaining brown sugar, oats, butter, and flour in a small bowl. 5. Combine the doughnuts and apple mixture. 6. Press Sauté. Use your hands to crumble the oat mixture over the apple mixture. Let the crisp bubble away for 2 minutes. 7. Press Cancel. Let the crisp cool for 5 minutes before spooning into bowls and topping with the vanilla ice cream.
Per Serving: Calories 337; Fat: 10g; Sodium 81mg; Carbs: 63g; Sugars: 42g; Protein 3g

Easy Cranberry-Pear Crisp

Prep Time: 5 minutes | Cook Time: 5 minutes | Serves: 6

3 large Anjou pears, peeled, cored and diced
1 cup (100g) fresh cranberries
1 tbsp. (13g) granulated sugar
2 tsp (5g) ground cinnamon
½ tsp ground nutmeg
½ cup (120ml) water
1 tbsp. (15ml) pure maple syrup

6 tbsps. (90g) unsalted butter, melted
1 cup (80g) old-fashioned rolled oats
⅓ cup (75g) dark brown sugar
¼ cup (30g) all-purpose flour
½ tsp sea salt
½ cup (50g) pecans, toasted (optional)
Vanilla ice cream, for serving (optional)

1. Combine the pears and cranberries in the Instant Pot, then top with the sugar. After sitting for a few minutes, sprinkle with the cinnamon and nutmeg. Add the maple syrup and water over top. 2. Combine the oats, brown sugar, flour, salt, and melted butter in a medium basin. 3. In the Instant Pot, spoon the mixture over the fruit. 4. Put the steam valve in the seal position and fasten the lid. Choose Pressure Cook, and then cook for 5 minutes at high pressure. After timer beeps, use a rapid release on the vent position. 5. Serve hot after spooning into separate dishes. Add the pecans and vanilla ice cream on top (if using).
Per Serving: Calories 336; Fat: 15.17g; Sodium 220mg; Carbs: 52.87g; Sugars: 27g; Protein 5g

Lemony Raspberry Curd

Prep Time: 5 minutes | Cook Time: 5 minutes | Serves: 2

12 oz. (340g) fresh raspberries
¾ cup (150g) sugar
2 tbsps. (30ml) fresh lemon juice

1 tsp lemon zest
2 large egg yolks
2 tbsps. (28g) unsalted butter

1. Combine the raspberries, sugar, lemon juice, and zest in the Instant Pot. 2. Put the steam valve in the sealed position and fasten the lid. Choose Pressure Cook, then cook for 1 minute at high pressure. 3. For at least 10 minutes, use a natural release on the seal position. Let off any lingering steam on the vent position. 4. Take off the lid. Blend the ingredients using an immersion blender or in a blender, then pulse until it's smooth. If it has been taken out, put the mixture back in and choose sauté. 5. Whisk the egg yolks together in a small dish in the meanwhile. Add them gradually to the raspberry mixture. Stir the mixture continuously until it boils, then choose Cancel. Add the butter. 6. Transfer to a glass or other airtight, heatproof container and let cool to room temperature. Refrigerate until the curd is completely set. Serve chilled. 7. Store this recipe in the fridge for up to 2 weeks.
Per Serving: Calories 363; Fat: 13g; Sodium 16mg; Carbs: 60g; Sugars: 44g; Protein 5g

Simple Honey Lemon Curd

Prep Time: 5 minutes | Cook Time: 10 minutes | Serves: 2

4 large eggs
⅓ cup (80ml) honey
Zest of 3 lemons

½ cup (120ml) fresh lemon juice
7 tbsps. (99g) grass-fed butter, melted and cooled
1 cup (237ml) water

1. Combine the eggs, honey, lemon zest, lemon juice, and melted butter in a blender. Blend them on low speed for 30 seconds, or until well combined. 2. Fill the 1 ½-quart (1.5-L) casserole dish that fits inside the Instant Pot with the lemon mixture. Cover the casserole dish with the glass lid. If the dish you're using doesn't have a glass lid, you may line the top with unbleached parchment paper, then cover it with foil and fasten it around the sides. 3. Add the water to the Instant Pot and put the steam rack inside. Place the covered casserole dish carefully on the rack. 4. Close the lid. For 5 minutes, press Pressure Cook while setting the pressure to high. 5. When the timer beeps, select Cancel or keep warm. When the timer beeps, allow the steam to naturally release for 15 minutes on the seal position. Perform a fast release while holding an oven mitt. Allow any remaining steam to release on the vent position then open the lid. 6. Carefully remove the casserole dish from the Instant Pot using an oven mitt, then remove the glass cover. Pour the curd into your preferred half-pint (250ml) glass jars, ramekins, or single glass airtight container after whisking it continuously until the mixture is perfectly smooth, or just leave it in the casserole dish. Refrigerate the lemon curd so that it can solidify. 7. Let chill for a minimum of 5 hours, or until fully chilled. Serve chilled.
Per Serving: Calories 309; Fat: 9g; Sodium 22mg; Carbs: 56g; Sugars: 50g; Protein 6g

Hot Spiced Apple-Cranberry Cider

Prep Time: 5 minutes | Cook Time: 10 minutes | Serves: 1.5L

6 apples, peeled, cored and quartered
2½ cups (590ml) filtered water, plus more as needed
3 cups (300g) frozen or fresh cranberries
Zest and juice of 2 medium oranges
⅓ cup (80ml) honey or pure maple syrup

1 (1" [2.5-cm]) piece fresh ginger, peeled and sliced
3 cinnamon sticks
13 whole cloves
Vanilla ice cream, for serving (optional)

1. Put the apples and water in a powerful blender and process until completely smooth and liquefied. 2. Through a fine-mesh filter, add the apple juice to the Instant Pot. 3. Add the cranberries, orange zest and juice, ginger, cinnamon sticks, and cloves. Add the extra filtered water until the liquid level reaches the "5 cup" mark on the Instant Pot's inside. 4. Press sauté to start boiling the ingredients. Press Cancel to stop the Instant Pot once the cider begins to boil. 5. Close the lid. Set the cooking time to 10 minutes and press Pressure Cook at high pressure. 6. When the timer beeps, select Cancel or keep warm. When the timer beeps, allow the steam to naturally release for 15 minutes on the seal position. Perform a fast release while holding an oven mitt. Allow any remaining steam to escape on the vent position until the float valve lowers, and then carefully lift the lid. 7. Into a very big bowl or a sizable heatproof pitcher, very gently spoon or pour the extremely hot spiced cider using an oven mitt. If extra straining is required to get rid of all the fruit pulp, do so. 8. Serve right away in your preferred cup and top with a scoop of vanilla ice cream for an added touch of luxury (if using).
Per Serving: Calories 180; Fat: 1g; Sodium 19mg; Carbs: 44g; Sugars: 34g; Protein 1g

Delicious Dulce De Leche

Prep Time: 5 minutes | Cook Time: 30 minutes | Serves: 1 cup

1½ cups water plus 3 tablespoons warm water
½ teaspoon baking soda

One 14-ounce can full-fat sweetened condensed milk

1. Fill the Instant Pot with 1 ½ cups of water. In the pot, place the steam rack. In a 2-quart, high-sided, round soufflé dish, combine the baking soda with the remaining 3 tablespoons warm water. Until smooth, whisk in the condensed milk. Lock the lid and place this bowl on the steam rack. 2. Select Pressure Cook on high. Set time to 30 minutes. 3. After the time has done cooking, switch it off and wait for around 15 minutes for the pressure to naturally release on the seal position. Open the lid. Use an immersion blender inside the insert to make the dulce de leche sauce extremely smooth, or whisk until smooth. Place the sauce in a small bowl and refrigerate for 1 to 2 hours. For up to 5 days, cover and refrigerate before serving, reheat tiny amounts in the microwave to help them soften.
Per Serving: Calories 865; Fat: 40g; Sodium 344mg; Carbs: 65g; Sugars: 14g; Protein 68.39g

Banana Cake with Almonds

Prep Time: 5 minutes | Cook Time: 25 minutes | Serves: 8

⅔ cup sliced almonds
⅔ cup graham cracker crumbs
½ cup plus 2 tablespoons granulated white sugar
3 tablespoons butter, melted and cooled, plus additional butter for greasing the pan
1-pound regular cream cheese
1 small very ripe banana

⅓ cup packaged, dehydrated, crisp, unsweetened, unsalted banana chips
2 large eggs
1 tablespoon all-purpose flour
½ teaspoon almond extract
1½ cups water

1. Butter a 7-inch round springform pan well on the inside. In a medium bowl, combine the melted butter, 2 tablespoons sugar, almond slices and graham cracker crumbs. Stir to combine well. To create a crust, press this mixture firmly into the bottom and halfway up the edges of the pan. 2. In a food processor, combine the remaining ½ cup sugar, cream cheese, banana, and banana chips (if using), cover, and process for approximately a minute or until smooth. One at a time, add the eggs and process each one until smooth. Add the flour and almond extract after opening the machine and cleaning the interior. Process while covered until smooth. Fill the prepared crust in the pan with this mixture. Do not cover the pan with foil. 3. Fill the Instant Pot with the water. In the cooker, place the steam rack. Make a sling out of aluminum foil, place the full springform pan on it, and then drop it into the pot using the sling. To prevent the sling's ends from coming in contact with the cheesecake mixture in the pan, fold them down. Lock lid. 4. Select Pressure Cook on high for 25 minutes. 5. After the cooking is finished, switch it off and wait for around 20 minutes for the pressure to naturally return to normal. Open the lid. Move the heated springform pan to a wire rack using the sling. After 15 minutes of cooling, refrigerate for 1 hour. For at least another hour or up to 2 days, cover and keep the food in the fridge. 6. To serve, take the cake out of the pan and slice it with a small knife. To remove the cake from the pan, unlatch the sides and pry it open. If desired, slice the cake from the pan's bottom with a long, thin knife before transferring the cheesecake to a serving tray with a big metal spatula.
Per Serving: Calories 282; Fat: 22g; Sodium 291mg; Carbs: 16g; Sugars: 11g; Protein 5g

Creamy Brownie Pudding

5 ounces semi-sweet chocolate, chopped; or 6 ounces semi-sweet morsels (about 1 cup)
½ ounce unsweetened chocolate, chopped (half of a 1-ounce square of standard baking chocolate, or about 1½ tablespoons chopped unsweetened chocolate)
1 cup whole milk

½ cup heavy cream
4 large egg yolks
Up to 2 teaspoons vanilla extract
¼ teaspoon salt
1½ cups water

1. Put both kinds of chocolate in a large dish that can withstand heat. Place aside. 2. Place the milk and cream in a medium bowl that can withstand the microwave. Heat for 1 to 2 minutes on high until steaming. After adding the chocolate to the boiling milk mixture, steep for 1 minute. Until melted and smooth, stir. While whisking intermittently, let cool for 5 minutes. 3. Mix in the salt, vanilla, and egg yolks well. Divide this mixture into four 1-cup ramekins that can withstand pressure and heat. Wrap each in aluminum foil securely. Fill the Instant Pot with the water. Stack the ramekins on the steam rack with three on the bottom and one in the center, on their edges, on top of the pot. Close lid. 4. Select Pressure Cook on high. Set time to 8 minutes. 5. After the cooking is finished, switch it off and wait for around 20 minutes for the pressure to naturally release on the seal position. Open the pot's lid by unlatching it. Move the heated covered ramekins to a wire rack, uncovered, and allow to cool for 15 minutes. Serve warm or cover once more and store in the refrigerator for up to 4 days or at least 2 hours until cooled.
Per Serving: Calories 399; Fat: 26g; Sodium 197mg; Carbs: 37g; Sugars: 32g; Protein 6g

Savory Butterscotch Pudding

3 tablespoons butter
½ cup packed dark brown sugar
1½ cups whole milk
½ cup heavy cream

6 large egg yolks
¼ teaspoon vanilla extract
⅛ teaspoon salt
1½ cups water

1. Select sauté. 2. Melt the butter in a 6- or 8-quart pot. For about 3 minutes, after smoothing out the brown sugar, boil the mixture while continuously bubbling. Add the milk and cream and stir until the sugar mixture smooths out and melts once more. After turning off the SAUTÉ function, pour the contents of the hot insert into a nearby big basin. Let cool for 15 minutes. Return the insert to the machine after cleaning and drying it in the interim. 3. Blend the milk mixture by whisking in the egg yolks, vanilla, and salt. Distribute this mixture equally into four 1-cup ramekins that can withstand pressure and heat. Wrap them all with aluminum foil. 4. Fill the instant pot with the water. Put the steam rack in pot. Stack the ramekins on the rack. Close lid. 5. Select Pressure Cook on high. Set time to 10 minutes. 6. After the cooking is finished, switch it off and wait for around 20 minutes for the pressure to naturally release on the seal position. Open the lid. Move the heated covered ramekins to a wire rack, uncovered, and allow to cool for 15 minutes. Serve hot or cover once more and store in the fridge for at least two hours or up to four days.
Per Serving: Calories 342; Fat: 23g; Sodium 206mg; Carbs: 25.87g; Sugars: 24g; Protein 7g

Sugar Tapioca Pudding

3 cups whole, low-fat, or fat-free milk
½ cup granulated white sugar
½ cup instant tapioca
1 teaspoon vanilla extract

¼ teaspoon table salt
1½ cups water
1 large egg, at room temperature
1 large egg yolk, at room temperature

1. In a 2-quart, high-sided, round, pressure- and heat-safe soufflé dish, whisk the milk, sugar, tapioca, vanilla, and salt until the sugar dissolves. Never cover. 2. Fill the Instant Pot with the water. Put the steam rack in pot. Close lid. 3. Select Pressure Cook on high. Set time to 5 minutes. 4. After the cooking is finished, switch it off and wait for around 20 minutes for the pressure to naturally return to normal. Open the cooker by releasing the lid clasp. In the baking dish, whisk the heated liquid until it is smooth, scraping up any clumps of tapioca formed there. 5. In a medium dish, combine the egg and egg yolk and whisk to mix. When all of the hot milk mixture has been added, continue whisking in tiny amounts of the hot tapioca custard into the eggs. After chilling for 2 hours, serve immediately, or cover and keep in the refrigerator for up to four days.
Per Serving: Calories 265; Fat: 13g; Sodium 232mg; Carbs: 29g; Sugars: 12.03g; Protein 7g

Vanilla Rice Pudding

Prep Time: 5 minutes | Cook Time: 17 minutes | Serves: 6

1 tablespoon butter
¾ cup raw white Arborio rice
One 12-ounce can whole or low-fat evaporated milk (1½ cups)
½ cup water
½ cup granulated white sugar

Up to 2 teaspoons vanilla extract
¼ teaspoon table salt
1 large egg, at room temperature
1 large egg yolk, at room temperature
⅓ cup heavy cream

1. Select Sauté function. 2. Melt the butter in the Instant Pot. For approximately a minute, while continually stirring, add the rice, cooking it until the tips of the grains become translucent. Add the salt, water, vanilla, sugar, and evaporated milk and stir until the sugar dissolves. Lock the lid on the pot and deactivate SAUTÉ. 3. Select Pressure Cook on high and set time to 10 minutes. 4. After the cooking is finished, switch it off and wait for around 15 minutes for the pressure to naturally release on the seal position. Open the lid. Repeatedly stir the rice mixture. 5. In a big bowl, combine the cream, egg, and egg yolk and whisk to combine well. Once the mixture is smooth, stir the remaining rice mixture in the pot along with about 1 cup of the leftover rice mixture on Sauté function. After 5 minutes, either serve warm or spoon into a large, clean dish and chill for about an hour. The pudding may be stored in the fridge for up to 2 days when covered.
Per Serving: Calories 270; Fat: 21.17g; Sodium 481mg; Carbs: 19g; Sugars: 5g; Protein 8g

Sweet Coconut Rice with Fresh Mango

Prep Time: 5 minutes | Cook Time: 17 minutes | Serves: 6

One 14-ounce can full-fat coconut milk or coconut cream (but not cream of coconut)
½ cup granulated white sugar
½ teaspoon vanilla extract

½ teaspoon table salt
3½ cups water
1½ cups raw, sweet, glutinous white rice
3 medium ripe mangos, peeled, pitted, and cut into bite-size chunks

1. Select Sauté function. 2. In the Instant pot, combine the sugar, vanilla, coconut milk, and salt. Cook for about 4 minutes, stirring often until bubbling. Scrape all of the coconut mixture into a large basin and turn off the SAUTÉ feature and then remove the heated insert from the appliance. Place aside. 3. Place the steam rack inside the pot after adding 1½ cups of water. In a 2-quart, high-sided, round soufflé dish, combine the rice with the remaining 2 cups water. Place this dish on the rack and tighten the pot's lid. 4. Select Pressure Cook on high for 12 minutes. 5. Quickly release the pressure on the vent position. Then wait 10 minutes, open the pot. Take the heated dish out of the rack. 6. Combine the cooked rice with all except ⅓ cup of the coconut milk mixture. Warm rice is served in the bowls with the mango slices scattered on top. The leftover coconut milk mixture is drizzled over the servings as desired.
Per Serving: Calories 367; Fat: 16.17g; Sodium 254mg; Carbs: 35g; Sugars: 6g; Protein 23g

Classic Sugar Flan

Prep Time: 5 minutes | Cook Time: 17 minutes | Serves: 4

½ plus ⅓ cup granulated white sugar
1½ cups plus 3 tablespoons water
3 large eggs
1¼ cups heavy cream

¾ cup whole milk
2 teaspoons vanilla extract
⅛ teaspoon table salt

1. In the Instant Pot on Sauté, melt the ½ cup sugar and 3 tablespoons water until amber or even somewhat darker. Stir regularly until the sugar melts, then let it sit undisturbed for 4 to 6 minutes, depending on the color you want. Four 1-cup ramekins, ideally Pyrex custard cups, that are heat- and pressure-safe should be filled evenly with the boiling sugar syrup. To slightly coat the sides of the cups, turn them this way and that while holding them with hot pads or oven mitts. Cool for 15 minutes at room temperature. 2. In a medium bowl, combine the eggs, milk, vanilla, cream, salt, and the remaining ⅓ cup sugar. Whisk the ingredients well to combine. Divide this mixture evenly into the covered custard cups. 3. Add the final 1½ cups of water to the Instant Pot. Place the steam rack inside the pot, then arrange the custard cups—possibly three below and one perched in the middle on the rims on the rack. Close the lid. 4. Select Pressure Cook on high and set time to 10 minutes. 5. After the cooking is finished, switch it off and wait for around 20 minutes for the pressure to naturally release on the seal position. Open the lid. Move the hot custard cups to a wire rack, unveiled, and allow to cool for 10 minutes. Next, place them in the refrigerator to chill for an hour. For at least one further hour or up to 3 days, cover and keep chilling. To release the custard and sugar sauce from within, flip one upside down on a serving platter and shake it a little.
Per Serving: Calories 266; Fat: 18g; Sodium 120mg; Carbs: 20g; Sugars: 19g; Protein 4g

Buttery Caramel Pears

Prep Time: 5 minutes | Cook Time: 15 minutes | Serves: 4

½ cup (1 stick) butter, cut into four or five pieces
⅔ cup packed light brown sugar
1 teaspoon ground cinnamon
¼ teaspoon grated nutmeg
¼ teaspoon baking soda

¼ teaspoon table salt
½ cup unsweetened apple juice or cider
4 large firm ripe pears, peeled, cored, and each cut into 4 to 6 wedges
2 teaspoons cornstarch
2 teaspoons water

1. Select Sauté function. 2. In the Instant Pot, combine the butter, brown sugar, cinnamon, nutmeg, baking soda, and salt. Stir until the butter is melted. After thoroughly incorporating the apple juice, add the pears and mix one more. Lock the lid on the pot and turn off SAUTÉ function. 3. Select Pressure Cook on high for 6 minutes. 4. When the cooking is finished, turn it off and let pressure return to normal naturally on the seal position, about 15 minutes. Unlatch the lid. 5. Select Sauté function. 6. Stir the cornstarch and water in a small bowl until completely smooth while the sauce comes to a boil. Add this slurry to the sauce and pears. For approximately a minute, stir continually until the mixture somewhat thickens. Remove the heated insert from the machine and turn off the SAUTÉ function. Allow to sit for 5 to 10 minutes before serving.
Per Serving: Calories 244; Fat: 23g; Sodium 422mg; Carbs: 7g; Sugars: 3g; Protein 1g

Traditional Noodle Kugel

Prep Time: 5 minutes | Cook Time: 25 minutes | Serves: 6

6 ounces wide egg noodles (3 cups)
1½ quarts (6 cups) water
2 large eggs
6 tablespoons granulated white sugar
6 tablespoons regular or low-fat sour cream
6 tablespoons regular or low-fat cream cheese

¼ cup regular or low-fat evaporated milk
2 tablespoons butter, melted and cooled, plus more butter as needed
½ teaspoon ground cinnamon
½ teaspoon vanilla extract
¼ teaspoon table salt
¼ cup raisins

1. Put the noodles into the Instant Pot and pour in the water. Close lid. 2. Select Pressure Cook on high for 4 minutes. 3. To restore the pot's pressure to normal, use the quick-release technique. Open the lid. Remove the noodles from the hot insert and place in a colander in the sink. Clean the insert, then put it back in the pot. Cool the noodles for 10 minutes, sometimes being tossed to prevent sticking. 4. In the meantime, grease a 7-inch round springform pan. In a blender, combine the eggs, sugar, sour cream, cream cheese, evaporated milk, melted butter, cinnamon, vanilla, and salt. Cover the container and mix until well combined, pausing the blender at least once to scrape the inside. 5. Pour the egg mixture into a large bowl, then combine it with the noodles and raisins. Pour this mixture and scrape into the prepared springform pan (if not tightly). Wrap with aluminum foil firmly. 6. Place the steam rack inside the pot after adding 1½ cups of water. Place the covered springform pan on a sling made of aluminum foil. Lower the pan onto the rack using the sling and tuck the ends of the sling into the pot. Close lid. 7. Select Pressure Cook on high for 20 minutes. 8. After the cooking is finished, switch it off and wait for around 20 minutes for the pressure to naturally return to normal. Open the lid. To remove the heated springform pan from the pot, use the foil sling. After 10 minutes, transfer on a wire rack to cool. Remove the springform pan by unlatching the ring. Slice into the wedges and serve warm after another 5 minutes of cooling, or let cool to room temperature, cover in the plastic wrap, and keep in the fridge for up to 3 days.
Per Serving: Calories 191; Fat: 10g; Sodium 277mg; Carbs: 18g; Sugars: 10g; Protein 4.39g

Quick Vanilla Custard

Prep Time: 5 minutes | Cook Time: 8 minutes | Serves: 4

4 large eggs
2 cups whole milk
3 tablespoons granulated white sugar

½ teaspoon vanilla extract
¼ teaspoon table salt
1½ cups water

1. In a large bowl, combine the milk, sugar, vanilla, eggs, and salt and whisk until very creamy. Distribute this mixture equally among four pressure- and heat-safe One-cup ramekins. Place a little piece of aluminum foil over each ramekin. 2. Fill the instant pot with the water. Add a steam rack to the pot. Then place the ramekins on the rack (probably 3 on the rack and then one balanced in the middle on the edges of the three below). Close the lid. 3. Select Pressure Cook on high. Set time to 8 minutes. 4. After the cooking is finished, switch it off and wait for around 15 minutes for the pressure to naturally release on the seal position. Open the lid. Move the heated covered ramekins to a wire rack, uncover, and allow to cool for 15 minutes. Serve warm or cover once more and store in the refrigerator for up to 4 days or at least two hours.
Per Serving: Calories 190; Fat: 8g; Sodium 209mg; Carbs: 22.87g; Sugars: 21.03g; Protein 6g

Fluffy Eggnog Cheesecake

Prep Time: 5 minutes | Cook Time: 25 minutes |Serves: 8

1½ cups vanilla wafer cookie crumbs
¼ cup (½ stick) butter, melted and cooled, plus additional butter for greasing the pan
2 tablespoons confectioners' sugar
1-pound regular cream cheese
½ cup granulated white sugar
1 large egg, at room temperature

3 large egg yolks, at room temperature
3 tablespoons brandy
3 tablespoons heavy cream
2 tablespoons all-purpose flour
½ teaspoon grated nutmeg
¼ teaspoon salt (optional)
1½ cups water

1. Butter a 7-inch round springform pan well on the inside. In a medium bowl, combine the cookie crumbs, melted butter, and confectioners sugar until well-combined. Pour into the prepared pan. To create a crust, press this mixture firmly into the bottom and halfway up the edges of the pan. 2. Combine the cream cheese and sugar in a food processor; cover the machine and pulse for approximately a minute, or until smooth. Process the egg until smooth after adding it. Add the egg yolks, one at a time, and process before being added to the mixture. 3. Remove the machine's cover, clean the interior, and then pour in the brandy and cream. Process while covered until smooth. Add the salt, nutmeg, and flour (if using). Process once more until seamless. Pour the mixture into the prepared crust in the pan. Do not cover the pan with foil. 4. Fill the Instant Pot with the water. In the pot, place the steam rack. Make a sling out of aluminum foil, place the full springform pan on it, and then drop it into the pot using the sling. To prevent the sling's ends from coming in contact with the cheesecake mixture in the pan, fold them down. Lock the lid. 5. Select Pressure Cook on high for 25 minutes. 6. After the cooking is finished, switch it off and wait for around 20 minutes for the pressure to naturally return to normal. Open the lid. Move the heated springform pan to a wire rack using the sling. After 15 minutes of cooling, refrigerate for 1 hour. For at least another hour or up to 2 days, cover and keep the food in the fridge. 7. To serve, remove the cake from the pan and slice it with a small knife. To remove the cake from the pan, unlatch the sides and pry it open. Using a spatula, remove the cheesecake from the pan and if preferred, slice the cake off the pan's base.
Per Serving: Calories 374; Fat: 31g; Sodium 432mg; Carbs: 18g; Sugars: 11g; Protein 6.39g

Soft Lemon Sponge Cake

Prep Time: 5 minutes | Cook Time: 25 minutes |Serves: 8

1½ cups water
Flour-and-fat baking spray
⅔ cup granulated white sugar
1 large egg, at room temperature
1 large egg white, at room temperature
5½ tablespoons butter, melted and cooled to room temperature
¼ cup regular sour cream (do not use low-fat or fat-free)

¼ cup fresh lemon juice
1 teaspoon vanilla extract
½ teaspoon lemon extract
1 cup all-purpose flour
½ teaspoon baking powder
½ teaspoon baking soda
¼ teaspoon table salt

1. In the Instant pot, pour the water. Insert a steam rack that is pressure- and heat-safe in the pot. Spray baking spray liberally into a 7-inch Bundt pan, making sure to get the fat and flour into every nook and cranny. Create a sling out of aluminum foil, then place the pan in the center of it. 2. In a food processor, combine the egg, egg white, sugar, melted butter, sour cream, lemon juice, and vanilla and lemon extracts. Process while covered until smooth. Stop the device and clean it inside out. Add the salt, baking powder, baking soda, and flour. Process until smooth. 3. Spoon and stir this mixture into the prepared pan. Lower the pan into the pot using the sling. Fold the ends of the sling down to fit inside without touching the batter. Place a large paper towel on top of the Bundt pan. Lock the lid. 4. Select Pressure Cook on high for 25 minutes. 5. After the cooking is finished, switch it off and wait for around 20 minutes for the pressure to naturally return to normal. Open the pot's lid by unlatching it. Take the paper towel off. Transfer the heated Bundt pan to a wire cooling rack using the sling. When the cake has cooled for 5 minutes, flip the pan onto a cutting board to release it. Before cutting into wedges to serve, transfer it from the board to the cooling rack and let it cool for at least another 15 minutes.
Per Serving: Calories 190; Fat: 12g; Sodium 230mg; Carbs: 12.87g; Sugars: 16.03g; Protein 3.39g

Sugar Chocolate Cakes

½ cup (1 stick) butter, cut into small chunks, plus more for greasing the ramekins
8 ounces bittersweet chocolate, preferably 70% cocoa solids, chopped
1 cup confectioners' sugar
3 large eggs, at room temperature
1 large egg yolk, at room temperature
6 tablespoons all-purpose flour
¼ teaspoon table salt
1½ cups water

1. In a large dish that fits the microwave, combine the chocolate and butter. Cook for 10 second intervals on high, stirring thoroughly between each, until little over half the butter has melted. Take out of the microwave and whisk continuously until smooth. 2. After 20 minutes, stir the chocolate mixture regularly while it cools to room temperature. Meanwhile, liberally butter the inside of four 1-cup ramekins that are both heat- and pressure-safe. 3. Smoothly combine the confectioners' sugar with the chocolate mixture. Before adding the second egg, fully integrate the first one by stirring it in. Mix in the egg yolk thoroughly and add the flour and salt. Divide this mixture equally among the ramekins that have been ready. Uncover the ramekins. 4. Pour the water in Instant the pot. Set the steam rack in the pot, then stack the four ramekins on the rack, placing three on the bottom layer and one on the top, balanced on the three below. Close lid. 5. Select Pressure Cook on high for 10 minutes. 6. After the cooking is finished, switch it off and wait for around 20 minutes for the pressure to naturally return to normal. Open the lid. To cool for 15 minutes, move the heated ramekins to a wire rack. Serve them warm or in their ramekins while covered and chilled in the refrigerator for up to a day.
Per Serving: Calories 556; Fat: 28g; Sodium 379mg; Carbs: 72g; Sugars: 52g; Protein 5g

Tasty Orange Pecan Cake

⅓ cup orange marmalade
½ cup (1 stick) cool butter, cut into chunks, plus additional for greasing the pan and the foil
¼ cup granulated white sugar
¼ cup packed light brown sugar
2 large eggs, at room temperature
3 tablespoons Triple Sec or Grand Marnier
1 tablespoon vanilla extract
¾ cup finely ground pecans
½ cup all-purpose flour
¼ teaspoon table salt
1½ cups water

1. Butter a 2-quart, high-sided, round soufflé dish liberally on the interior. Cover the whole bottom of this plate with the marmalade. 2. In a large basin, beat the butter, white, and brown sugars for about 5 minutes at medium speed with an electric mixer. One at a time, beat in the eggs, making sure the first is well absorbed before continuing. 3. Wipe the bowl's inside clean. Mix in the grand Marnier and vanilla well. Beat the flour, salt, and crushed pecans into the mixture on a low speed just until combined. Smooth the top of the batter before pouring it into the prepared pan. Use a piece of aluminum foil with butter on one side to cover the dish, butter side up. Tightly seal this foil over the baking dish. 4. Pour the water into the Instant pot. Set the steam rack in the pot. Make a foil sling, set the baking dish on it, and use the sling to lower the dish onto the trivet. Fold down the ends of the sling and lock the lid on the pot. 5. Select Pressure Cook on high for 35 minutes. 6. After the cooking is finished, switch it off and wait for around 20 minutes for the pressure to naturally return to normal. Open the lid. Transfer the heated baking dish to a wire rack using the sling. Remove the lid and let the food cool for 5 minutes. To remove the cake, carefully run a flatware knife along the dish's inside edge. Over the baking pan, place a big plate or cake stand. Turn everything upside down, then shake and hit the baking dish to loosen the cake. After approximately an hour, serve warm or cool to room temperature. For around 3 hours, the cake can be left unattended at room temperature.
Per Serving: Calories 885; Fat: 64g; Sodium 1204mg; Carbs: 40g; Sugars: 15g; Protein 35.39g

Vanilla Date Nuts Cakes

Prep Time: 5 minutes | Cook Time: 35 minutes | Serves: 4

½ cup chopped baking dates
½ teaspoon baking soda
⅓ cup boiling water
1 large egg, at room temperature
¼ cup whole or low-fat milk (do not use fat-free)
3 tablespoons butter, melted and cooled, plus more for greasing the ramekins and the foil
2 tablespoons bourbon, whiskey, or rum
⅔ cup all-purpose flour

¼ cup finely chopped walnuts
1 teaspoon baking powder
½ teaspoon ground dried ginger
½ teaspoon ground cinnamon
1¼ cups plus ½ teaspoon granulated white sugar
½ teaspoon table salt
2 cups water
1 cup heavy cream
1 teaspoon vanilla extract

1. In a small dish, evenly combine the baking soda and dates for baking. After adding the boiling water, stir briefly to let the mixture cool to room temperature (approximately 30 minutes). Meanwhile, liberally butter the inside of four 1-cup ramekins that are both heat- and pressure-safe. 2. In a large bowl, stir together the egg, milk, melted butter, and bourbon for about 2 minutes, until the mixture is homogenous and smooth. Add the flour, walnuts, baking soda, ginger, cinnamon, ½ teaspoon sugar, and ¼ teaspoon salt. Whisk until combined. Mix thoroughly after adding the date mixture. Divide this batter among the four prepared ramekins. 3. Use the greased side of four little pieces of aluminum foil to close the ramekins. Add 1 ½ cups of water to the Instant Pot. Set the steam rack inside the pot. Stack the four filled ramekins on the rack, using three for the first layer and balancing the remaining in the center on the edges of the three below. Close lid. 4. Select Pressure Cook on high for 35 minutes. 5. Make the caramel sauce in the interim: In a medium saucepan over medium heat, stir the remaining 1 ¼ cups sugar, the remaining ½ cup water, and the remaining ¼ teaspoon salt until the sugar melts. It will take 5 to 6 minutes of undisturbed cooking for the mixture to turn amber. As low as you can, lower the heat. Whisk in the cream and vanilla while being careful since the mixture may bubble up. Whisk continuously until smooth. After turning off the heat, let the pan cool for up to 2 hours at room temperature while whisking every so often. 6. After the cooking is finished, switch it off and wait for around 20 minutes for the pressure to naturally return to normal. After removing the foil lids, place the heated ramekins to a wire rack. Invert the ramekins onto serving plates when they have cooled for 5 minutes. Gently tap and shake the ramekins to release the cakes within. Warm the caramel sauce and drizzle some over each.

Per Serving: Calories 388; Fat: 24g; Sodium 559mg; Carbs: 37g; Sugars: 16g; Protein 5g

Maple Apple Cake

Prep Time: 5 minutes | Cook Time: 35 minutes | Serves: 6

1 cup all-purpose flour
1 teaspoon baking powder
1 teaspoon ground cinnamon
9 tablespoons (1 stick plus 1 tablespoon) butter, plus more for greasing the pan
¼ cup maple syrup
2 medium baking apples, preferably McIntosh apples, peeled, cored,

and thinly sliced
1½ cups water
½ cup granulated white sugar
2 large eggs, at room temperature
2 teaspoons vanilla extract
3 tablespoons whole milk

1. Whisk the flour, baking powder, and cinnamon in a medium bowl. Set aside. Generously butter the inside of one 2-quart, high-sided, round soufflé dish. 2. Press sauté. 3. In the Instant Pot, melt two tablespoons of the butter. When the maple syrup is heated, add it and stir. Cook the apples for approximately 5 minutes, stirring frequently, until tender. Fill the baking dish with the whole contents of the heated insert, smoothing the apple mixture into an equal layer. 4. After drying and cleaning, put the insert back into the machine. Fill the pot with the water. Place the steam rack inside that is heat- and pressure-safe. 5. In a large bowl, whisk the remaining 7 tablespoons butter and sugar for about 4 minutes on medium speed with an electric mixer. One at a time, beat in the eggs, ensuring sure the first is well mixed in before adding the second. Add the vanilla extract after lowering the mixer's speed. Just until combined, add the flour mixture. When adding the milk, beat it in well. Over the apples in the prepared pan, pour this batter. Wrap with aluminum foil firmly. 6. Construct a foil sling. Place the trivet on top of the baking dish after setting it on the sling. Before locking the lid onto the pot, fold the ends of the sling down so they don't contact the batter. 7. Select Pressure Cook on high for 35 minutes. 8. After the cooking is finished, switch it off and wait for around 20 minutes for the pressure to naturally return to normal. Open the lid. Transfer the heated baking dish to a wire rack using the sling. Remove the lid and let the food cool for 5 minutes. To remove the cake, carefully run a flatware knife along the dish's inner edge. Over the baking pan, place a big plate or cake stand. Turn everything upside down before tapping and jiggling the baking dish to loosen the cake and allow the apple "sauce" to flow over it. Cool for 15 minutes, serve warm.

Per Serving: Calories 352; Fat: 22g; Sodium 140mg; Carbs: 36g; Sugars: 16g; Protein 3.9g

Pumpkin Spice Cheese

Crust

2 tbsp. (28g) grass-fed butter or ghee, melted, plus more butter for pan

2 tbsp. (19g) maple sugar

1 cup (100g) superfine blanched almond flour

Cheesecake

16 oz. (455g) cream cheese, softened

1 cup (245g) pure pumpkin puree

2 large eggs, at room temperature

½ cup (76g) maple sugar

1 tbsp. (8g) cassava flour

1 tsp pure vanilla extract

Zest of 1 orange

2 tsp (5g) ground cinnamon

½ tsp ground ginger

½ tsp ground cloves

½ tsp ground allspice

¼ tsp sea salt

1 cup (237ml) water

Homemade whipped cream or coconut whipped cream, for garnish (optional)

Ground cinnamon, for garnish (optional)

1. Get the crust ready. Butter an Instant Pot-compatible 6- or 7-inch (15- or 18.5-cm) round springform pan. Place aside. 2. Combine all the crust ingredients in a bowl and well mixed with clean hands. Pour the mixture into the prepared springform pan, pressing it down to create a dense bottom crust. Don't let the pan's sides fill up too much. Place the pan in the freezer for 15 minutes to cold. 3. Get the cheesecake ready. Combine the cream cheese, pumpkin, eggs, maple sugar, cassava flour, vanilla, orange zest, cinnamon, ginger, cloves, allspice, and salt in a blender. Process slowly until everything is well-blended and smooth. Incorporate the frozen crust with the cheesecake filling. 4. Place the steam rack into the Instant Pot after adding the water. Place the springform pan carefully on the rack and cover with a glass casserole lid. Put the steam vent in the sealed position and fasten the lid. 45 minutes of high pressure are set by pressing Pressure Cook. 5. Open the lid when the timer goes off. When the timer beeps, allow the steam to naturally release for 15 minutes on the seal position. Perform a fast release while holding an oven mitt. Allow any remaining steam to escape until the float valve lowers, and then carefully lift the lid. 6. Carefully lift the rack and springform pan out of the Instant Pot after removing the cover. Employ oven mitts. With the glass top still on, let the cheesecake to cool to room temperature. Remove the lid once it has cooled completely, being careful not to drop any moisture onto the cheesecake's top. When you're ready to take the cheesecake from the pan, gently run a knife over the edges to release them. Return the lid on the cheesecake after thoroughly wiping away all of the dampness. Transfer to the refrigerator and refrigerate for at least 6 hours, ideally overnight. 7. Serve cold. If you choose, top the dish with the homemade whipped cream, coconut whipped cream, or cinnamon powder.

Per Serving: Calories 415; Fat: 32g; Sodium 409mg; Carbs: 23g; Sugars: 10g; Protein 11g

Yummy Key Lime Cake Soufflé

Butter for greasing the pan and foil

1½ cups water

3 large eggs, separated and at room temperature

¾ cup granulated white sugar

1 cup regular cultured buttermilk

1 tablespoon finely grated lime zest, preferably from key limes

4½ tablespoons bottled or fresh key lime juice (from 3 to 4 key limes)

2 teaspoons vanilla extract

½ teaspoon table salt

6 tablespoons all-purpose flour

1. Butter a 2-quart, high-sided, round soufflé dish liberally on the interior. Fill a 6- or 8-quart pot with water. Place a trivet inside the pot that is both pressure- and heat-safe. 2. In a medium bowl, whip the egg whites with an electric mixer on high speed for about 3 minutes, or until soft peaks form when a spatula is inserted into the mixture. For approximately 2 minutes, or until the mixture is thick and can form silky peaks that keep their shape on a spatula, add ¼ cup of sugar in a steady, slow stream. 3. Wash the beaters and dry them. Beaten the egg yolks and remaining ½ cup sugar for about 4 minutes, or until thick and pale yellow. After cleaning the interior of the bowl, beat the buttermilk, lime juice, lime zest, and vanilla until creamy. Remove the beaters and scrape the surface. 4. Stir the flour into the egg yolk mixture with a rubber spatula until just moistened. Gently fold the egg whites in until they are combined but not quite dissolved. The batter ought to have white flecks in it. 5. Spoon the batter into the baking dish as carefully as possible. Grease aluminum foil lightly and use to loosely encase the cake, buttered side down. Create a foil sling, place the baking dish in the middle of the sling, and then lower the sling onto the rack to place the baking dish. Fold down the ends of the sling so they don't touch the batter, then lock the lid onto the pot. 6. Select Pressure Cook on high for 20 minutes. 7. After the cooking is finished, switch it off and wait for around 20 minutes for the pressure to naturally return to normal. Open the lid. Transfer the heated baking dish to a wire rack using the sling. Remove the lid and let the food cool for at least 10 or even up to an hour. Serve in the bowls or on small plates with large spoonful.

Per Serving: Calories 140; Fat: 7g; Sodium 281mg; Carbs: 13g; Sugars: 5g; Protein 4.39g

Conclusion

The Instant Pot Duo mini appliance has two programs: Pressure cooking and Non-pressure cooking. Pressure cook, steam, rice, porridge, bean/chili, meat/stew, and soup/stock are included in pressure cooking. In non-pressure cooking, sauté, slow cook, and yogurt are included. It comes with a cooker base, inner pot, stealing ring, and steam-release valve, float valve, condensation collector, and pressure lid. This cookbook is filled with delicious pressure cooking and non-pressure cooking recipes. It is a wonderful appliance because you can cook food in very little time. You didn't need to purchase separate appliances. You can select your favorite recipe, adjust the pressure level, cooking time, and temperatures, put ingredients, close the lid and start cooking. It has user-friendly operating buttons. The cleaning process is pretty simple. The install and removal process of accessories are super easy. Thank you for reading this book.

Stay safe and happy cooking!

Appendix 1 Measurement Conversion Chart

VOLUME EQUIVALENTS (LIQUID)

US STANDARD	US STANDARD (OUNCES)	METRIC (APPROXIMATE)
2 tablespoons	1 fl.oz	30 mL
¼ cup	2 fl.oz	60 mL
½ cup	4 fl.oz	120 mL
1 cup	8 fl.oz	240 mL
1½ cup	12 fl.oz	355 mL
2 cups or 1 pint	16 fl.oz	475 mL
4 cups or 1 quart	32 fl.oz	1 L
1 gallon	128 fl.oz	4 L

VOLUME EQUIVALENTS (DRY)

US STANDARD	METRIC (APPROXIMATE)
⅛ teaspoon	0.5 mL
¼ teaspoon	1 mL
½ teaspoon	2 mL
¾ teaspoon	4 mL
1 teaspoon	5 mL
1 tablespoon	15 mL
¼ cup	59 mL
½ cup	118 mL
¾ cup	177 mL
1 cup	235 mL
2 cups	475 mL
3 cups	700 mL
4 cups	1 L

TEMPERATURES EQUIVALENTS

FAHRENHEIT (F)	CELSIUS(C) (APPROXIMATE)
225 °F	107 °C
250 °F	120 °C
275 °F	135 °C
300 °F	150 °C
325 °F	160 °C
350 °F	180 °C
375 °F	190 °C
400 °F	205 °C
425 °F	220 °C
450 °F	235 °C
475 °F	245 °C
500 °F	260 °C

WEIGHT EQUIVALENTS

US STANDARD	METRIC (APPROXINATE)
1 ounce	28 g
2 ounces	57 g
5 ounces	142 g
10 ounces	284 g
15 ounces	425 g
16 ounces (1 pound)	455 g
1.5pounds	680 g
2pounds	907 g

Appendix 2 Recipes Index

A

Apple and Pork Curry 74

Apple Cinnamon Crumb Muffins 15

Apple Sauce with Pear and Sweet Potato 89

Apple Strawberry Sauce 32

Asian Fish and Vegetables 66

Asian Short Ribs with Sesame 79

Authentic Adobo Chicken Drumstick 60

Authentic Alaskan Wild Cod 65

Authentic Carrot Potato Soup with Broccoli 39

Authentic Cincinnati-Style Chili 46

Authentic Spanish Omelet 24

B

Baked Sweet Potatoes with Marshmallows 31

Balsamic Pork Chops with Pears and Figs 80

Banana Cake with Almonds 92

Basic Chicken Thighs 53

BBQ Pulled Chicken Sandwiches 55

Beef and Mushroom Stew with Egg Noodle 75

Best Nutty Zucchini Bread 19

Best Pot Roast 84

Best Whole Chicken 55

Broccoli and Cheese Soup 42

Buttered Lobster Claws 69

Buttery Caramel Pears 95

C

Cajun Shrimp Boil 72

Cheese and Sausage Egg Muffins 15

Cheese Buffalo Potatoes 27

Cheese Spinach Frittatas 22

Cheese Summer Squash and Zucchini 26

Cheesy Beany Pasta 45

Cheesy Carrot and Broccoli Soup 40

Cheesy Corn Zucchini Casserole 34

Cheesy Ham and Egg Muffins 15

Cheesy Italian Sausage and Peppers 82

Cheesy Leek and Asparagus Frittata 23

Cheesy Rice and Chicken Thighs 53

Cheesy Yellow Squash Frittata 14

Cheesy Zucchini Fritters 30

Chicken Thighs with Carrot and Cherry Tomato 55

Chickpea Curry with Patota 62

Chocolate Cookies Cheesecake 87

Chocolate-Hazelnuts French Toast Casserole 19

Chuck Roast with Vegetables 78

Cider-Braised Brussels Sprouts 35

Cinnamon Raisin-Filled Apples 87

Classic Beef Biryani 83

Classic Beef Chili 45

Classic Chicken Pesto 53

Classic Chickpea Tagine 28

Classic French Toast-Cinnamon Roll Casserole 18

Classic Heart Healthy Soup 39

Classic Huevos Ranchero 23

Classic Italian Soup 38

Classic Lasagna Soup 43

Classic Middle Eastern Baked Eggs 24

Classic Sugar Flan 94

Classic Tomato-Poached Halibut 64

Coconut Banana Bread with Chocolate Chips 89

Coconut Banana Oat Cake 22

Coconut Beef Fajitas 79

Coconut Creamed Kale 35

Coconut Milk Crabs 68

Coconut Tomato Chicken Curry 51

Creamy Baked Potato Soup 43

Creamy Brownie Pudding 93

Creamy Buttermilk Corn Bread 19

Creamy Chicken Cajun Pasta 53

Creamy Chicken Rice Soup 40

Creamy Mashed Cauliflower 33

Creamy Onion Soup 37

Creamy Strawberry Oats 20

Creamy Tomato Soup with Basil 40

Cubano Sloppy Joe Wraps 82

Curried Coconut Chicken with Potatoes 59

D

Delicious Beef Noodle Soup 42

Delicious Dulce De Leche 92

Delicious Flank Steak Taco 78

Delicious Manchester Stew 62

Delicious Maple and Cinnamon Cereal Bowls 21

Delicious Mediterranean Squid 69

Delicious Shrimp Paella 72

E

Easy Chicken Breast in Sauce 57

Easy Cob-Styled Corn 29

Easy Cranberry-Pear Crisp 91

Easy Curried Cauliflower 32

Easy Oysters with Butter 68

Easy Salsa Verde Chicken 58

Easy Shredded Chicken Breast 50

Easy Stuffed Peppers 65

Easy Traditional Shakshuka 22

F

Flavorful Chicken Fajitas 57

Flavorful Chili Macaroni and Cheese 47

Flavorful Pork Chops and Sauerkraut 78

Fluffy Eggnog Cheesecake 96

Fresh Mixed Fruit 21

Fresh Salmon Fillets with Dill 66

Fresh Spiced Beets 28

Fresh Tomato Basil Soup 41

G

Garlic Buttered Mashed Potatoes 26

Garlic Ham and Black-Eyed Peas 28

Garlicky Bacon and Cabbage Soup 37

Garlicky Broccoli 32

Gingered Orange Cod Fillets 67

Greek Quiche with Kalamata Olives 14

Green Beans with Shallot 27

Ground Beef Chili with Beans 45

H

Ham and Split Pea Soup 38

Hawaiian Pulled Pork 77

Healthy Barley Soup with Beans 39

Healthy Carnitas Lettuce Wraps 74

Healthy Chicken Sandwich with Bacon Ranch 51

Healthy Mixed-Berry Syrup 20

Healthy Seafood Gumbo 70

Healthy Vegetable and Beef Soup 38

Hearty Fish Stew 64

Herbed Poached Salmon with Carrots 63

Homemade Chicken Hawaiian 50

Homemade Chicken Wings 56

Homemade Corn Bread 33

Homemade Delicious Gravy 16

Homemade Honey Sriracha Chicken Breast 58
Homemade Meat Pie 85
Homemade Peaches Steel-Cut Oats 18
Homemade Pork Chops with Cherry 84
Homemade Tomato Lentil Soup 42
Honey Chicken Thighs with Ketchup 58
Honey Garlic Chicken Thighs 52
Honey-Glazed Carrots 27
Hot Spiced Apple-Cranberry Cider 92

I

Italian Sausage and Peppers Hoagies 81
Italian-Style Asparagus 35

K

Kale Tomato Tortellini Soup with Parsley 43

L

Lemon-Dill Fish 67
Lemony Artichoke with Dipping Sauce 31
Lemony Butter Cod Fillets 67
Lemony Butter Crab Legs 68
Lemony Garlic Squid 66
Lemony Raspberry Curd 91
Lemony Shredded Chicken and Rice Soup 41
Lentil Stew with Rice 63
Limey Honey Chicken Wings 57

M

Maple Apple Cake 98
Maple Sea Scallops 69
Mexican Stuffed Peppers 83
Mini Monkey Breads with Cereal 88
Mini Quiches with Cheese and Mushroom 24
Mouthwatering Bean Soup 47
Mushroom Pork Ragout 75
Mushrooms and Goat Cheese Frittata 14
Mussels in White Wine 71
Mustard Pork Chops 74
Mustard Tilapia with Almond 67

N

Nutritious Congee with Chicken 52
Nutritious Salsa Chicken Tacos 50
Nutritious Seafood Gumbo 70
Nutty Chocolate Banana Quinoa 17

P

Parmesan Haddock Fillets 68
Peanut Butter and Raisin Granola Bars 21
Peanut Butter and Strawberry Jelly Oatmeal 16
Pecan and Apple Oatmeal 16
Perfect Chicken Enchilada Soup 44
Perfect Chocolate Cake 90

Perfect Clam Sauce 64
Pinto Bean and Tortilla Soup 41
Pork Chops and Acorn Squash 84
Pork Roast with Apples and Plums 77
Potato and Chicken Thigh Casserole 52
Primavera Spaghetti Squash with Peas 34
Pumpkin Cheesecake with Granola 87
Pumpkin Spice Cheese 99

Q

Quick Salty Potatoes 29
Quick Vanilla Custard 95

R

Red Beans and Ham Hocks with Rice 77
Refreshing Balsamic-Maple Parsnips 35
Refreshing Chicken Piccata 60
Rosemary Pork Tenderloin 85

S

Salsa Chicken Nachos 59
Savory Butterscotch Pudding 93
Savory Chicken Enchiladas 54
Savory Chipotle Beer Chili 46
Savory Goat Cheese and Bacon Muffins 17
Savory Red Potato Salad 30
Seafood Plov with Cranberries 70
Simple and Quick Meatloaf 76
Simple Chai Spice Rice Pudding 88
Simple Chicken Puttanesca 60
Simple Honey Lemon Curd 91
Simple Lemon Octopus 69
Simple Mongolian beef 82
Simple Shrimp and Grits 71
Simple Sicilian Steamed Leeks 26
Simple Steamed Tilapia 65
Simple Sweet Potatoes 29
Simple Thai Chicken 58
Simple Vegetarian Chili 48
Smoked Ham and White Beans 29
Soft Lemon Sponge Cake 96
Soft-Boiled Eggs with Lemony Shredded Kale 20
Sour and Sweet Chicken Breast 51
Southwest Chili with Black Beans and Corn 48
Spice Trade Beans and Bulgur 63
Spiced Baby Back Pork Ribs 79
Spiced Hoisin Short Ribs 80
Spicy Barbecued Pork 85
Spicy Cacciatore Chicken 59
Spicy Chicken Wings 56
Spicy Red Chili 44

Spicy Whole Chicken 50
Spicy Worcestershire Chicken Breast 57
Steamed Fish with Cherry Tomatoes and Olives 65
Steamed Lemony Artichokes 26
Steamed Mussels with Pepper 62
Sticky Asian Sesame Chicken 56
Stir-Fried Chicken and Vegetables 54
Sugar Chocolate Cakes 97
Sugar Tapioca Pudding 93
Summer Vegetable Tian 34
Super-Easy Sweet Potatoes 32
Sweet Apple Crisp Doughnut 90
Sweet Bananas Corn Muffins 18
Sweet Bread Pudding with Pomegranates 88
Sweet Coconut Rice with Fresh Mango 94
Sweet Strawberry Jam with Chia Seeds 20
Swiss Steak with Potato and Carrot 83

T

Tasty Barbecued Ribs 81
Tasty Chicken Alfredo 54
Tasty Marinara Meatballs 81
Tasty Orange Pecan Cake 97
Tasty Pork and Squash Ragu 75
Tasty Rice Pilaf with Mushrooms 27
Tasty Satay Pork with Rice Noodles 76
Tender Mixed Seafood with Rice 71
Teriyaki Pork Roast 80
Tomato-Based Spaghetti Squash with Olives 30
Traditional Beef and Sweet Potato Chili 46
Traditional Noodle Kugel 95
Traditional Shrimp Scampi 72
Traditional Sweet Corn Tamalito 33

V

Vanilla Date Nuts Cakes 98
Vanilla Pudding Cups 89
Vanilla Raisin Muffins with Pecans 17
Vanilla Rice Pudding 94
Vegetable and Chicken Noddle Soup 37

W

Wisconsin Brats and Cheddar Chowder 44

Y

Yummy Bacon Corn Grits 16
Yummy Buffalo Chicken Chili 47
Yummy Coconut Brownies 90
Yummy Homemade Dressing 31
Yummy Huevos Rancheros Casserole 23
Yummy Key Lime Cake Soufflé 99
Yummy Pork Tacos with Mango Salsa 76

Made in United States
Troutdale, OR
01/03/2025

27570417R00065